Reading Activities & Resources That Work

Reading Activities & Resources That Work

Phyllis J. Perry

Highsmith PRESS
Fort Atkinson, Wisconsin

Published by Highsmith Press LLC
W5527 Highway 106
P.O. Box 800
Fort Atkinson, Wisconsin 53538-0800

1-800-558-2110

Photographs by David L. Perry
Cover design by Frank Neu

The paper used in this publication meets the minimum requirements of
American National Standard for Information Science —
Permanence of Paper for Printed Library Material.
ANSI/NISO Z39.48-1992.

Library of Congress Cataloging-in-Publication Data

Perry, Phyllis Jean.
    Reading activities & resources that work / Phyllis J. Perry.
       p.   cm.
    Includes bibliographical references and index.
    ISBN 0-917846-94-X (pbk. : alk. paper)
    1. Reading–Aids and devices. 2. Children–Books and reading.
  3. Storytelling. 4. Education, Elementary–Activity programs.
  I. Title.
  LB1573.39.P536 1997
  372.41–dc21   97-9859
                                         CIP

While it isn't possible to thank all the teachers and students who shared with me the excitement of trying out ideas and resources that enrich the elementary school curriculum, I would like to thank two outstanding educators and dear friends. For their support throughout the years, I am deeply indebted to Chuck Cassio and Sid Weathermon.

Contents

1

Introduction

*T*eachers, parents, librarians and other adults involved in working with youth in the broad field of elementary language arts make excellent use of a wide variety of books. Some are fiction. Some are nonfiction. They are written by many authors on countless topics, because children, like adults, enjoy choices as to which of these books they will read.

Using fiction and nonfiction to teach reading, writing, speaking, listening, and viewing, and to develop research skills is basic to language arts instruction. Students and their teachers respond to these materials in unique and interesting ways. Today's classrooms, as well as organized activities at home and in many types of youth groups, reflect this excitement for interdisciplinary learning.

For example, reading and writing skills are important tools in studying science, in following directions for arts and crafts, and in learning about customs and special holidays around the world. When first graders prepare a fairy tale musical to share with parents, reading, writing, speaking, listening, viewing, math, social studies, art, and music may all be involved as students write programs, learn parts, carry out research, measure for costumes, and paint and build sets. The same range of skills might be tapped in many scouting and church activities.

This sourcebook provides a listing of a rich collection of print and nonprint material as well as hands-on ideas for an integration of the curriculum bringing together bits and pieces of information in a meaningful whole. Students find practical uses for the application of skills that they have mastered. Reasons for learning information and interrelationships between and among branches of knowledge are discovered as students are involved in cross-curricular activities in school and in other youth activities.

Teachers are also faced with new challenges, because in addition to an integrated and multicultural curriculum, today's education is also individualized or personalized. Just as classes of students may no longer use a single basal reader, they also may not use a single social studies or science textbook. Independent research and small group projects add to the common core of learning for students in most classrooms.

When teachers help their students plan a unit of study, they need to have available both ideas for hands-on activities to interest and engage the class, and an extensive collection of trade books and other materials such as videocassettes and computer software programs that will assist in further unique explorations to be carried out by individuals and small groups.

Adults who work with youth listen to the individual voices of children and follow their interests and curiosity in planning lessons and activities. When a child says, "I want to know more about...," the teacher pounces on the moment and uses appropriate resources to encourage further investigation.

In a whole language classroom, instruction and exploration is not limited to the use of books, magazines, and other print materials. It is common place in elementary school classrooms to see teachers of elementary language arts using creative movement and dance, listening centers, peer and cross-grade tutoring and critique groups, computer centers, videocassettes, flannel boards, filmstrips, dramatic presentations, games, and puppet stages to mention only a few possibilities.

Reading Activities and Resources That Work provides teachers with activities in a number of areas and gives an extensive annotated bibliography of over 1,000 recent trade books, all published in the last dozen years, that will prove valuable in finding activities and resources quickly. Such materials allow individual students opportunities to delve more deeply into a subject area or to follow an interesting sidelight. These additional investigations might occur in school or they might take place at home or in other youth group settings.

Since the titles included in this book are recent ones, they should be available from publishers and producers. Many titles will also be available in most large libraries and bookstores. (International Standard Book Numbers (ISBN) are included whenever they were available.) Suggestions are also included for using magazines, videos, audio cassettes, kits, and computer programs that might be both appropriate and easily accessible.

Since kids are curious, and since a large number of trade books, magazines, and other materials exist, it might appear that, provided sufficient monies have been budgeted, there's not a problem in having all that's needed for studying and enjoying the language arts and for investigating a variety of topics at school and at home. But there is a problem.

The problem is time. Time is a precious commodity. Teachers and parents never have enough of it. They can't afford to spend days at a library scouring through the shelves or using the computer catalog to check through a number of databases to find out what contemporary titles are both appropriate and available to meet student needs. The listings in *Reading Activities and Resources That Work* save educators hours of time in searching out materials.

This book is not designed to be read from cover to cover. Teachers, parents, librarians, and other interested adults should dip into it when a section would provide information useful for a general activity or when a listing of materials is needed to enable a student to pursue research. Topics included are: Storytelling and Puppetry; Arts & Crafts; Creative Dramatics; Poetry; Folktales, Fables, Myths, and Legends; Music and Movement; Holidays Around the World; Doing Research; and Games.

Reading Activities and Resources That Work provides ideas and sources of material for adults who work with children in any aspect of the language arts to promote learning that is relevant, challenging, and fun!

2

Storytelling and Puppetry

In one Native American tribe, someone is designated as "The Keeper of the Old Things." It is the task of that venerated person to remember and recount the important events of the past and to find a suitable person to train so that there will remain an unbroken chain of memory.

In most of today's families, it often falls to older relatives to take on this role of historian and family storyteller, while in school settings many teachers and librarians are noted for their storytelling abilities. Through listening to and telling stories, children learn many valuable language arts skills.

Some people are natural storytellers and can hold an audience fascinated with nothing but their memories and their voices. Others may require props such as a collection of mementos or a family photograph album. Still others may enjoy working with puppets to share a story with a room full of students or with one special child.

Storytelling activities at home and at school help the young child acquire some concept of time. At first, the child may be simply astonished to realize that the tiny baby in a photograph that he is looking at is actually his father, or that the girl proudly smiling at the top of the playground slide before beginning a perilous descent is his mother. Even more surprising may be the realization that the pretty young woman pushing the swing in the playground is his familiar grandmother.

Directions for Ideas That Work

GUESS WHO?: A simple school activity involving photographs also provides some interesting bulletin boards. The teacher sends a letter to staff members asking that they loan a baby picture to the teacher to put up on a hall bulletin board under the caption "Guess Who?" Each photo should be given to the teacher in an envelope with the subject's name on the envelope. The pictures are pinned up but are not identified except by a number. Students and other staff members may try to guess the identity of the subjects. After a week, the identity of the subjects can be posted. A teacher could send a similar letter to parents of students in the class asking that parents send a baby picture of the student in an envelope to school. In the classroom, a "Guess Who?" bulletin board will lead to a lot of puzzling over the identity of the subjects which can later be revealed.

Storytelling can work together with photographs or mementos to immortalize events that tend to "humanize" teachers, parents and other family members. The ideas below will help to get you started.

◆ A photo showing the fifth grade teacher at age ten with her broken leg in a cast after tumbling out of the apple tree in an attempt to peek in a just-out-of-reach bird's nest is proof positive that today's serious adults as well as today's adventurous children have been involved in accidents. And a picture of Uncle Jim, wearing his baseball uniform in a city league at the ball park, establishes a feeling of continuity with today's Little Leaguer.

◆ Mementos add to the child's store of knowledge about family history. In a scrapbook, there may be a certificate of award acknowledging a spelling bee champ, a school program announcing a violin solo, a newspaper clipping detailing a player's contributions to the team at a state basketball tournament, or a photo showing a trophy won at a horse show. If some adult in a family saves these special tangibles from the past and enjoys sharing them, there will be opportunity for good family discussions.

◆ When a child lives some distance from grandparents who still reside in the same town or house where the child's parents grew up, visits and excursions to the old "homesite" and favorite spots may add to the storytelling tradition. The child may see where her mother or father attended school and the park where the family used to picnic. Within the home may be a prized bookcase that the child's mother or father made in a crafts class.

Such storytelling is a priceless tradition that can be shared across the generations. Nor does the storyteller have to worry about taking up too much time with his or her audience. A child who becomes bored will show it. An interested child will have countless questions to ask. These none too subtle clues will be a good guide to the storyteller.

Just as storytelling about relatives in the home helps to build language skills, many teachers, librarians, scout masters, church fellowship leaders, and other adults also have a facility for making up "characters," putting them in situations, and telling creative stories with ongoing escapades. Interested children will beg for more of these adventures.

Many adults in different settings will have special tales to tell. These may be favorite nursery rhymes and poems, tall tales, stories told around a scouting campfire, or legends associated with particular holidays or natural phenomena. "Old Timers" in the community may be asked to come to school and share their knowledge of some significant event in the town that happened 50 years ago. The fun of such tales is that each telling is unique. The teller may embellish or edit to suit the particular occasion.

The classroom is a wonderful place to practice storytelling. Students learn a great deal about plot, character, and setting from these oral experiences. Many young students find oral storytelling frees them from constraints they may face when writing stories using their limited spelling and punctuation skills.

Directions for Ideas That Work

PASS THE BUTTON STORIES: A simple group story technique is to thread a large button on a string. The string needs to be long enough so that the whole class can sit in a circle and each can hold a piece of string loosely in his or her lap.

The "story starter" takes the button in hand and begins to tell a story. The teacher or adult leader of the group is a good choice for the story starter who should introduce the setting as well as a couple of the characters. For example, the story starter might say, "One dark Halloween night, Robbie and Kim were out trick-or-treating. They had wandered far from their homes and found themselves in a strange neighborhood. They saw a huge house that was all dark except for a

Illus. 2.1. Pass the button stories: Students sit in a circle. They hold a string on which a button is threaded. The story starter, holding the button, begins to tell a tale. At an exciting moment, the story starter passes the button to the right. The person to the right, takes the button, picks up the story, and goes on.

Jack-o'-lantern that was shining in one downstairs window. They boldly walked up to the door and knocked. When the door cracked open..."

At this point, the person telling the story passes the button along the string to the person on his/her right. The person who gets the button continues with the story for a few sentences, stops at an exciting point, and then passes the button to the right.

Some hilarious adventure stories can result from this add-on-to-the-story technique. When the group is familiar with the process, anyone in the group might be the story starter. The teacher might also consider running a tape recorder so that the story is preserved.

Although it is fun to sit around a circle in the classroom or around a campfire on a family or scout outing and tell spooky tales, a word of caution is needed. Frightening a young child is never a good idea. Be sure that you know your group of children well and that they are comfortable with the activity so that fears and nightmares don't result.

There are also tall tales or wildly exaggerated stories that some adults tell especially well. Children of a certain age particularly enjoy these Paul Bunyan-type tales. It's a great time to discuss what distinguishes fact from fancy and to discuss the various kinds of humor. After reading a number of these stories and discussing the elements of tall tales, a follow-up classroom activity might be to write original stories.

Directions for Ideas That Work

TALL TALES: Prepare a blank book for each child to fill in before the class or story time. Rather than the typical shape, these books should be tall and narrow. Taking $8\frac{1}{2}$" x 11" typing paper and cutting it in half lengthwise will make good-sized filler sheets. Use two staples to fasten together twenty-four of these pages inside a construction paper cover. The two staples should be placed at the top of the tall tale book. Explain that each student will write an original tall tale in the blank book.

Those who wish to do so, may illustrate their tall tales. Allow some time for volunteers to share their tall tales with the class or with another group of students.

One of the simplest techniques is to tell a story using felt pieces which have been cut out and are then placed onto a flannel board at appropriate times during the storytelling. Such boards can be purchased or they can easily be made by simply stretching a piece of flannel cloth over a frame.

The use of flannel boards should not be restricted to language arts. Math vocabulary such as **over, under, above, beside, beneath**, etc. can be taught to young children by using figures on a flannel board and encouraging students to place objects on the board in specific positions. Science cycles can be shared by showing the water cycle during a flannel board presentation or by showing the development of a frog from frog eggs, to legless tadpole, to two-legged and then four-legged tadpoles, and finally to a full-grown frog.

Making and using puppets in storytelling

Storytelling can lead quite naturally into puppetry. While not everyone is a puppeteer, for those even slightly interested, puppets can add many exciting opportunities to storytelling. Most gift and toy shops are well-supplied with a variety of hand puppets depicting real and fantastic animals and people.

The storyteller may want to slip on one of these hand puppets before telling a tale. Older students might want to get actively involved in putting on puppet shows and in making their own puppets, props, and a puppet theatre.

Making puppets does not have to be difficult. There are patterns to knit puppets; puppets can also be fashioned from gloves and socks; simple puppets can be cut from pieces of felt; or cut like paper dolls and taped to a dowel stick or ruler. Puppets can even be made from peanuts!

Directions for Ideas That Work

PEANUT PUPPETS: An easy way to make tiny finger puppets is to buy some peanuts in the shell. Cut or break the shells in half and take out the nuts. Half of an empty peanut shell fits nicely on a child's fingertip.

The peanut can be transformed into a person or an animal by using a very few supplies. Colored pencils or inks can be used to draw on eyes, a nose and a mouth. A bit of felt cut in a circle will make a full-length dress for a peanut lady. Two oval pieces of white felt can be cut and glued for a rabbit's ears. A piece of black construction paper can make a top hat. Bits of yarn can be turned into braids. Thread can make a cat's whiskers. Tiny feathers, scraps of lace, and sequins can result in grand costumes.

Illus. 2.2. Peanut puppets: Puppets come in all shapes and sizes! Favorites, just right for little fingers, are these peanut puppets. They are simple to dress and to decorate.

Once you have created a set of peanut puppets, the class will probably want to make a number of tiny puppet stages so that they can create and present peanut puppet shows at school and at home.

When the stage is ready, a student can put the shoe box on a table top, sit on the floor, and reach up and work the peanut puppets in the miniature stage. After the show, the puppets and props can be stored in the empty box.

Directions for Ideas That Work

PEANUT PUPPET STAGE: A shoe box makes an effective peanut puppet stage. Ask students to bring in empty shoe boxes. (If a few children bring in two or three boxes, they will help to supply students who may not have an empty shoe box at home.)

Take the lid and cut the center away leaving just a one-inch border on all four sides. Turn the empty shoe box on its side and tape the lid securely on top and along the open side of the shoe box. Students may keep any small props inside the open shoe box, and there will be a few inches of "stage" right in front of the puppets where tiny bits of scenery can be placed.

Illus. 2.3. Peanut puppet stage: An easy-to-make stage for peanut puppets can be created from a shoe box. By cutting out the inside of the lid of the shoe box, and attaching it as shown, the stage is just the right size for peanut-sized performers.

Those who find that puppetry is a good way for students to practice language arts skills can get more deeply involved. Dividing a class into groups of four to six children and having them plan a puppet show involves many skills. The students will have to agree on what puppets are needed and what the story line will be. Then they need to write or record the story making effective use of dialogue and being certain that they have a beginning, middle and ending to their plot.

Students may want to do the show "live" or they may want to tape their story with dialogue and sound effects and simply play the recorded story for the audience to hear while the actors manipulate the puppets. Any type of puppets can be used, but papier-mache puppets are very effective for a class presentation.

Equipped with a set of puppets, students may want to present not only their original stories but some favorite nursery rhymes or tales for

Directions for Ideas That Work

PAPIER-MACHE PUPPETS: Each student will wad up a double-sized sheet of newspaper into a ball about the size of a soft-ball. Use strips of masking tape to wrap around the wad of paper to keep the round shape. Insert, well up into the paper ball, a tube of tagboard that is five inches long and just big enough to fit around the neck of a large soda pop bottle. Tape the tube securely into place and then put the tube which is now supporting the paper ball onto the neck of an empty pop bottle.

At this point, be sure to add any special features that the puppet will need. You might cut pointed cat ears from newspaper and tape those on top of the ball or you might tape long floppy ears for a donkey onto the ball.

To do the next step, you can purchase a sack of wheat paste at any hardware store. Pour some wheat paste into an empty coffee can or a large plastic bucket containing several inches of water. Stir while pouring until the mixture is thick and smooth like pancake batter.

Tear up strips of paper towels or newspapers. Strips should be eight to ten inches long and an inch wide. Dip a strip of paper into the wheat paste mixture, wiping off the excess by pulling the strip between two fingers held over the can or bucket. Then place the strip of paper across the newspaper ball. Continue until the ball is covered with strips of paper. Be sure that papier-mache is used to make a smooth neck connecting the tube to the head. Leave the puppet heads on their pop bottles over-night to dry.

Illus. 2.4. Papier-mache puppets: Papier-mache is easy to work with. A ball of newspaper forms the puppet head. Strips of newspaper dipped in a wheat-paste mixture drape on easily and form smooth heads that dry fast. Tempera paint and bits of yarn complete the effect for Tigger and Eeyore.

The next day, each student can paint the puppet's face an appropriate color with tempera paint and can add features such as eyes and mouth. When the paint is dry, students can add yarn hair or whiskers, and can make a simple costume from felt and glue it to the neck tube.

other primary grade classes. Puppets can unleash an enormous amount of artistic and linguistic creativity.

Storytelling, including family histories and favorite tales, as well as opportunities to explore familiar tales and original stories through the use of flannel boards and puppets can all be successful language arts activities in the school, at home, and in other youth settings.

Resource books

A B C Puppets: Patterns for Cut-and-Paste Projects.
Marilynn G. Barr. Palo Alto, CA: Monday Morning Books, 1989. 64 pp. Contains patterns for simple puppets to be made by children ages three to six. [alphabet]

Artstarts: Drama, Music, Movement, Puppetry and Storytelling Activities.
Martha Brady. Englewood, CO: Teacher Ideas Press, 1994. 217 pp. ISBN 1-56308-148-2. Good resource for cross-disciplinary arts projects. For all elementary grades. [creative dramatics; movement; music; puppets]

Awakening the Hidden Storyteller: How to Build a Storytelling Tradition in Your Family.
Robin Moore. Boston, MA: Shambhala, 1991. 153 pp. ISBN 0-87773-599-9. Information on storytelling techniques with references. Suitable for all parents and teachers. [creative dramatics; storytelling]

Bedtime Stories.
Don Ferguson, Nikki Grimes, & Betty Birney. Greenwich, CT: Twin Books, 1991. 112 pp. ISBN 1-879991-04-7. Contains a good collection of bedtime stories. Appropriate for preschool through grade 3. [bedtime stories]

Best-Loved Stories Told at the National Storytelling Festival.
Jonesborough, TN: National Storytelling Press, distributed by August House Publishers, 1991. 223 pp. Contains 37 folk and fairy tales. Suitable for all elementary grades. [storytelling]

Beyond Words: Great Stories for Hand and Voice.
Valerie Marsh. Fort Atkinson, WI: Alleyside Press, 1995. 82 pp. ISBN 0-917846-49-4. A collection of twenty folktales and original tales with sign language diagrams. Suitable for all ages. [sign language; folklore]

Bible Crafts: Grades 1 & 2.
Sandra J. Stone, ed. San Diego, CA: Rainbow Books, 1992. 64 pp. ISBN 0-9372-82-27-8. Describes many different craft projects. [Bible crafts; puppets]

Bible Crafts: Grades 3 & 4.
Sandra J. Stone, ed. San Diego, CA: Rainbow Books, 1992. 64 pp. ISBN 0-937282-28-6. Describes many different craft projects including the making of puppets. [Bible crafts; puppets]

Bible Crafts: Grades 5 & 6.

Sandra J. Stone, ed. San Diego, CA: Rainbow Books, 1992. 64 pp. ISBN 0-937282-29-4. Gives directions for making puppets as well as other craft projects. [Bible crafts; puppets]

The Big Book of Things to Make and Play With: Toys, Games, Puppets.

Highlights for Children, eds. Honesdale, PA: Boyds Mills Press, 1995. 79 pp. ISBN 1-56397-473-8. Contains suggestions for many craft activities including the making of puppets. For all elementary grades. [games; puppets; toys]

Bookplay: 101 Creative Themes to Share With Young Children.

Margaret Read MacDonald. North Haven, CT: Library Professional Publications, 1995. 225 pp. In addition to themes, includes bibliographical references. Appropriate for preschool through grade 3. [themes]

Campfire Tales: Ghoulies, Ghosties, and Long-Leggety Beasties.

Merrillville, IN: ICS Books, 1989. 163 pp. ISBN 0-934802-50-5. Contains a collection of scary stories along with large print outlines to be read by firelight. [campfire stories; ghosts]

Caroline Feller Bauer's New Handbook for Storytellers: With Stories, Poems, Magic, and More.

Caroline Feller Bauer. Chicago: American Library Association, 1993. 550 pp. ISBN 0-8389-0613-3, ISBN 0-8389-0664-8 paper. A manual for all storytellers. [poetry; magic; storytelling]

Celebrate the World: Twenty Tellable Folktales for Multicultural Festivals.

Margaret Read MacDonald. Bronx, NY: H. W. Wilson, 1994. 225 pp. ISBN 0-8242-0862-5. Contains twenty stories and bibliographic references. For all elementary grades. [folklore; multicultural; storytelling]

Chalk in Hand: The Draw and Tell Book.

Phyllis Noe Pflomm. Metuchen, NJ: Scarecrow Press, 1985. ISBN 0-8108-1921-X. Shows how to tell stories while drawing at the chalkboard. For all elementary grades. [chalk talk stories; draw-and-tell stories]

Chalk Talk Stories.

Arden Druce. Metuchen, NJ: Scarecrow Press, 1993. 146 pp. ISBN 0-8108-2781-6. Explains how to use the blackboard as an aid to storytelling. For all elementary grades. [chalk talk stories]

Crazy Gibberish: And Other Story Hour Stretches from a Storyteller's Bag of Tricks.

Naomi Baltuck. Hamden, CT: Linnet Books, 1993. 152 pp. ISBN 0-208-02336-4, ISBN 0-208-02337-2 paper. Includes stories, games, music, and tongue twisters. For all elementary grades. [games; music; tongue twisters]

Creative Fun Crafts for Kids.

Jennie Mackenzie. Menlo Park, CA: Sunset Publications, 1993. 77 pp. ISBN 0-376-04296-6. Among other crafts, explains how to make puppets. Suitable for all elementary grades. [crafts; puppets]

Christian Crafts Paper Bag Puppets.

Susan J. Stegenga. Carthage, IL: Shining Star Publications, 1990. 64 pp. ISBN 0-86653-552-7. Contains Christian-oriented activities involving simple puppets for children aged four to ten. [crafts; Christian activities; puppets]

Draw Me a Story.

Barbara Freedman. Fayetteville, NC: Feathered Nest Productions, 1989. 56 pp. Contains a dozen stories to draw and tell for tiny tots. Suitable for preschoolers through grade 2. [draw-and-tell stories]

Earthmaker's Tales: North American Indian Stories About Earth Happenings.

Gretchen Mayo. New York: Walker & Co., 1989. 96 pp. ISBN 0-8027-6839-3. Contains black and white illustrations to go along with many North American Indian tales. For all elementary grades. [Indians of North America]

Every Child a Storyteller: Handbook of Ideas.

Harriet R. Kinghorn and Mary Helen Pelton. Englewood, CO: Teacher Ideas Press, 1991. 211 pp. ISBN 0-87287-868-6. Contains ideas for storytelling. Includes bibliographic references. Appropriate for all elementary grades. [storytelling]

An Exchange of Gifts: A Storyteller's Handbook.

Marion V. Ralston. Markham, Ont: Pippin Publishing, 1993. 88 pp. Helpful storytelling handbook. Appropriate for storytellers of all ages. [storytelling]

Family Storytelling Handbook: How to Use Stories, Anecdotes, Rhymes, Handkerchiefs, Paper, and Other Objects to Enrich Your Family Traditions.

Anne Pellowski. New York: Macmillan, 1987. 150 pp. ISBN 0-02-770610-9. Contains tips on storytelling. Suitable for storytellers of all ages. [parent resources; storytelling]

Fantastic Theater: Puppets and Plays for Young Performers and Young Audiences.

Judy Sierra. Bronx, NY: H. W. Wilson Co., 1991. 249 pp. ISBN 0-8242-0809-9. Includes 30 puppet plays and chapters on using rod and other types of puppets and puppet stages. For elementary students grade 3 and up. [plays; puppets]

Flannel Board Fun: A Collection of Stories, Songs and Poems.

Diane Briggs. Metuchen, NJ: Scarecrow Press, 1992. 143 pp. ISBN 0-8108-2616-X. Simple stories for flannel board presentation with bibliographic references. Suitable for preschool through grade 3. [flannel board stories]

The Flannel Board Storybook.
  Frances S. Taylor and Gloria G. Vaughn. Atlanta, GA: Humanities Ltd., 1986. 219 pp. ISBN 0-89334-206-8, ISBN 0-89334-093-6 paper. Contains flannelgraphs for storytelling. Appropriate for preschool through grade 3. [flannel board stories; storytelling]

Flannel Graphs: Flannel Board Fun for Little Ones.
  Jean Stangl. Belmont, CA: David S. Lake, Pub., 1986. ISBN 0-8224-3060-6. Good stories to use for preschool to grade 3. [flannel board stories]

Fold and Cut Stories.
  Jerry J. Mallett and Timothy Ervin. Hagerstown, MD: Alleyside Press, 1993. 56 pp. ISBN 0-913853-26-7. Introduces new storytelling techniques. For all elementary grades. [fold-and-cut stories]

Folding Paper Toys.
  Shari Lewis. Lanham, MD: Scarborough House, 1993. 84 pp. ISBN 0-8128-1953-5. Gives directions for making, flying, and sailing paper toys and for making puppets. For all elementary grades. [boats; airplanes; puppets]

Folding Stories: Storytelling and Origami Together As One.
  Christine Petrell Kallevig. Newburgh, IN: Storytime, Inc., 1991. 93 pp. ISBN 0-9628769-0-9. Contains stories to tell and instructions for doing origami with them. Suitable for elementary students grade 2 and up. [origami; storytelling]

From Wonder to Wisdom: Using Stories to Help Children Grow.
  Charles A. Smith. New York: New American Library, 1989. 304 pp. Contains a helpful bibliography. For all elementary grades. [storytelling]

The Ghost & I: Scary Stories for Participatory Telling.
  Jennifer Justice, ed. Cambridge, MA: Yellow Moon Press, 1993. 126 pp. ISBN 0-938756-37-0. A source of spooky tales. For elementary grades. [ghosts; storytelling]

Holiday Hoopla: Flannel Board Fun: Rhyming Flannel Board Stories With Learning Activities.
  Kathy Darling. Palo Alto, CA: Monday Morning Books, 1990. 64 pp. ISBN 1-8782279-14-9. Simple holiday stories to be told by using a flannel board. For preschool through grade 3. [flannel board stories; holidays]

I Can Make Puppets.
  Mary Wallace. Toronto: Greey de Pencier Books, 1994. 32 pp. ISBN 1-895689-24-8. ISBN 1-895688-20-5 paper. Explains simple puppet making. For all elementary grades. [puppets]

Imagination: At Play With Puppets and Creative Drama.
  Nancy Frazier and Nancy Renfro. Austin, TX: Nancy Renfro Studios, 1987. 96 pp. ISBN 0-931044-16-2. Contains good ideas for presenting simple plays. For all elementary grades. [creative dramatics; puppets]

Is Your Storytale Dragging?

Jean Stangl. Belmont, CA: Fearon Teacher Aids, 1989. 76 pp. ISBN 0-8224-3904-2. Contains creative activities for storytelling. For all elementary grades. [storytelling]

Jim Henson's "The Storyteller."

Anthony Minghella. New York: Knopf, 1991. 179 pp. Contains nine traditional European folk and fairy tales based on the Emmy-award-winning TV program. For all elementary grades. [folklore; fairy tales]

Juba This & Juba That.

Virginia Tashjian, ed. Boston, MA: Little, Brown, 1995. 106 pp. ISBN 0-316-83234-0. An anthology of rhymes and songs to sing and play as well as stories and riddles. Suitable for the elementary grades. [riddles; songs]

Jump Up and Say: A Collection of Black Storytelling.

Linda Goss and Clay Goss. New York: Simon & Schuster, 1995. 301 pp. ISBN 0-684-81090-5. ISBN 0-684-81001-8 paper. Stories and a bibliography of references. For all elementary grades. [African American–stories]

The Little Pigs' Puppet Book.

N. Cameron Watson. Boston, MA: Little, Brown, 1990. 32 pp. ISBN 0-316-92468-7. As three pigs decide to put on a show, they provide step-by-step directions about writing a script, putting up a stage, making scenery, etc. Suitable for preschool through grade 3. [creative dramatics; pigs; puppets]

Look Back and See: Twenty Lively Tales for Gentle Tellers.

Margaret Read MacDonald. Bronx, NY: H. W. Wilson, 1991. 178 pp. ISBN 0-8242-0810-2. Contains 20 stories for storytelling. Appropriate for the elementary grades. [storytelling]

Look What We've Brought You from Vietnam: Crafts, Games, Recipes, Stories, and Other Cultural Activities from New Americans.

Phyllis Shalant. New York: Julian Messner, 1988. 48 pp. ISBN 0-671-65978-2. ISBN 0-671-65978-2 paper. Filled with ideas for Vietnamese crafts. Suitable for students in grades 2–6. [cookery; crafts; gifts; Vietnam]

The Make Something Club: Fun With Crafts, Food, and Gifts.

Frances W. Zweifel. New York: Viking, 1994. 32 pp. Describes how to build such things as bird feeders, necklaces, and sock puppets. Suitable for grade 2 and up. [cookery; crafts, gifts; puppets]

Make Your Own Performing Puppets.

Teddy Cameron Long. New York: Sterling Publishing Co. Inc., 1995. 96 pp. ISBN 1-895569-32-X. Gives explanation for making a variety of simple puppets. Suitable for students in grades 4–7. [puppets]

Mississippi River Tales: From the American Storytelling Tradition.

Frank McSherry, Charles G. Waugh, and Martin H. Greenberg, eds. Little Rock, AR: August House, 1988. 203 pp. ISBN 0-87483-067-2. Contains stories from the Mississippi River area. Appropriate for elementary grades. [Mississippi River; storytelling]

Multicultural Folktales: Stories to Tell Young Children.

Judy Sierra and Robert Kaminski. Phoenix, AZ: Oryx, 1991. 126 pp. ISBN 0-89774-688-0. Contains folktales and a bibliography. For all elementary grades. [folklore; multicultural stories]

Musical Story Hours: Using Music With Storytelling and Puppetry.

William M. Painter. Hamden, CT: Library Professional Publications, 1989. 158 pp. ISBN 0-208-02205-8. Contains ideas for blending music and stories. For all elementary grades. [music; puppets; storytelling]

My Best Bedtime Book.

Ella Baker. New York: Gallery Books, 1988. 95 pp. Contains many fairy tales. Suitable for preschool through second grade. [bedtime stories; fairy tales]

Mystery-Fold: Stories to Tell, Draw, and Fold.

Valerie Marsh. Hagerstown, MD: Alleyside Press, 1993. 73 pp. ISBN 0-913853-31-3. Explains how to tell stories with dynamic drawings, and using paper folding to mask and reveal picture parts. Suitable for preschool to grade 5. [fold-and-tell stories]

Once Upon a Felt Board.

Roxane Chadwick. Carthage, IL: Good Apple, 1986. 124 pp. ISBN 0-86653-338-9. Ideas for storytelling using a felt board for children preschool through grade 4. [flannel board stories; storytelling]

1-2-3 Puppets: Simple Puppets to Make for Working With Young Children.

Jean Warren. Everett, WA: Warren Publishing, 1989. 77 pp. ISBN 0-911019-21-9. Tells how to make a variety of simple puppets. For preschool through grade 1. [puppets]

Ozark Ghost Stories.

Richard and Judy Dockrey Young, eds. Little Rock, AR: August House, 1995. 186 pp. ISBN 0-87483-410-4. Provides ghost stories and includes a bibliography. Suitable for grade 2 and up. [ghosts; Ozarks]

Paper-Cutting Stories for Holidays and Special Events.

Valerie Marsh. Fort Atkinson, WI: Alleyside Press, 1994. 63 pp. ISBN 0-91746-42-7. Contains creative activities to enhance stories. For preschool through grade 5. [fold-and-tell stories; holidays]

Papier-Mache.

Barry Caldecott. New York: Franklin Watts, 1992. 48 pp. Provides step-by-step instruction on how to use papier-mache to create a vase, hobby horse, and puppets. Includes bibliographic references. Suitable for all elementary grades. [papier-mache; puppets]

The Parent's Guide to Storytelling: How to Make Up New Stories and Retell Old Favorites.
    Margaret Read MacDonald. New York: HarperCollins, 1995. 118 pp. ISBN 0-06-446180-7. Helpful guide for adults with bibliographic references. [parent resources; storytelling]

Picture Book Storytelling: Literature Activities for Young Children.
    Janice J. Beaty. Fort Worth, KS: Harcourt Brace College Pub., 1994. 261 pp. ISBN 0-15-500486-7. Filled with suggestions for a variety of literature activities. Contains bibliographic references. For adults who work with elementary children. [picture books; storytelling]

A Piece of the Wind and Other Stories to Tell.
    Ruthilde Kronberg and Patricia A. McKissack. San Francisco: Harper & Row, 1990. 164 pp. Contains a collection of stories from around the world. Gives tips, including how to vary voice patterns and use body expression for storytelling. For teachers of all elementary grades. [storytelling]

Pint-Sized Puppets and Poems.
    Cara Bradshaw. Carthage, IL: Good Apple, 1994. 46 pp. ISBN 0-86653-785-6. Contains activities using puppets that will appeal to preschoolers through grade 2. [poetry; puppets]

Plays for Young Puppeteers: 25 Puppet Plays for Easy Performances.
    Lewis Mahlmann and David Cadwalader. Boston: Plays, Inc., 1993. 328 pp. ISBN 0-8238-0298-1. Contains a collection of plays with notes on costuming, special effects and presentation. Suitable for grade 2 and up. [creative dramatics; plays; puppets]

Puppet and Theater Activities: Theatrical Things to Do and Make.
    Beth Murray, ed. Honesdale, PA: Boyds Mills Press, 1995. 32 pp. ISBN 1-56397-333-2. Gives instructions for making puppets, scenery, masks and staging the recording of a radio show. Suitable for preschool through grade 2. [creative dramatics; puppets]

The Puppet Book: How to Make and Operate Puppets and Stage a Puppet Play.
    Clair Buchwald. Boston: Plays, Inc., 1990. 125 pp. ISBN 0-8238-0293-0. Gives six plays and tips about the stage, props, puppets, and sets. Appropriate for grade 2 and up. [plays; puppets]

Puppet Plays Plus: Hand Puppet Plays for Two Puppeteers.
    Phyllis Noe Pflomm. Metuchen, NJ: Scarecrow Press, 1994. 244 pp. ISBN 0-8108-2738-7. Contains two-character, simple plays and also has bibliographic references. For all elementary grades. [plays; puppets]

Puppets.

  Helen and Peter McNiven. New York: Thomson Learning, 1994. 32 pp. A simple introduction to puppet making. For all elementary grades. [puppets]

Puppets.

  Denny Robson and Vanessa Bailey. New York: Gloucester Press, 1991. 32 pp. Explains how to make puppets and how to operate them during a puppet show. For all elementary grades. [puppets]

Puppets.

  Lyndie Wright. New York: Franklin Watts. 1989. 48 pp. Discusses puppet making. Suitable for all elementary grades. [puppets]

Puppets and Masks.

  Nan Rump. Worcester, MA: Davis Publications, 1996. 184 pp. ISBN 0-87192-298-3. Describes how to make puppets and present puppet plays. Suitable for all elementary grades. [masks; puppets]

Puppets, Poems, & Songs.

  Julie Catherine Shelton. Carthage, IL: Fearon Teacher Aids, 1993. 288 pp. ISBN 0-8224-5152-2. Includes songs, poems and patterns for step-by-step assembly of puppets. Suitable for preschool through grade 3. [poetry; puppets; songs]

Ready-to-Tell Tales: Surefire Stories from America's Favorite Storytellers.

  David Holt and Bill Mooney, eds. Little Rock, AR: August House, 1994. 224 pp. ISBN 0-87483-380-9. Contains a multicultural collection of tales that are favorites of 40 different storytellers. Suitable for all elementary grades. [multicultural stories; storytelling]

Shadow Theater.

  Denny Robson and Vanessa Bailey. New York: Gloucester Press, 1991. 32 pp. Contains step-by-step instructions for presenting a hand shadow show. Appropriate for grade 2 and up. [shadow theater]

Showkits: Whole Language Activities: Patterns for Making Puppets, Costumes to Use With Picture Book Characters.

  Candy Jones and Lea McGee. Palo Alto, CA: Monday Morning Books, 1991. 64 pp. Gives lots of ideas for making and dressing puppets and includes bibliographic references. Suitable for all elementary grades. [picture books; puppets]

60 Art Projects for Children: Painting, Clay, Puppets, Prints, Masks, and More.

  Jeannette Mahan Baumgardner. New York: Clarkson Potter, 1993. 112 pp. Explains how to carry out a number of craft projects including the making of puppets. Includes a bibliographic reference. For all elementary grades. [clay projects, crafts; masks; painting; printmaking]

Story Hours With Puppets and Other Props.

William M. Painter. Hamden, CT: Library Professional Publications, 1990. 187 pp. ISBN 0-208-02284-8. Directions for telling stories using puppets. For all elementary grades. [puppets; storytelling]

Storytellers: Folktales and Legends from the South.

John A. Burrison, ed. Athens, GA: University of Georgia Press, 1989. 261 pp. ISBN 0-8203-1099-9. ISBN 0-8203-1267-3 paper. Contains materials for storytelling. For all elementary grades. [folklore–Southern U.S.; storytelling]

The Storyteller's Start-up Book: Finding, Learning, Performing, & Using Folktales Including Twelve Tellable Tales.

Margaret Read MacDonald. Little Rock, AR: August House, 1993. 215 pp. ISBN 0-87483-304-3. ISBN 0-87483-305-1 paper. Explains storytelling with folktales and includes bibliographic references. Suitable for the elementary grades. [folklore; storytelling]

Storytelling: Art and Technique.

August Baker and Ellin Greene. New York: Bowker, 1987. 182 pp. ISBN 0-8352-2336-1. Discusses the art of storytelling. Appropriate for the elementary grades. [storytelling]

The Storytelling Coach: How to Listen, Praise, and Bring Out People's Best.

Doug Lipman. Little Rock, AR: August House, 1995. 250 pp. ISBN 0-87483-435-X. ISBN 0-87483-434-1 paper. Provides tips on how to help others improve on their storytelling techniques. Suitable for adults. [storytelling]

Storytelling Folklore Source Book.

Norma J. Livo and Sandra A. Rietz. Englewood, CO: Libraries Unlimited, 1991. 384 pp. ISBN 0-87287-601-2. A source for storytellers. Includes an extensive bibliography. Appropriate for all elementary grades. [folklore; storytelling]

Storytelling for the Fun of It: A Handbook for Children.

Vivian Dubrovin. Masonville, CO: Storycraft Pub., 1994. 142 pp. ISBN 0-9638339-0-1. Useful handbook with bibliographic references. Appropriate for grades 4–7. [storytelling]

Storytelling for Young Adults: Techniques and Treasury.

Gail de Vos. Englewood, CO: Libraries Unlimited, 1991. 169 pp. ISBN 0-87287-832-5. Contains tips on storytelling effectively. Appropriate for adults and young adults. [storytelling]

Storytelling from the Bible: Make Scripture Live for All Ages Through the Art of Storytelling.

Janet Litherland. Colorado Springs, CO: Meriwether Pub., 1991. 181 pp. ISBN 0-916260-80-1. Contains many stories from the Bible. For all ages. [Bible stories; storytelling]

The Storytelling Handbook: A Young People's Collection of Unusual Tales and Helpful Hints On How to Tell Them.
>   Anne Pellowski. New York: Simon & Schuster Books for Young Readers, 1995. 122 pp. ISBN 0-689-80311-7. Contains pointers on effective story-telling and includes a bibliographic reference. Appropriate for elementary grades. [storytelling]

Storytelling Made Easy With Puppets.
>   Jan M. Van Schuyver. Phoenix, AZ: Oryx, 1995. 147 pp. ISBN 0-89774-732-1. Gives information on hand puppets and puppet plays. For all elementary grades. [puppets; storytelling]

Storytelling Step-by-Step.
>   Marshall Cassady. San Jose, CA: Resource Publications, 1990. 156 pp. ISBN 0-89390-183-0. Provides a guide to storytelling techniques. Suitable for the elementary grades. [storytelling]

Storytelling With Music, Puppets, and Arts for Libraries and Classrooms.
>   William M. Painter. North Haven, CT: Library Professional Publications, 1994. 164 pp. ISBN 0-208-02372-0. Ideas for teachers and librarians on using puppets. Includes a bibliographic reference. Appropriate for adults. [music; storytelling]

Storytelling With Puppets.
>   Connie Champlin and Nancy Renfro. Chicago: American Library Association, 1985. 293 pp. Tips on storytelling using puppets. Appropriate for the elementary grades. [puppets; storytelling]

Storytelling World: All About Pockets: Storytime Activities for Early Childhood.
>   Christine Petrell Kallevig. Broadview Heights, OH: Storytime Ink International, 1993. 127 pp. Contains two-minute stories, poems, games, riddles, and songs with patterns for use with storytelling aprons. Suitable for preschoolers and grades K and 1. [games; riddles; poetry; storytelling]

The Storytime Sourcebook: A Compendium of Ideas and Resources for Storytellers.
>   Carolyn N. Cullum. New York: Neal-Schuman, 1990. 177 pp. ISBN 1-55570-067-5. Contains ideas and resources for storytellers. Suitable for elementary grades. [storytelling]

Super Story Telling: Creative Ideas Using Finger Plays, Flannel Board Stories, Pocket Stories, and Puppets With Young Children.
>   Carol Elaine Catron and Barbara Catron Parks. Minneapolis, MN: T. S. Denison, 1986. 239 pp. ISBN 0-513-01793-3. Effective stories for use with preschool children. [finger plays; flannel board stories; puppets; storytelling]

Talk That Talk: An Anthology of African-American Storytelling.
>   Linda Goss and Marian E. Barnes, eds. New York: Simon & Schuster, 1989. 52 pp. ISBN 0-685-28304-6. A collection for Afro-American storytelling.

Contains a bibliography. Appropriate for elementary grades. [African American stories; storytelling]

Telling Stories to Children.

Marshall Shelley. Batavia, IL: Lion Pub. Co., 1990. 122 pp. ISBN 0-7459-1903-0. Tips on telling stories to children. Suitable for use with the elementary grades. [storytelling]

Telling Your Own Stories: For Family and Classroom Storytelling, Public Speaking and Personal Journaling.

Donald D. Davis. Little Rock, AR: August House, 1993. 127 pp. ISBN 0-87483-235-7. A manual to help develop storytelling skills. For adults to improve oral presentations. [parent resources; storytelling]

Terrific Paper Toys.

E. Richard Churchill. New York: Sterling Publishing Co. Inc., 1991. 128 pp. Shows how to make a variety of paper flowers, toys, and puppets. Suitable for use with all elementary grades. [crafts; puppets; toys]

A Treasury of Flannelboard Stories.

Jeanette Graham Bay. Fort Atkinson, WI: Alleyside Press, 1995. 191 pp. ISBN 0-917846-51-6. Good source of flannelboard stories and contains bibliographic references. For use with preschool and primary grade students. [flannel board stories]

Twenty Tellable Tales: Audience Participation Folktales for the Beginning Storyteller.

Margaret Read MacDonald. Bronx, NY: H. W. Wilson, 1986. 220 pp. ISBN 0-8242-0719-X. ISBN 0-8242-0822-6 paper. Contains twenty stories for storytelling. Suitable for use in the elementary grades. [folklore]

Twenty-two Splendid Tales to Tell from Around the World.

Pleasant DeSpain. Seattle, WA: Merrill Court Press, 1990. 1 vol. ISBN 0-87483-340-X. Contains tales for storytelling. Suitable for use in the elementary grades. [multicultural stories; storytelling]

Twice Upon a Time: Stories to Tell, Retell, Act Out, and Write About.

Judy Sierra and Robert Kaminski. Bronx, NY: H. W. Wilson, 1989. 232 pp. ISBN 0-8242-0775-0. Contains stories for telling, acting out, and as springboards to spark writing. Suitable for use in the elementary grades. [creative writing; storytelling]

Waiting-for-Christmas Stories.

Bethany Roberts. New York: Clarion, 1994. 32 pp. ISBN 0-395-67324-0. Includes seven bedtime stories for Christmas Eve. Suitable for preschool and primary-aged students. [Christmas]

The Way of the Storyteller.
> Ruth Sawyer. New York: Penguin, 1987. 356 pp. ISBN 0-14-004436-1. Originally published in 1962, this is a favorite source book for storytelling. Suitable for use in the elementary grades. [storytelling]

When the Lights Go Out: Twenty Scary Tales to Tell.
> Margaret Read MacDonald. Bronx, NY: H. W. Wilson, 1988. 176 pp. ISBN 0-8242-0770-X. ISBN 0-8242-0823-4 paper. Contains scary stories for adults to tell to kids. [ghosts]

Wonder Tales from Around the World.
> Heather Forest. Little Rock, AR: August House, 1995. 155 pp. ISBN 0-87483-427-9. Includes twenty-seven folktales from Europe, Asia, Africa, India, the Arctic and the Americas. Suitable for use in the elementary grades. [folklore]

Other resources

You might want to contact a local or state chapter of the National Storytelling Association. *The National Storytelling Directory* of the National Storytelling Association is published in Jonesborough, Tennessee.

Adventure Through African Storytelling.
> Dylan Pritchett. Community Video Center. Colorado Springs, CO: Pikes Peak Library, 1995. 1 videocassette, 60 minutes. Dylan Pritchett tells stories using music and movement. Suitable for elementary grades. [Africa–stories; movement; music]

Introduction to Puppet Making.
> Bogner Entertainment and Jim Gamble Puppet Productions. Bogner Entertainment, 1992. 1 videocassette, 30 minutes. Discusses finger, book, and rod puppets and introduces marionettes. Suitable for use in the elementary grades. [puppets]

Just Grandma and Me.
> Mercer Mayer. Fort Atkinson, WI: NASCO. Macintosh CD-ROM, SB 25501J. For use in a thematic unit on grandparents. Suitable for use in the elementary grades. [grandparents]

Making and Using Puppets in the Primary Grades.
> Susan Barthel and Bruce Chesse. Oregon Puppet Theatre. Portland, OR: Puppet Concepts Publications, 1992. 1 videocassette, 30 minutes. Teaches the use of puppets as instructional devices. Suitable for use in the elementary grades. [puppets]

Martha's Attic: Puppet Shows, Puppet Fun.
> Martha Lambert and James Bryce. S. I. Listening Library, Inc. 1986. 1 videocassette. 60 minutes. Martha Lambert teaches puppet making. Suitable for use in the elementary grades. [puppets]

More Preschool Power.

Bethesda, MD: Concept Association, 1991. 1 videocassette, 30 minutes. Teaches songs and a variety of activities such as learning to tie shoes and brush teeth. Also includes section on shadow puppets. Suitable for use in the elementary grades. [puppets]

My First Activity Video.

Sony Music Entertainment, Inc. Sony Kids Video, 1992. 1 videocassette, 50 minutes. Gives easy to follow instructions for making puppets, masks, and other crafts. Suitable for use in the elementary grades. [crafts; puppets]

My Shadow.

Robert Lewis Stevenson. Lincoln, NE: Great Plains National Instructional Television Library. 1 videocassette, 30 minutes. After presenting the poem, LeVar Burton talks about shadow puppets. Suitable for use in the elementary grades. [shadows; puppets]

Puppets, How They Happen.

Kate Amend, ed. Evanston, IL: FilmFair Communications, 1987. 1 videocassette, 18 minutes. A demonstration of how to make and use puppets that is appropriate for students through the primary grades. [puppets]

Storytelling for Young Children.

Kaminski Media Arts Prod. Ashland, OR, 1993. 1 videocassette, 35 minutes. Judy Sierra & Bob Kaminski use flannel board, puppets, and song in storytelling. Suitable for use in the primary grades. [flannel board stories; storytelling]

Traditions: A Potpourri of Tales.

Jackie Torrence. Cambridge, MA: Rounder Records, 1994. 1 sound cassette. Contains six tales; African, African-American, Euro-American, and Appalachian. Suitable for use in the elementary grades. [folklore]

The World Is a Storytellers Village.

Milbre Burch. Pasadena, CA: Kind Crone, 1994. 1 sound cassette, 81 min. Contains thirteen tales. Suitable for use in the elementary grades. [storytelling]

The Writing Adventure.

Blacklick, OH: SRA. 2 computer disks, User's Guide, and Reference Chart 16791, Apple II family. Has word processing possibilities for note taking, editing, and printing stories along with a proofing aid. Suitable for use in the upper elementary grades. [creative writing]

3

Arts and Crafts

*A*s a teacher, librarian, parent, or other adult who works with children, perhaps when you hear the words "arts and crafts," you shudder and maintain you can't do anything the least bit artistic. This is simply not true. While it's a fact that not everyone is a great painter, and not everyone can make a fabulous quilt or sketch a life-like galloping horse, it is a rare individual indeed who does not have some skill that will be useful in arts and crafts.

Can you trace your hand? Fold a piece of paper? Take a photo? Sew on a button? Glue something on a pine cone? Cut out an airplane wing? If so, there are crafts you can do! And if you can do them, you can teach others to do them too.

During such teaching/learning, students acquire and use many language arts skills. They learn to listen, to be able to sequence activities, to read directions, and to explain steps to others in their groups. By watching a crafts video, they increase their viewing skills and visual literacy. They may be involved in library research to learn more about the historical importance of a craft in another culture or to uncover periodi-

Directions for Ideas That Work

A CLOTHESPIN AIRPLANE: Take a wooden clothespin. Cut from light weight cardboard the wing for an airplane. Decorate the wing with your favorite designs or paint it a bright color.

Slide the decorated airplane wing into the clothespin and wedge it into place with a toothpick or bits of cardboard. Have fun seeing how far it will glide. Experiment with different lengths and widths of wing. Look at books of airplanes. Experiment with making paper airplanes. Describe how it feels to fly. Write a poem or story in which something (plane, leaf, butterfly) is sailing through the air. Read a biography about an early aviation pioneer.

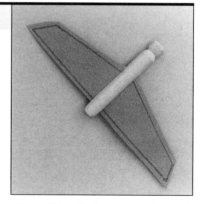

Illus. 3.1. Clothespin airplane: A clothespin holds a cardboard airplane wing. Other airplanes can be folded from plain or decorated paper. In this way, arts and crafts can be blended with science activities.

cals with helpful and informative articles. The crafts that follow are examples of easy-to-do projects that reap learning benefits for children.

For a teacher and students to enjoy some crafts together can take a minimum of materials and skill. Many books show step-by-step directions for making a greeting card using glue and colored paper. Making a special thank you card to send to someone who visited and shared in your classroom could be a great alternative to the usual thank you letter.

Although some of these products may be not as "creative" or as "original" as you'd like, following some directions from craft books will build up both confidence and expertise. In turn, these initial experiences may help teachers and students to sail out into brand new and completely original directions.

Directions for Ideas That Work

SHADOW PORTRAITS: Shadow portraits are both easy and fun to make. Tape a piece of white construction paper to the wall. Have the subject sit in a chair in front of the paper with one shoulder toward the paper.

Shine a bright light on the subject so that a sharp shadow of his or her silhouette falls on the paper. Turn off the other lights in the room. Trace the shadow onto the paper.

Then put a piece of black construction paper underneath the white sheet on which you've drawn the outline. Cut through both sheets of paper. You will now have a black silhouette which can be signed, dated, and framed. It makes a great gift for a child to give a special friend or relative!

Link the art project with science. Use a flashlight to make large shadows. How can you make the shadows smaller? Use different colored cellophane over three flashlights and produce red, blue, and green light. By shining all the colors from three flashlights onto one spot, can you produce white light? Link the art project with reading and writing. Read and write some shadow poems. Write an original short story in which a spooky shadow plays a significant role.

Illus. 3.2. Shadow portraits: Making shadow portraits is a simple activity. Signed, dated, mounted on a sheet or tagboard, a child's silhouette makes a valued gift.

Children often are quicker than adults to use one idea as a springboard for another. Encourage these far-ranging artistic explorations. Providing the time and materials and a place to work may be the adult's main contribution to truly creative arts and crafts projects.

And let's face it; arts and crafts can be messy. It's a good idea to have some boxes where basic supplies are kept. A sturdy cardboard box can hold such items as: scissors, rulers, needles and thread, stapler, gummed tape, paste, glue, tape measure, etc. Putting balls of yarn in another box with a lid, punching a number of holes in the lid, and threading the yarn out through the holes, makes a variety of colored yarns easily available without a tangle of knots. Yet another box may be home for ribbons, buttons, pine cones, nut cups, corks, walnut shells, etc.

Directions for Ideas That Work

FEELY BOOKS: Many primary grade students like to write picture books. Older elementary students may enjoy writing a picture book to take to a kindergarten or first grade classroom to share. Such books are short and most students will enjoy writing them. When you begin the project, encourage students to bring "valuable junk" from home to put in the arts and crafts box. This might include pieces of felt, yarn, sequins, buttons, foil, colored tissue paper, etc.

Once students have written their stories and been through a proof-reading and editing process, have students staple together sheets of white paper in sufficient quantity for the number of pages in their picture book. Nine-inch by twelve-inch white art paper is good for this purpose. Next, have each student print the words of the picture book onto the blank paper. (Study picture books first to show students that words sometimes appear at the top of a page, at the bottom of a page, or go clear across the page.) If children have the skills, they might want to use a computer word processing program to print the words to their story on their book pages.

Illus. 3.3. Feely Books: On the pages of a "feely book" there are many things for a young reader to touch. A king may wear a crown with a "jewel" glued on it. The picket fence may be make of toothpicks. Even the cover of the book has special items to touch. Sally's hair is made of yellow yarn, the cat's head is a cotton ball, and the dog is cut from brown felt.

Once the words of the picture book are printed, have children illustrate their books using markers or crayons or colored pencils.

Encourage them to include something "feely" on each page. This might mean pasting on a cotton ball cloud, gluing on a picket fence of toothpicks, using a sequin and some foil to make a king's crown, or pasting a yarn beard on a giant.

When the "feely books" are shared, young listeners or readers can be encouraged to touch and feel objects on each page.

Providing labels on these boxes builds reading and vocabulary skills in young children.

A box or drawer where large paper can be stored flat may also prove helpful. Packages of 12" x 18" colored construction paper, packages of crepe paper, and pieces of cardboard can be stored in the box. Tempera paints, brushes, and quantities of magic markers are also useful supplies to have on hand.

If having all of these supplies on hand sounds disheartening to you, don't despair! Many of the resources listed require items that can commonly be found around the house such as egg cartons, clothes pins, empty food containers, toothpicks, popcorn, etc. Other projects require things that can be found on a hike in the woods.

Directions for Ideas That Work

COIL POTS: Some teachers and students enjoy working with clay. Although many fine ceramics require baking in a kiln and special glazes, there are also simple clay crafts to make.

Students can make coil pots decorated with tempera paint and filled with dried wild flowers. Modeling clay can be used over and over to form and re-form zoo animals. There may be a potters' guild in your town or city where you could go on a field trip to see wheels and kilns. Perhaps a speaker from one of these groups is available to visit the classroom.

Making a coil pot is an easy clay activity. First, cut a round base of self-hardening clay to form the bottom of the pot. Place the base on a sheet of cardboard so that it will not stick to the table. Next, roll out a piece of clay into a long "snake." Coil this long strip around the base. (If the strip cracks or breaks, your clay is too dry and you need to add a little water.)

When one coil strip ends, push an opening, like a "mouth" into the coil end you've been using, and insert the tapered end of the new coil strip into the "mouth." Moisten the spot where the two pieces come together. Continue coiling until you reach the desired height.

You can make your pot go straight up, or curve in or out depending on how you place the coil strips.

Once the basic pot is made, you can leave the coils showing or smooth the sides until the coil strips blend together. If it is self-hardening clay, it is ready to be set aside to dry and then to be painted.

This would be a great time to share Byrd Baylor's beautiful book, *When Clay Sings*. The book describes the daily life and customs of prehistoric southwest Indian tribes traced from the designs and remains of their pottery.

Illus. 3.4. Coil pots: All pottery does not need to be fired and glazed. Everyone succeeds in making a simple coiled pot. Filled with dried weeds and flowers, the clay pot can make a beautiful decoration.

Directions for Ideas That Work

FALL MOBILE: Take a small group of children on a nature hike. Encourage each student to find seven small objects and put them carefully in their back packs to take home with them. These "finds" should be things whose removal will not greatly impact the environment. (Children should not dig things up or break branches from trees.) A beautiful colored leaf, a small twig covered in bark or with an interesting shape, a seed pod, a little rock that sparkles, or a leaf with interesting veins or toothed edges are all examples of "treasures."

After the hike, have the children tie each of their treasures to a piece of black carpet thread and tie the thread to the bottom arm of a black coat hanger. Then have them hang the coat hanger from its hook and move the objects along the arm so that the coat hanger stays in balance. The finished work can be taken home and hung as a Fall Mobile.

As a result of their walk, encourage students to write observations in their journals, make sketches of interesting things they saw, write a fall poem, or write a story about a bird, ant, squirrel, or other animal that they saw.

Remember that arts and crafts can be as simple or as complicated as you want, and they provide wonderful tie-ins to the language arts. Shoe boxes and straws provide raw materials that are easy to work with, but that can still produce delightful results.

You, or one of your students, may be especially interested in photography, film strip making, or video recording. Some "other resources" are

Directions for Ideas That Work

CIRCUS TRAIN: Make a circus train using shoe boxes, straws and stuffed animals. Cut a "window" in the lid of a shoe box, cutting an inch from the edge on all sides. Turn the shoe box on its side, and put the small stuffed animals (or paper cut-outs) into the shoe box.

Then use striped plastic straws to make "bars" for the cage. Cut the straws so that they are one-inch taller than the shoe box. Flatten the ends of the straws and tape them at the top and bottom at two-inch intervals in front of the stuffed animals or the paper cut-outs.

Put the lid back on the box and tape it in place. Make several, and you'll have a circus train! Pin them onto a bulletin board. Add clowns or a ring master. Now you're ready to write poems and stories about when the circus comes to town!

Illus. 3.5. Circus train: This circus train makes a colorful and exciting bulletin board. Stories, poems, and articles which the students write about various wild animals can be displayed along with the train.

listed at the end of the chapter that may be helpful in expanding on these artistic hobbies.

Today we also find a lot of "wearable art." You may want your students to use pens with washable inks to decorate a skirt or shirt or to experiment with knots and dyes to create a fabulous t-shirt. These can contain slogans and messages that the students create.

Other chapters in this book contain information for exploring arts and crafts. The chapter on Storytelling and Puppets contains a listing of books that describe how to make a variety of puppets from papier-mache, peanuts and Styrofoam and various puppet stages and costumes.

The chapter on Creative Dramatics includes information about creating simple props, scenery, special make-up, and costumes. And many of the books listed in the chapter on Holidays Around the World contain craft suggestions.

Resource books

Adventures in Art: Art and Craft Experiences for 7-11-year-olds.

Susan Milord. Charlotte: VT: Williamson Publishing Co., 1990. 158 pp. ISBN 0-913589-54-3. Contains historical information and one hundred activities involving printmaking, wearable art, portraiture, and sculpture. [history; wearable art]

American Pueblo Indian Activity Book.

Walter D. Yoder. Santa Fe, NM: Sunstone Press, 1994. 48 pp. ISBN 0-86534-219-9. Contains 40 Indian craft activities. Suitable for grade 3 and up. [Indians of North America]

Ancient Egyptians.

Fiona Macdonald. Hauppauge, NY: Barron's, 1993. 57 pp. ISBN 0-8120-6378-3. Gives information about Egyptian civilization including their arts and crafts. Suitable for use in the elementary grades. [Egypt]

Artists and Artisans.

Irene M. Frank. New York: Facts On File, 1987. 213 pp. Explores the occupations related to painting, sculpting, glassblowing, and pottery-making in history. Suitable for students in grade 3 and up. [artists]

The Art of Embroidery.

Julia Barton. London: Merehurst Press, 1989. 144 pp. ISBN 1-85391-016-3. Tips and discussion on embroidery. Appropriate for students in grade 3 and up. [embroidery]

Balloon Sculpting: A Fun and Easy Guide to Making Balloon Animals, Toys & Games.

Bruce Fife. Colorado Springs, CO: Picadilly, 1994. 95 pp. ISBN 0-941599-25-6. Contains easy-to-follow directions for making toys, etc. from balloons. Suitable for use in all elementary grades. [animals; balloons; games]

Batik and Tie-Dye.

Susie O'Reilly. New York: Thomson Learning, 1993. 32 pp. Gives simple techniques and instructions for a variety of projects. Appropriate for students in grade 3 and up. [batik; tie-dye]

Bats, Butterflies, and Bugs.

St. Clair Adams Sullivan. Boston, MA: Little, Brown, 1990. 79 pp. Includes instructions for making toys that look like bats, butterflies and bugs. Appropriate for elementary students in grade 2 and up. [bats; insects; toys]

Block Printing.

Susie O'Reilly. New York: Thomson Learning, 1993. 32 pp. Explains relief printing techniques. For use in all elementary grades. [printmaking]

Cards.

Clare Beaton. New York: Warwick Press, 1990. 24 pp. Gives step-by-step instructions for making a variety of greeting cards. For use in all elementary grades. [greeting cards]

Cartooning.

Anthony Hodge. New York: Gloucester Press, 1992. 32 pp. Introduces step-by-step through simple projects a range of cartooning techniques. Suitable for use with upper elementary students. [cartoons]

Chalk Talks: The Magical Art of Drawing With Chalk.

Osmond McGill. Brookfield, CT: Millbrook Press, 1995. 80 pp. ISBN 1-56294-669-2. Explains how to present chalk drawings on boards or felt-tipped drawings on easels. For students in grades 3–6. [chalk talk stories]

Child's Play: 200 Instant Crafts and Activities for Preschoolers.

Leslie Hamilton. New York: Crown, 1989. 206 pp. ISBN 0-517-57171-4. Contains a collection of crafts, games, and activities. Suitable for all elementary grades. [games]

Clay.

Jeannie Hull. New York: Franklin Watts, 1989. 48 pp. Gives step-by-step instructions, shown through photographs, of how to prepare clay and make pots. Suitable for use in all elementary grades. [clay projects]

Clayworks: Colorful Crafts Around the World.

Virginia Fowler. New York: Prentice-Hall Books for Young Readers, 1987. 150 pp. Gives instructions on making clay objects from cultures both ancient and modern. For use in all elementary grades. [clay projects]

Collage.

Anthony Hodge. New York: Gloucester Press, 1991. 32 pp. Explains simple projects involving a variety of collage techniques. Suitable for use in all elementary grades. [collage]

Collage.

Sue Stocks. New York: Thomson Learning, 1994. 32 pp. A first introduction to collage. Suitable for use in all elementary grades. [collage]

A Collage of Crafts.

Charlie Guerrier. New York: Ticknor & Fields, 1994. 56 pp. ISBN 0-395-68377-7. Shows how to make crafts using leaves, shells, newspapers, and cardboard. Suitable for use in all elementary grades. [collage]

The Color Purple and All That Jazz!

Carole Marsh. Historic Bath, NC: Gallopade Publishing, 1989. 31 pp. ISBN 1-55609-315-2. ISBN 1-55609-314-4 paper. Describes the contributions of Afro-Americans to the arts. Suitable for use in all elementary grades. [African Americans]

Craft Painting Fun.

Carolyn Davis. Tustin, CA: Walter Foster Publishing, 1991. 63 pp. ISBN 1-56010-071-0. Describes painting craft objects. Suitable for use in the elementary grades. [painting]

Crafts for Decoration.

Caroline Bingham and Karen Foster, eds. Brookfield, CT: Millbrook Press, 1993. 48 pp. ISBN 1-56294-098-X. Explains many activities including designing a necklace, decorating a letter, stenciling, tie-dying, etc. For use with students in grades 2–6. [stenciling; tie-dye]

Crafts for Everyday Life.

Caroline Bingham and Karen Foster, eds. Brookfield, CT: Millbrook Press, 1993. 48 pp. ISBN 1-56294-097-X. Describes such crafts as candle-making, quilting, woodworking, and calligraphy in an historical context. For use with upper elementary students. [calligraphy; candle-making; quilting; woodworking]

Crafts for Play.

Caroline Bingham and Karen Foster, eds. Brookfield, CT: Millbrook Press, 1993. 48 pp. ISBN 1-56294-096-1. Describes toys, games and dolls from other cultures and gives instructions for making some of these. For use in grades 2–6. [games; toys; multicultural crafts]

Creating Milk Carton Crafts.

Nancy Giles. Carthage, IL: Good Apple, 1991. 64 pp. Gives step-by-step instructions and has many holiday ideas. For use in the elementary grades. [holidays; milk cartons]

Creative Egg Carton Crafts.

Nancy McClure and Janis Rhodes. Carthage, IL: Good Apple, 1991. 64 pp. ISBN 0-86653-471-7. Describes how to turn egg cartons into dinosaurs and caterpillars. Appropriate for use in preschool through grade 2. [caterpillars; dinosaurs; egg cartons]

Creative Food Box Crafts.

Nancy Giles. Carthage, IL: Good Apple, 1991. 64 pp. ISBN 0-86653-475-X. Contains ideas for making simple gifts and musical instruments. For use in preschool through grade 3. [gifts; musical instruments]

Design.

Catherine McDermott. Austin, TX: Steck-Vaughn, 1991. 48 pp. Explores the history of design from the Industrial Revolution to the present. Suitable for upper elementary students. [design]

Doing the Days: A Year's Worth of Creative Journaling, Drawing, Listening, Reading, Thinking, Arts & Crafts Activities for Children Ages 8-12.

Lorraine M. Dahlstrom. Minneapolis, MN: Free Spirit Publications, 1993. 231 pp. ISBN 0-915793-62-8. Many activities using the language experience approach. [creative writing]

Draw, Design and Paint: Projects Designed to Foster Individual Expression in the Visual Arts.

Jan Barry. Carthage, IL: Good Apple, 1990. 140 pp. ISBN 0-86653-536-5. An activity book filled with art projects. Suitable for use in grades 2–6. [drawing]

Draw 50 Trees, Flowers, and Other Plants.

Lee J. Ames. New York: Doubleday, 1994. 60 pp. ISBN 0-385-47004-5. ISBN 0-385-47150-5 paper. Step-by-step instructions for drawing plants and trees. Suitable for use in the elementary school. [drawing; plants]

Drawing.

Anthony Hodge. New York: Gloucester Press, 1991. 31 pp. Gives a variety of opportunities for projects on line, light, and shadow, and personal expression. Appropriate for elementary students. [drawing]

Drawing.

Sue Stocks. New York: Thomson Learning, 1994. 32 pp. Explains various drawing techniques. Suitable for elementary students in grade 3 and up. [drawing]

Drawing Life in Motion.

Jim Aronsky. New York: Lothrop, Lee & Shepard, 1984. 46 pp. ISBN 0-688-03803-4. ISBN 0-688-07076-0 paper. Shows how to give the effect of motion to your drawings. Suitable for upper elementary students. [drawing]

Drawing Prehistoric Animals.

Jerome Goyallon. New York: Sterling Publishing Co. Inc., 1995. 80 pp. ISBN 0-8069-0931-5. ISBN 0-8069-0979-X paper. Shows how prehistoric animals and fossils are drawn. Appropriate for grades 3–7. [drawing; animals]

Eco-Arts and Crafts.

Stuart A. Kallen. Edina, MN: Abdo & Daughters, 1993. 46 pp. ISBN 1-56239-208-5. ISBN 1-56239-421-5 paper. Gives instructions for craft projects using recycled materials and things found around the house. Appropriate for students in grades 3–4. [recycled materials]

Endangered Animals.

Beverly Armstrong. Santa Barbara, CA: The Learning Works, 1994. 32 pp. ISBN 0-88160-228-0. Creative art activities in drawing animals for all ages, grades 1–6. [endangered species]

50 Nifty Origami Crafts.

Andrea Urton. Los Angeles, CA: Lowell House, 1992. 80 pp. ISBN 1-56565-011-5. Describes eight basic origami forms and gives step-by-step directions for making 50 figures. Appropriate for elementary students grade 3 and up. [origami]

Free and Inexpensive Arts & Crafts to Make and Use.

Nancee McClure. Carthage, IL: Good Apple, 1987. 112 pp. ISBN 0-86653-387-7. Contains at least ten craft ideas for each month of the year. Suitable for students in grades 2–6. [seasons]

Good Earth Art: Environmental Art for Kids.

Mary Ann F. Kohl. Bellingham, WA: Bright Ring, 1991. 223 pp. Describes over two hundred projects involving painting, drawing, mobiles, sculpture, collage, printing & weaving. Appropriate for all elementary grades. [collage; ecology projects; mobiles; printmaking; weaving]

Handicrafts.

Rosie Wermert. New York: Random House, 1989. 32 pp. Contains twenty fun and easy projects you can make by simply tracing your hand. Suitable for all elementary grades. [hands]

Hand-Shaped Gifts: Handmade Gifts from Little Fingers.

Diane Bonica. Carthage, IL: Good Apple, 1991. 138 pp. ISBN 0-86653-612-4. This is a craft book for PK–4th graders using hands as the basis for crafts. [hands]

Holiday Patterns.

Jean Warren. Everett, WA: Warren Publishing, 1991. 237 pp. ISBN 0-911019-45-6. This is a guide to a variety of handicrafts including paper work and decorations. For all elementary grades. [holidays]

How to Draw Cartoon Animals.

Christopher Hart. New York: Watson-Guptill, 1995. 144 pp. ISBN 0-8230-2360-5. An instructional guide to cartooning. For use in upper elementary grades. [animals; cartoons]

How to Draw Indian Arts and Crafts.

John Meiczinger. Mahwah, NJ: Watermill Press, 1989. 32 pp. ISBN 0-8167-1537-8. ISBN 0-8167-1515-7 paper. Contains instructions on how to make a tepee, baskets, feather headdress, and pottery. For use in grades 2–6. [Indians of North America]

How to Make Your Own Video.

Perry Schwartz. Minneapolis, MN: Lerner, 1991. 72 pp. ISBN 0-8225-9588-5. Tells how to use a camcorder and make home videos. For use in upper elementary grades. [video production]

The Incredible Clay Book.

Sherri Haab and Laura Torres. Palo Alto, CA: Klutz Press, 1994. 80 pp. ISBN 1-878257-73-0. Tells how to make and bake many clay creations. For use in all elementary grades. [clay projects]

Incredibly Awesome Crafts for Kids.

Sara Jane Treinen, ed. Des Moines, IA: Better Homes & Gardens Books, 1992. 168 pp. ISBN 0-696-01924-8. ISBN 0-696-01984-1 paper. Includes a variety of creative crafts including toys and decorations. For use in all elementary grades. [toys]

Kids Create: Arts and Crafts Experiences for 3–9-year-olds.

Laurie Carlson. Charlotte, VT: Williamson Publishing Co., 1990. 158 pp. ISBN 0-913589-51-9. Contains easy-to-follow instructions for 150 different craft activities. For use in the primary grades.

Kidvid: Fun-damentals of Video Instruction.

Kaye Black. Tucson, AZ: Zepher Press, 1989. 96 pp. ISBN 0-913705-44-6. Shows and explains to children in nine lessons the basics of video production. For use with students in grades 4–12. [video production]

The Little Hands Art Book.

Judy Press. Charlotte, VT: Williamson Publishing Co., 1994. 156 pp. ISBN 0-913589-86-1. Explores various arts and crafts designed to be done with children ages two to six. [games]

Make Crafts!

Kim Solga. Cincinnati, OH: North Light Books, 1993. 48 pp. ISBN 0-89134-493-4. Explains projects such as basketry, weaving, and leather tooling. For preschoolers. [basketry; leather; weaving]

Make Sculptures!

Kim Solga. Danbury, CT: Grolier Educational Corp., 1993. 48 pp. ISBN 0-89134-420-9. Describes projects for ages six to eleven using clay, papier-mache, and household items. [clay projects; papier-mache; sculpture]

Make Your Own Animated Movies and Videotapes: Film And Video Techniques from the Yellow Ball Workshop.

Yvonne Anderson. Boston, MA; Little, Brown, 1991. 176 pp. ISBN 0-316-03941-1. Contains instructions for making animated movies, operating a camera, and synchronizing sound. For use with grade 6 and older. [motion picture production; video production]

Make Your Own Performing Puppets.

Teddy Cameron Long. New York: Sterling Publishing Co. Inc., 1995. 96 pp. ISBN 1-895569-32-X. Many ideas for puppet making. Suitable for use in upper elementary grades. [puppets]

Making Masks.

Helen and Peter McNiven. New York: Thomson Learning, 1995. 32 pp. Directions for making simple masks. Suitable for students in grade 2 and up. [masks]

Making Models.

Diana Craig. Brookfield, CT: Millbrook Press, 1993. 92 pp. ISBN 1-56294-204-2. Explains various techniques for projects in making jewelry, piggy banks, and edible pastry faces. For use in grades 3–6. [edible art; jewelry]

Making Presents.

Juliet Bawden. New York: Random House, 1994. 46 pp. ISBN 0-679-93-495-2. ISBN 0-679-83495-8 paper. Explains how to make such presents as clay buttons, picture frames, magnets, and clay pots. For use in grades 1–5. [clay projects; gifts]

Making Toys and Gifts.

Stefan Lemke. Chicago: Children's Press, 1991. 64 pp. ISBN 0-516-49259-4. Gives instructions for many projects for kids who are age eight or older. [gifts]

Marine Life.

Beverly Armstrong. Santa Barbara, CA: The Learning Works, 1994. 32 pp. ISBN 0-88160-227-2. Creative drawing fun with marine fauna for all ages. [drawing; marine life]

Market Guide for Young Artists and Photographers.

Kathy Henderson. White Hall, VA: Shoe Tree Press, 1990. 191 pp. ISBN 1-55870-176-1. Contains one hundred listings of markets and contests for kids eighteen and under. For use in grade 2 and up. [contests]

Masks.

Clare Beaton. New York: Warwick Press, 1990. 24 pp. ISBN 1-887238-02-6. Gives instructions on how to make masks. For use with grade 2 and up. [masks]

Meet Matisse.

Nelly Munthe. Boston, MA: Little, Brown, 1983 45 pp. Provides an introduction to cut-outs with instructions for several different techniques. For use with upper elementary students. [Matisse]

Modeling.

Susie O'Reilly. New York: Thomson Learning, 1993. 32 pp. Explains sculpture techniques. For use with students in grade 2 and up. [sculpture]

The Modeling Book.

Annie Owen. New York: Simon & Schuster Books for Young Readers, 1991. 30 pp. Explains how to make a variety of things from different kinds of clay. For use in all elementary grades. [clay projects]

Models.

Helen McNiven. New York: Thomson Learning, 1994. 32 pp. Describes model making. For use with upper elementary students. [models]

Month-by-Month Arts & Crafts: December, January, February.

Marcia Schonzeit, ed. New York: Scholastic Professional Books, 1991. 72 pp. ISBN 0-590-56093-X. Provides ideas for seasonal handicrafts for grades 1–6. [months]

Month-by-Month Arts & Crafts: March, April, May.

Marcia Schonzeit, ed. New York: Scholastic Professional Books, 1991. 72 pp. ISBN 0-590-56093-X. Provides ideas for seasonal handicrafts for grades 1–6. [months]

Month-by-Month Arts & Crafts: September, October, November.

Marcia Schonzeit, ed. New York: Scholastic Professional Books, 1991. 72 pp. ISBN 0-590-56093-X. Provides ideas for seasonal handicrafts for grades 1–6. [months]

More Than Sixty Projects for Kids.

Pat Roberts. Scotts Valley, CA: Mark Publishing, 1991. 72 pp. This is a guide for parents/teachers to assist kids in making 60 projects. Suitable for use in the elementary school. [holidays]

My First Camera Book.

Anne Kostick. New York: Workman Pub., 1989. 51 pp. ISBN 0-89480-381-6. Gives tips for taking pictures, making postcards, etc. through a story of how Teddy Bear Bialosky shares. For use in the primary grades. [photography; postcards]

Needlecraft.

Susie O'Reilly. New York: Thomson Learning, 1994. 32 pp. Explains how to do embroidery and quilting. For use with upper elementary students. [needlework]

Painting.

Anthony Hodge. New York: Gloucester Press, 1991. 32 pp. Describes painting techniques and explores portraiture, still life, landscapes, and surrealism. For use with upper elementary students. [painting]

Painting and Sculpture.

Jillian Powell. Austin, TX: Steck-Vaughn, 1990. 48 pp. Describes, with examples, the history of painting and sculpture from cave paintings to present. Includes Oriental, Islamic, African, American, and European examples. For use with upper elementary students. [painting; sculpture]

Paper.

Erica Burt. Vero Beach, FL: Rourke Enterprises, 1990. 32 pp. ISBN 0-86592-488-0. Gives instructions for projects using paper or cardboard and folding, curling, cutting, or tearing. For use grades 2–6. [paper projects]

Paper Craft.

Denny Robson. New York: Gloucester Press, 1993. 32 pp. ISBN 0-531-17428-X. Provides step-by-step directions for making pop-up cards, book jackets, and origami flowers. For use in upper elementary grades. [origami; paper projects]

Papercrafts: Origami, Papier-Mache, and Collage.

Judith Hoffman Corwin. New York: Franklin Watts, 1988. 72 pp. Provides instructions for many paper projects. For use in all elementary grades. [collage; origami; papier-mache]

Paper Kaleidoscopes.

Kay Leonard. Joplin, MO: Pelona Press, 1989. 40 pp. ISBN 0-685-26430-0. Gives directions for making paper kaleidoscopes. For use in the upper elementary grades. [kaleidoscopes]

Papermaking.

Susie O'Reilly. New York: Thomson Learning, 1993. 32 pp. Surveys the history of uses of paper and describes how to make paper pulp and various paper art projects. For use in upper elementary grades. [papermaking]

Paper Sculpture.

John Lancaster. New York: Franklin Watts, 1989. 48 pp. ISBN 0-531-10758-2. Provides step-by-step directions for projects involving tearing, folding, and weaving paper. For use in grades 3–6. [paper projects; sculpture]

Papier-Mache.

Miranda Innes. New York: Dorling Kindersley, 1995. 96 pp. ISBN 0-7894-0335-8. Explains many craft projects using papier-mache. For use in all elementary grades. [papier-mache]

Papier-Mache.

Deri Robbins. New York: Kingfisher Books, 1993. 40 pp. ISBN 1-85697-692-0. Gives step-by-step instructions on how to make such things as bowls, masks, and animals from papier-mache. Suitable for use in grade 3 and up. [papier-mache]

Patriotic Fun.

Judith Hoffman Corwin. New York: Julian Messner, 1985. 64 pp. ISBN 0-671-50799-0. Describes customs and suggests crafts for eight patriotic holidays including Flag Day. For use in grade 3 and up. [holidays; patriotism]

Photography.

David Cumming. Austin, TX: Steck-Vaughn Library, 1989. 48 pp. Gives an overview of British and American photography as art and discusses photography as a career. For use in the upper elementary grades. [photography]

Photography.

Duncan Fraser. New York: Bookwright, 1987. 32 pp. Tells how cameras were invented, their history, and how to choose a camera. For use with upper elementary students. [photography]

Photography: Take Your Best Shot.

Terri Morgan and Samuel Thaker. Minneapolis, MN: Lerner, 1991. 72 pp. ISBN 0-8225-2302-7. Gives practical techniques for photography and discusses dark-room skills. For use with students in grade 5 and up. [photography]

Pint-Sized Puppets and Poems.

Cara Bradshaw. Carthage, IL: Good Apple, 1994. 46 pp. ISBN 0-86653-785-6. An activity book for children preschool through grade 2. [poetry; puppets]

Playing With Plasticine.

Barbara Reid. New York: Morrow Junior Books, 1988. 95 pp. ISBN 0-688-08415-X. ISBN 0-688-08414-1 paper. Explains how to turn plasticine into flat pictures and three-dimensional objects. For use in all elementary grades. [plasticine crafts]

Printing.

Sue Stocks. New York: Thomson Learning, 1994. 32 pp. Discusses printing techniques and stencil work. For use in all elementary grades. [printmaking]

Projects for Autumn and Holiday Activities.

Joan Jones. Ada, OK: Garrett Educational Corp., 1989. 31 pp. Contains autumn arts and crafts projects. For use in all elementary grades. [autumn; holidays]

Puppets.
   Helen and Peter McNiven. New York: Thomson Learning, 1994. 32 pp. A
   simple introduction to puppetry. For use in all elementary grades.
   [puppets]

Quilting by Machine.
   Cy DeCose, ed. Minneapolis, MN: Cy DeCose, Inc., 1990. 128 pp. ISBN 0-
   86573-253-1. ISBN 0-86573-254-X paper. Tells how to use a machine to
   quilt. For use in all elementary grades. [quilting]

Recyclables Fun: Creative Craft Ideas.
   Diane Cherkerzian. Honesdale, PA: Boyds Mills Press, 1995. 48 pp. ISBN 1-
   56397-275-1. Explains how to make many crafts using scraps and cartons.
   For use in preschool through grade 2. [recycled materials]

Rediscovering Papier-Mache.
   Susanne Haines. New York: Holt, 1993. 96 pp. ISBN 0-8050-2618-5. A book
   on contemporary crafts. For use in all elementary grades. [papier-mache]

Sewing Kid's Stuff: Fun Things for Kids to Wear and Share.
   Cindy Kacynski, ed. Peoria, IL: PJS Publications, 1991. 175 pp. ISBN 0-
   9621148-3-9. Filled with information on sewing. For use with upper
   elementary students. [sewing]

Sketching Outdoors in Autumn.
   Jim Aronsky. New York: Lothrop, Lee & Shepard, 1988. 48 pp. ISBN 0-688-
   06288-1. Contains ideas for outdoor fall sketching. For use with students in
   grade 5 and up. [drawing; seasons]

Stencils and Screens.
   Susie O'Reilly. New York: Thomson Learning, 1993. 32 pp. Explains the
   process of using screens for printing and stencil work. For use with students
   in grade 2 and up. [printmaking; stenciling]

Television and Video.
   Ian Graham. New York: Gloucester Press, 1991. 32 pp. Tells how TV and
   various pieces of video equipment work. For use with upper elementary
   students. [television production; video production]

Terrific Paper Toys.
   Elmer Richard Churchill. New York: Sterling Publishing Co. Inc., 1991.
   128 pp. Tells how to make items from paper such as toys, hats, puppets, and
   flowers. For use in all elementary grades. [puppets; toys]

Things to Do.
   Editors of Time-Life Books. Alexandria, VA: Time-Life Books, 1989. 87 pp.
   ISBN 0-8094-4898-X. Filled with projects to make such things as seashell
   mobiles, paper airplanes, and peanut puppets done in a question/answer
   format. For use in grades 1–4. [airplanes; puppets]

Time Out Together: A Month-by-month Guide to Activities to Enjoy With Your Children.

Jan Brennan. Little Rock, AR: August House, 1990. 173 pp. ISBN 0-87483-103-2. Contains creative activities and ideas for adults who work with elementary children. [months; parent resources]

Toys and Games.

Helen and Peter McNiven. New York: Thomson Learning, 1995. 32 pp. ISBN 1-56847-213-7. Discusses paper toy making and provides bibliographical references. For use in the elementary grades. [games; toys]

Toys Made Out of Clay.

Hannelore Schal. Chicago: Children's Press, 1990. 64 pp. Describes a variety of projects and games that can be made from clay. For use in the elementary grades. [clay projects; toys]

Treasured Time With Your Toddler: A Monthly Guide to Activities.

Jan Brennan. Little Rock, AR: August House, 1991. 189 pp. ISBN 0-87483-127-X. Contains a variety of creative activities for use with preschoolers. [months; parent resources]

You Can Make It! You Can Do It! 101 E-Z Holiday Craft-tivities for Children.

Ann Peaslee and Julien Kille. Union City, CA: Heian International, 1990. 128 pp. ISBN 0-89346-337-X. Explains how to make a variety of holiday decorations, crafts, and includes creative activities. For use in grades 3–6. [holidays]

VCRs.

Carolyn E. Cooper. New York: Franklin Watts, 1987. 96 pp. Explains how to use videotape and VCRs with instructions for audio dubbing. For upper elementary students. [video production]

Weaving.

Susie O'Reilly. New York: Thomson Learning, 1993. 32 pp. Describes hand weaving and gives directions for projects in paper, tapestry, and ikat weaving. For students grade 3 and up. [weaving]

Weepeople: A Unique Adventure in Crafts and Americans.

Ed and Stevie Baldwin. New York: Putnam, 1983. 160 pp. Describes doll making and soft sculpture. For use with upper elementary students. [doll making; soft sculpture]

Wood.

Graham Carrick. Vero Beach, FL: Rourke Enterprises, 1990. 32 pp. ISBN 0-86592-484-8. Explains a variety of projects made by constructing or carving wood. For use with students in grades 2–6. [woodworking]

Other resources

These magazines might prove useful to consult for craft ideas: *Crafts 'n Things, American Craft, Ceramics Monthly, Art News,* and *School Arts.*

Art Lessons for Children. Vol. 6. Plants of the Rain Forest.

Donna Hugh, Instructor. Fallbrook, CA: Coyote Creek Productions, 1994. 1 videocassette, 48 minutes. Uses water colors, white tempera paint, black crayon and paper to demonstrate techniques for drawing plants. For use with upper elementary students. [rain forests; drawing]

Chinese New Year.

Bala Cynwyd, PA: Schlessinger Video Productions, 1994. Fabian-Baber Communications. 1 videocassette, 30 minutes. Combines music, folktales, arts & crafts in exploring the Chinese New Year. For grades K–4. [Chinese New Year]

Christmas.

Bala Cynwyd, PA: Schlessinger Video Productions, 1994. Fabian-Baber Communications. 1 videocassette, 30 minutes. Combines music, folktales, arts & crafts in exploring symbols of Christmas. For grades K–4. [Christmas]

E-Z Bread Dough Sculpture.

Torrance, CA: Morris Video, 1988. 1 videocassette, 20 minutes, My Fun Pack, #416. For ages 4–8. Shows bread dough craft. [dough sculpture]

Halloween.

Bala Cynwyd, PA: Schlessinger Video Productions, 1994. Fabian-Baber Communications. 1 videocassette, 30 minutes. Combines music, folktales, arts & crafts in exploring symbols of Halloween. For grades K–4. [Halloween]

Kid Pix (R) 2

Fort Atkinson, WI: NASCO. Four Macintosh diskettes and a teacher guide, packaged in a 3-ring binder. Allows students to create multimedia reports and animation with sound effects. For PreK–grade 12. [animation; multimedia]

Hanukkah; Passover.

Bala Cynwyd, PA: Schlessinger Video Productions, 1994. Fabian-Baber Communications. 1 videocassette, 30 minutes. Combines music, folktales, arts & crafts in exploring symbols of Hanukkah and Passover. For grades K–4. [Hanukkah; Passover]

Let's Create Art Activities.

Ann Felice. Parsippany, NJ: Let's Create, Inc., 1990. 1 videocassette, 51 minutes. Explains a variety of simple craft ideas. For ages 5–10. [clay projects; masks]

Making Playthings.

Los Angeles, CA: Concord Video, 1985. 1 videocassette, 60 minutes, VHS CU 512. Shows how to make playthings for kids. Suitable for use with elementary students. [toys]

Painting Without a Brush.

Julie Abowett. Torrance, CA: Morris Video, 1988. 1 videocassette, 20 minutes. Shows how to paint with string, sponges, etc. For ages 4–8. [painting]

Shape Starship.

Includes teacher's guide and 64K computer diskette for Apple II, II Plus, IIe, IIc, IIgs. SB19520J. Fort Atkinson, WI: NASCO. Involves shapes and patterns. For grades K–3. [shapes]

4

Creative Dramatics

*W*hen adults think of exploring drama, they may be frightened off by awful images of stage-door mothers and fathers forcing precocious children into being miserable screen stars. There also may be lingering memories of nervously having to recite something in front of a group of relatives, giving an oral report before a critical class, entering a speech contest, or singing a musical solo before an audience.

The anxiety associated with such performance, the butterflies in the stomach, feelings of embarrassment and being put on the spot, seem to remain forever. Many highly successful adults still cite having to stand and speak before a group as their greatest fear. Feeling they have somehow survived performance situations and reached this point in their lives, adults may be unwilling to expose children to what they think might be similar ordeals.

But exploring creative dramatics, as it is intended in this book, is not meant to conjure up stressful and embarrassing situations. Drama can be fun. It can be a spur to creativity and an integral part of a dynamic language arts classroom. It can be as simple as holding a conversation with favorite friend as in the exercise described below.

Directions for Ideas That Work

STORYBOOK CHARACTER CONVERSATIONS: Invite students to write their names and the name of a favorite storybook character on a slip of paper. Pair characters and post these pairings. In this way, students know with whom they have been paired so that they have advance "think time" to plan what one character might have to say to another.

Allow time for the paired characters to hold their conversation in front of the class. Cinderella, for example might share her complaints about her stepmother and step-sisters with Snow White. The wolf from *The Three Little Pigs* might discuss his adventures with the wolf from *Little Red Riding Hood*. Henry Huggins from Beverly Cleary's *Henry and Ribsy* might discuss the problems that pets cause with Fern from E.B. White's *Charlotte's Web*. Students will take the part of their character and speak from a first person point of view.

Students will have the chance to share their understanding of book characters in this way while honing dramatic and oral language skills.

Creative dramatics can help develop confidence in children. A good rule to follow is to encourage but not push kids into performance situations. With friends at home and at school, creative drama can be like a game to many children. It can also lead to team building.

Directions for Ideas That Work

A CLASSY MACHINE: The whole class can work together to create a living machine. (This will work for a scouting group too.) First, the leader should explain that while machines are fascinating and complicated, and can make a variety of interesting sounds, all the parts must work smoothly together. Explain that the whole class will work together to create a smooth-running machine.

Demonstrate a simple movement. Stand with your hands on hips, and to a fairly slow count of 1, 2, 3, 4 bend over so that your head goes down on 1, 2, and is chest-high on 3. Then come upright again on the count of 4. When you come upright on the count of 4, exhale with a loud "ahh." Do this two or three times so that students see that you repeat the movement to the same count each time.

Then demonstrate another movement to the count of four. Extend your right arm to the side on the count of 1. Leave it extended for 2 and 3. Drop it to your side on the count of 4 and make a "ping" sound.

Once students have the idea, clear a space and build the machine. While the leader keeps the slow count of 1, 2, 3, 4, half the students will come up, one by one, and join the machine, adding their movement and sound. Then this half of the group can sit down and watch while the second half of the class makes its machine.

Creative dramatics is a broad area of language arts exploration. It can encompass delightful and simple finger plays for the very young. There are also opportunities for young students to "pretend" to be a various animals.

Directions for Ideas That Work

WHICH ANIMAL AM I?: Young children enjoy pretending to be animals. They need only their imaginations. With a small group of young children, you can turn this into an interesting guessing game. Have one child move across the carpet pretending to be a favorite animal. The child should not tell the others which animal he or she is pretending to be. The other children will watch the actions and movement and then try to guess.

Perhaps a child will join hands together and wave his arms like an elephant's trunk as he lumbers slowly across the carpet. Then another child may hop across the carpet as a rabbit or kangaroo. Yet another may "swim" like a turtle, by using her arms and legs to scoot across the carpet on her stomach.

During a unit of study on animals, this can lead to library research and an interesting discussion on how animals move. Students might want to find out how a seastar travels or explain the locomotion of a snail. A pair of students might want to find out how fast an ostrich can run or what is the fastest land animal. These interesting locomotion facts, printed out along with pictures, would make a great bulletin board.

Charades and various types of word games help build a rich vocabulary for students and also provide a lot of fun.

Directions for Ideas That Work

ACTING OUT ANTONYMS: A group of older children might like to act out antonyms. Divide your group into a Red Team and a Blue Team. Have each team huddle together and write down on slips of paper pairs of antonyms such as fast/slow, clean/dirty, friend/enemy, etc. Drop the slips of paper into a coffee can.

After each team has generated six pairs of antonyms, have a member of the Red Team draw a slip of paper from the Blue Team's coffee can. The Red Team member who drew the slip, then tries to act out nonverbally the pair of antonyms for his/her own team members. Set a timer. If the team can guess the antonyms in less than 1 minute, they earn 2 points. If they guess in more than 1 but less than 2 minutes, they earn 1 point. After two minutes, the team member reads out loud the pair of antonyms.

Then a member of the Blue Team draws a pair of antonyms from the Red Team's coffee can, and the procedure continues.

An interesting follow-up activity would be to have the students write a short story about two friends who in many ways are opposites. How can they show, rather than tell, this information in the story? Is there a way in the story for the two opposites to complement one another?

Improvisation and drama can be effective teaching tools in many content areas. Perhaps the students have seen a film or engaged in a discussion on personal safety. Volunteers might take the parts of a child on the playground who is approached by a stranger, or two children walking home from school who are offered a ride by someone they don't know. Improvising the conversation and appropriate action add another dimension to the learning.

If there have been a lot of petty squabbles on the playground over sharing equipment, etc., creative drama might be used as a means of showing how various conflict situations might be handled. These improvised conversations provide models that may result in improved conflict resolution.

At some point, children in third and fourth grades may feel that they are "too old" for folk and fairy tales. Such children, however, may really enjoy working on the presentation of a familiar story to present as a play to a kindergarten or first grade class.

Directions for Ideas That Work

FUN WITH FOLK AND FAIRY TALES: A small group of children will re-read a familiar tale such as "The Three Billy Goats Gruff." The size of the group should match the number of characters in the story. Have the children choose a part to act out. For this particular story you need four characters: a Troll, Little Billy Goat, Medium-Sized Billy Goat, and Great Big Billy Goat Gruff.

You might use a bench, a low table, and another bench for the "bridge." The goats will need to practice the way they "trip-trap" as they climb up and cross over the bridge. For example, Little Billy Goat needs to make less noise that Great Bill Billy Goat Gruff. The goats also need to practice using squeaky, medium-sized, and great big voices when they speak. The Troll might want to try out various "scary" voices. Costumes aren't essential, but the Billy Goats might want to wear "horns" and "beards," and the troll might wear a funny mask.

Considerable practice is needed for the dramatic moment when Great Big Billy Goat Gruff and the Troll engage in combat to assure that no one gets too rough and that no one is hurt. When the group is ready to act out the whole story for a kindergarten or first grade class, the players may want to hold a dress rehearsal in front of their own class first.

A follow-up activity might be to write "fractured fairy tales." Encourage individuals or groups of two to take a familiar tale and completely change it. Put it in a different setting. Have the princess rescue the prince from the dragon. Have little bear wander into Goldilock's house. Have the students write their new fairy tales and share them with the class.

Older students will enjoy being in a skit to celebrate holidays and special events in the church or synagogue, and inventing short, humorous skits to present at a scouting pack meeting or around a campfire. Teachers will also find that creative dramatics can add interest to social studies classes.

Instead of, or in addition to, having students prepare oral and written reports about famous American men and women, students might be asked to prepare a monologue in which they describe an incident, told in the first person, from the life and from the point of view of one of these characters.

Directions for Ideas That Work

HISTORICAL MONOLOGUES: Invite each student to research a man or woman that is appropriate to your unit of study. You might, for example, ask students to select from explorers, trappers, and traders who were influential in opening up the west. Or you might have each student choose significant figures from the history of transportation such as the Wright Brothers or Henry Ford.

Encourage them to find some interesting story or event in the life of their famous character. Then have the student relate that story or event, from the first person point of view, for the rest of the class. You might set the time for the monologue at two to three minutes.

Some of the resources listed in this chapter are for presenting readers' theatre which appeals to many children and adults more than acting. There are also ideas for those who might be interested in writing some original plays or adapting stories for dramatization.

Some authors and publishing companies now produce plays that fit nicely into units of study. You can find a play about the rain forest or a play about a famous inventor that might make a fine addition to a topic you are studying in science or social studies.

Other students might be interested in trying to record a "radio play." Professional ones are available on audio tapes, and students might enjoy listening to one of these before attempting their original efforts.

Once students have chosen a favorite story and have become familiar with it, they can plan to read it into a tape recorder. They will want to plan ahead of time possible musical backgrounds for certain sections and experiment with sound effects. They may even want to break up their story by including a humorous commercial or two. Mistakes can be easily erased and re-recorded. When finished, the students may want to share their finished product with their classmates.

For those students and adults who are really interested in the stage, there are additional resource materials for warm-ups, one-act plays, improvisations, two- and three-minute skits, and directions for making simple props and costumes. But even here, the stress should be on expressing and enjoying oneself, not on being frightened and worried about presenting a perfect production. When such plays are shared with parents and friends, spontaneity and enthusiasm are highly valued.

Remember that other chapters may also be useful in conjunction with this one. The section on storytelling and puppets contains many ideas for putting on dramatic puppet shows. The chapter on music contains resources for musical nursery rhymes, finger plays, and musical comedies. The chapter on arts and crafts contains suggestions for making masks, props, and costumes. Dip into the other chapters as needed and enjoy your exploration of creative dramatics.

Resource books

Acting & Theatre.
Cheryl Evans and Lucy Smith. London: Usborne, 1992. 64 pp. An introduction to acting and theatre. Suitable for use with elementary grades. [acting]

Acting Games: Improvisations and Exercises.
Marsh Cassady. Colorado Springs, CO: Meriwether Pub., 1993. 178 pp. ISBN 0-916260-92-5. Contains a wide range of acting exercises. For use in grade 6 and in middle and secondary schools. [acting; games]

Acting Natural: Monologs, Dialogs, and Playlets for Teens.
    Peg Kehret. Colorado Springs, CO: Meriwether Pub., 1991. 219 pp. ISBN 0-916260-84-4. Good source for short monologues and short plays. For use in grade 6 and in middle and secondary schools. [acting]

An Actor.
    Brooke Goffstein. New York: Harper & Row, 1987. 19 pp. A young actor shows the roles that he plays on the stage. For students in grade 3 and up. [acting]

Actors in Action: Creative Dramatic Activities for the Elementary School.
    Lee DiGiano. Minneapolis, MN: T. S. Denison, 1989. 72 pp. Contains ideas for children from kindergarten through sixth grade to engage in drama. [acting; creative dramatics]

American Dragons: Twenty-Five Asian American Voices.
    Laurence Yep, ed. New York: HarperCollins, 1993. 27 pp. ISBN 0-06-021494-5. Includes short stories, poems, and play excerpts. Suitable for use in the elementary school. [Asian Americans]

Aplauso! Hispanic Children's Theater.
    Joe Rosenberg, ed. Houston, TX: Piñata Books, 1995. 274 pp. ISBN 1-55885-127-5. This is a collection of plays for children written in English by Hispanic Americans. For grade 6 and up. [Hispanic American plays; plays]

Behind the Scenes: The Unseen People Who Make Theater Work.
    Walter Williamson. New York: Walker & Co., 1987. 156 pp. ISBN 0-8027-6703-6. Discusses ten types of essential backstage work. For use with upper elementary students. [acting]

Be Kind to Your Mother (Earth): An Original Play.
    Douglas Love. New York: HarperCollins, 1994. 55 pp. ISBN 0-694-00654-8. Explores whether children can travel back in time to prevent Earth's pollution. For use in grade 3 and up. [ecology projects]

Biblical Christmas Performances: Plays, Poems, Choral Readings. Stories and Songs.
    Compiled by Rebecca Daniel. Carthage, IL: Shining Star Publications, 1988. 96 pp. ISBN 0-86653-461-X. Contains drama ideas for children ages five to thirteen around the theme of Christmas. [Bible stories; Christmas]

Biblical Story Performance: Stories, Songs, Plays, Musicals.
    Compiled by Rebecca Daniel. Carthage, IL: Shining Star Publications, 1989. 96 pp. Contains instructions for presenting simple performances for children ages five to thirteen. [Bible stories]

The Big Book of Christmas Plays: 21 Modern and Traditional One-Act Plays for the Celebration of Christmas.

Sylvia E. Kamerman, ed. Boston, MA: Plays, Inc., 1988. 357 pp. ISBN 0-8238-0288-4. Contains twenty-one royalty-free plays for students in grade 4 through high school. [Christmas; plays]

The Big Book of Comedies: 25 One-Act Plays, Skits, Curtain Raisers, and Adaptations for Young People.

Sylvia E. Kamerman, ed. Boston, MA: Plays, Inc., 1989. 327 pp. ISBN 0-8238-0289-2. Contains plays for children who are in the middle grades through high school. [plays]

The Big Book of Folktale Plays: One-Act Adaptations of Folktales from Around the World, for Stage and Puppet Performance.

Sylvia E. Kamerman, ed. Boston, MA: Plays, Inc., 1991. 323 pp. ISBN 0-8238-0294-9. Contains a collection of 32 plays. Suitable for use in grades 3–7. [folklore; plays]

The Big Book of Holiday Plays, 31 One-Act Plays, Curtain Raisers, and Adaptations for the Celebration of Holidays and Special Occasions Round the Year.

Sylvia E. Kamerman, ed. Boston, MA: Plays, Inc., 1990. 329 pp. ISBN 0-8238-0291-4. Includes plays for such occasions as Book Week and Black History Month. [holidays; plays]

The Big Book of Large-Cast Plays: 27 One-Act Plays for Young Actors.

Sylvia E. Kamerman, ed. Boston, MA: Plays, Inc., 1994. 351 pp. ISBN 0-8238-0302-3. These plays features stories dealing with history and with fairy tales. Suitable for use in the elementary grades. [fairy tales; history; plays]

Black Fairy, and Other Plays for Children.

Useni Eugene Perkins. Chicago: Third World Press, 1993. 189 pp. ISBN 0-88378-077-1. These musical dramas for children emphasize Afro-American traditions and values. For use in the elementary grades. [African Americans–plays; plays]

Blame It On the Wolf: An Original Play.

Douglas Love. New York: HarperCollins, 1994. 45 pp. ISBN 0-694-00653-X. In this courtroom drama, the wolf stand trial for eating Grandma. For use in grade 3 and up. [plays; trials]

Boundless Imagination.

Jan Thurman-Veith. Palo Alto, CA: Monday Morning Books, 1986. 112 pp. Creative, dramatic play for children ages three to six. [creative dramatics]

Children's Plays for Creative Actors: A Collection of Royalty-free Plays for Boys and Girls.

Claire Boiko. Boston, MA: Plays, Inc., 1985. 372 pp. ISBN 0-8238-0267-1. Contains 35 one-acts. Appropriate for use in grades 3–7. [plays]

Child's Play: Quick and Easy Costumes.

Leslie Hamilton. New York: Crown, 1995. 168 pp. ISBN 0-517-88173-X. Directions for making simple costumes. Suitable for use in the elementary school. [costumes]

Christmas On Stage: An Anthology of Royalty-free Christmas Plays for All Ages.

Theodore O. Zapel, ed. Colorado Springs, CO: Meriwether Pub., 1990. 293 pp. ISBN 0-916260-68-2. Contains a collection of holiday plays for all ages. [Christmas plays]

Classics to Read Aloud to Your Children.

William F. Russell, ed. New York: Crown, 1984. 311 pp. ISBN 0-517-55404-6. Contains selections from poems and plays by well-known authors. To be read to children (preschool to grade 5) by adults. [plays]

Clown Skits for Everyone.

Happy Jack Feder. Colorado Springs, CO: Meriwether Pub., 1991. 170 pp. ISBN 0-916260-75-5. Contains 32 clown skits to be performed by one or two people. For all ages. [clowns]

Contemporary Scenes for Contemporary Kids.

Kat Sawyer-Young. Boston, MA: Baker's Plays, 1986. 50 pp. A collection of short, original scenes appropriate for students aged ten to seventeen. [plays]

Costumes.

Claire Beaton. New York: Warwick Press, 1990. 24 pp. Contains seven detailed ideas for making inexpensive costumes. Appropriate for use in all elementary grades. [costumes]

Costumes.

Danielle Sensier. New York: Thomson Learning, 1995. 48 pp. ISBN 1-56847-227-7. Shows traditional costumes from around the world. Appropriate for use in the elementary school. [costumes]

Creative Dramatics for Children.

Maureen M. Cresci. Glenview, IL: Scott Foresman, 1989. 56 pp. ISBN 0-673-38464-0. Suitable for use with children in grades 3–6. [creative dramatics]

Creative Dramatics for Young Children.

Lucy Townsend and Jane Belk Moncure. Elgin, IL: Child's World, distributed by Children's Press, 1986. 63 pp. Filled with drama ideas for use with young children. [creative dramatics]

The Curtain Rises.

Paula Gaj Sitarz. White Hall, VA: Shoe Tree Press, 1991. 2 vols. ISBN 1-55870-198-2. A good introduction to theatre history. Suitable for grades 5–9. [creative dramatics–history]

The Dressing-Up Book.

Wendy Baker and Diane James. Richmond Hill, Ont., Canada: Scholastic Canada, 1991. 46 pp. Describes how to create costumes using simple materials. Appropriate for use in the elementary school. [costumes]

Early Stages: The Professional Theater and the Young Actor.

Walter Williamson. New York: Walker & Co., 1986. 120 pp. ISBN 0-8027-6624-2. Discusses the history of theatre and the training necessary to be an actor. Profiles ten young performers. Suitable for grade 6 and up. [creative dramatics–history]

Easy Plays for Preschoolers to Third Graders.

Amorie Havilan and Lyn Smith. Brandon, MS: Quail Ridge Press, 1985. 150 pp. A collection of twelve plays suitable for various holidays for preschoolers to grade 3. [holidays; plays]

El Teatro.

Clarisa Bell. Torance, CA: Laredo Pub. Co., 1992. 24 pp. ISBN 1-56492-056-9. Text is in English and Spanish. Describes in rhyming text with illustrations such art forms as opera, tragedy, ballet, etc. For use with students in grades 2–6. [Spanish language]

Escape to Freedom: A Play About Young Frederick Douglass.

Ossie Davis. New York: Puffin, 1990. 89 pp. ISBN 0-14-034355-5. Tells how a slave endures many years before escaping to the North. For use in grades 4–7. [African Americans; Douglass, Frederick; history; plays]

Everyday Plays for Boys and Girls.

Helen Louise Miller. Boston, MA: Plays, Inc., 1986. 198 pp. ISBN 0-8238-0274-4. Contains fifteen one-act plays suitable for children twelve and under, grades 1–6. [plays]

Face Painting.

Clare Beaton. New York: Warwick Press, 1990. 24 pp. ISBN 0-531-1516-1. Discusses the materials needed to do face painting and gives step-by-step instructions for several designs. Appropriate for use with elementary students through grade 4. [face painting]

Face Painting and Dressing Up for Kids: Step-by-Step.

Petra Boase and Bettina Graham. New York: Smithmark, 1995. 96 pp. ISBN 0-8317-3077-3. Directions for 50 disguises. Suitable for use with elementary students in grades 3–6. [face painting]

Fantastic Theater: Puppets and Plays for Young Performers and Young Audiences.

Judy Sierra. Bronx, NY: H. W. Wilson, 1991. 249 pp. ISBN 0-8242-0809-9. Contains 30 plays. Suitable for use in grades 3–7. [plays; puppets]

First Plays for Children: A Collection of Little Plays for the Youngest Players.
   Helen Louise Miller Gotwalt. Boston, MA: Plays, Inc., 1988. 285 pp. ISBN 0-8238-0268-X. Contains 26 short plays with production notes. Suitable for use in the primary grades. [plays]

Funny Skits and Sketches.
   Terry Halligan. New York: Sterling Publishing Co. Inc., 1987. 128 pp. Contains 33 short, funny skits. For use with upper elementary grade students. [comedies]

Fun With Choral Speaking.
   Rose Marie Anthony. Englewood, CO: Teacher Ideas Press, 1990. 138 pp. Contains ideas for choral readings with children ages five to eight. [choral reading]

Great Scenes and Monologues for Children.
   Craig Slaight and Jack Sharrar, eds. Newbury, VT: Smith and Kraus, 1993. 175 pp. ISBN 1-880399-15-6. A collection of scenes suitable for use with children in grades 2–9. [acting]

Greek and Roman Plays for the Intermediate Grades.
   Albert Cullum. Carthage, IL: Fearon Teacher Aids, 1993. 287 pp. ISBN 0-86653-941-7. Contains adaptations of plays suitable for use with students in grades 4–8. [plays–Greek; plays–Roman]

Hamlet for Young People.
   Diane Davidson, ed. Fair Oaks, CA: Swan Books, 1993. 64 pp. ISBN 0-934048-24-X. An adaptation of William Shakespeare's play. Suitable for upper elementary students and middle school students. [Shakespeare, William]

Have You Ever… Bringing Literature to Life Through Creative Dramatics.
   Lois Kipnis and Marilyn Gilbert. Hagerstown, MD: Alleyside Press, 1994. 77 pp. ISBN 0-913853-33-X. Uses well-known stories and poems. Contains a bibliography. For use with all elementary students. [creative dramatics]

The Herbie Jones Reader's Theater.
   Suzy Kine. New York: Putnam, 1992. 177 pp. ISBN 0-399-22120-4. Contains twenty-one episodes from four *Herbie Jones* novels that have been adapted into scripts. For use in grades 2–6. [readers' theater]

Holiday in the Rain Forest: An Original Play.
   Douglas Love. New York: HarperCollins, 1994. 55 pp. ISBN 0-694-00657-2. A funny, suspenseful play in which the Kane family solves a rain forest mystery. For use with grade 3 and up. [mysteries; plays; rain forests]

Holiday Plays for Reading.
> Henry Gilfond. New York: Walker & Co., 1985. 156 pp. ISBN 0-8027-6601-3. A collection of plays to celebrate holidays. Suitable for use with grade 4 and up. [holiday plays; plays]

Holiday Programs for Boys and Girls.
> Aileen Fisher. Boston, MA: Plays, Inc., 1986. 393 pp. ISBN 0-8238-0277-9. Contains a collection of plays, poems, and skits for children to present on special occasions. Suitable for use in the grades 2–6. [holiday plays; poetry]

Humorous Plays for Teenagers.
> Christina Hamlett. Boston, MA: Plays, Inc., 1987. 237 pp. ISBN 0-8238-0276-0. Filled with curtain-raisers, melodramas, and one-act comedies for students in middle school and high school. [comedies; plays]

Improvisations in Creative Drama: A Program of Workshops and Dramatic Sketches for Students.
> Betty Keller. Colorado Springs, CO: Meriwether Pub., 1988. 175 pp. ISBN 0-916260-51-8. Ideas for working with student actors. Suitable for use with upper elementary students. [creative dramatics]

Just a Minute: Ten Short Plays and Activities for Your Classroom: With Rehearsal Strategies to Accompany Multi-Cultural Stories from Around the World.
> Irene N. Watts. Portsmouth, NY: Heinemann, 1990. 130 pp. ISBN 0-435-08602-2. Ideas for ten multicultural plays. Appropriate for use with upper elementary students. [multicultural plays]

Kabuki Gift: An Original Play.
> Douglas Love. New York: HarperCollins, 1994. 57 pp. ISBN 0-694-00658-0. This is a comedy presented in the ancient Japanese Kabuki-style for children. Appropriate for use with upper elementary students. [comedies; Japanese plays]

Kidzeye Theatre: a Collection of One-Act Plays for Performance by Young Actors.
> Chris Bernstein. Morrison. CO: Calbern Publishing, 1995. 280 pp. These one-acts are suitable for children ages eight to twelve. [plays]

Make Costumes: For Creative Play.
> Priscilla Hershberger. Danbury, CT: Grolier Educational Corp., 1993. 48 pp. ISBN 0-89134-450-0. Step-by-step costuming instructions using easy-to-find supplies for children in grades 4–7. [costumes]

Make Your Own... Videos, Commercials, Radio Shows, Special Effects, and More.
> The Fun Group. Illustrated by Ellen Sasaki. New York: Grosset & Dunlap, 1992. 94 pp. Simple explanations of making videos and radio shows. Appropriate for use in the upper elementary grades. [radio production; video production]

More Classics to Read Aloud to Your Children.

William F. Russell. New York: Crown, 1986. 264 pp. ISBN 0-517-56108-5. Contains a selection of poems and plays that groups can read aloud together. [plays; poetry; read alouds; parent resources]

Much Ado About Nothing for Young People.

Diane Davidson, ed. Fair Oaks, CA: Swan Books, 1994. 65 pp. ISBN 0-934048-25-8. An adaptation of William Shakespeare's play. For students in grades 5–8. [Shakespeare, William]

Mystery Plays for Young Actors.

John Murray. Boston, MA: Plays, Inc., 1984. 188 pp. Contains detective and mystery plays. Appropriate for use with upper elementary students. [mysteries; plays]

Newspaper Theatre: Creative Play Production for Low Budgets and No Budgets.

Alice Morin. Belmont, CA: Fearon Teacher Aids, 1989. 79 pp. ISBN 0-8224-6349-0. Ideas for inexpensive theatre productions. Suitable for use in the elementary school. [plays]

The No-Sew Costume Book.

Michaeline Bresnahen and Joan Gaestel Macfarlane. Lexington, MA: Greene Press, Pelham Books, 1990. 166 pp. Contains ideas on how to make simple costumes. Appropriate for use in the elementary school. [costumes]

Not So Dumb: Four Plays for Young People.

Toronto: Coach House Press, 1993. 204 pp. ISBN 0-88910-453-0. Contains four plays. Appropriate for use with upper elementary students. [plays]

Now Hiring: Theater.

Jane Richards Mason. New York: Crestwood, 1994. 48 pp. Discusses careers in the theatre. Appropriate for use with upper elementary students. [careers]

Onstage Backstage.

Caryn Huberman and Jo Anne Wetzel. Minneapolis, MN: Carolrhoda Books, 1987. 56 pp. A ten-year-old discusses what it's like to be associated with the Palo Alto Children's Theatre. Appropriate for use in the upper elementary grades. [theatre]

Party Rhymes.

Collected by Marc Brown. New York: Dutton, 1988. 47 pp. ISBN 0-525-44402-5. ISBN 0-14-050318-8 paper. Contains a collection of twelve finger plays or physical activities that can be set to music. Appropriate for preschoolers and primary grade students. [finger plays; music]

Patriotic and Historical Plays for Young People: One-Act Plays and Programs About the People and Events That Made Our Country Great.

Sylvia E. Kamerman, ed. Boston, MA: Plays, Inc., 1987. 230 pp. ISBN 0-8238-0285-X. Contains 25 one-act plays for children. Appropriate for students in grades 3–9. [history; patriotism; plays]

Playing Scenes: A Sourcebook for Performers.

Gerald Lee Ratliff. Colorado Springs, CO: Meriwether Pub., 1993. 428 pp. ISBN 0-916260-89-5. Hints for playing scenes along with suggestions for physical and vocal warm-up exercises. For use with upper elementary students through adults. [acting]

Plays.

Kate Haycock. Ada, OK: Garrett Educational Corp., 1990. 32 pp. ISBN 0-944483-98-4. Provides an inside look at theatre terminology. For use with students in grades 4–8. [acting; theatre]

Plays Children Love: Volume II: A Treasury of Contemporary and Classic Plays for Children.

Coleman A. Jennings and Aurand Harris, eds. New York: St. Martin's, 1988. 560 pp. ISBN 0-312-01490-2. Contains nineteen plays using child actors for young audiences. Suitable for use with upper elementary students. [plays]

Plays for Children and Young Adults: An Evaluative Index and Guide.

Rashelle S. Karp and June H. Schlessinger. New York: Garland, 1991. 580 pp. ISBN 0-8240-6112-8. A guide to children's plays. A good resource guide for adults. [plays]

Plays for Young Audiences: Featuring the Emerald Circle and Other Plays.

Max Bush. Colorado Springs, CO: Meriwether Pub, 1995. 383 pp. ISBN 1-56608-011-8. A collection of ten plays. Suitable for grades 4–12. [plays]

Plays from African Tales: One-act, Royalty-Free Dramatizations for Young People, from Stories and Folktales of Africa.

Barbara Winther. Boston, MA: Plays, Inc., 1992. 145 pp. ISBN 0-8238-0296-5. Includes such favorite tales as *Anansi, the African Spider* and *Ijapa, the Tortoise.* For use with elementary students. [Africa; plays]

Plays from Favorite Folk Tales: 25 One-Act Dramatizations of Stories Children Love.

Sylvia E. Kamerman, ed. Boston, MA: Plays, Inc., 1987. 293 pp. ISBN 0-8238-0280-9. Contains 25 one-act dramatizations. Suitable for use with elementary students, grade 2 and up. [folklore; plays]

Plays of Black Americans: Episodes from the Black Experience in America, Dramatized for Young People.

Sylvia E. Kamerman, ed. Boston, MA: Plays, Inc., 1987. 134 pp. ISBN 0-8238-0301-5. Contains a collection of plays focusing on the Black experience. Suitable for use with upper elementary students. [African Americans; plays]

Plays of Great Achievers: One-Act Plays About Inventors, Scientists, Statesmen, Humanitarians, and Explorers.

Sylvia E. Kamerman, ed. Boston, MA: Plays, Inc., 1992. 364 pp. ISBN 0-8238-0297-3. Contains twenty-three one-act plays. Suitable for students in upper elementary and middle school. [explorers; humanitarians; plays; scientists; statesmen]

Plays, Pageants and Programs for Schools, Camps, and Organizations.

John R. Carroll, Byron, CA: Front Row Experience, 1990. 89 pp. ISBN 0-915256-29-0. A collection of children's plays. Suitable for use by elementary school students. [plays]

Plays, Players, and Playing: How to Start Your Own Children's Theater Company.

Judith A. Hackbarth. Colorado Springs, CO: Piccadilly Books, 1994. 203 pp. ISBN 0-941599-29-9. Good ideas for beginning with play production. Also contains a bibliography. A resource for adults. [plays]

Plays to Play With Everywhere.

Sally-Anne Milgrim. New York: Samuel French, 1991. 138 pp. Contains six children's plays and a glossary of dramatic terms. Suitable for use in the elementary school. [plays]

Presenting Reader's Theatre: Plays and Poems to Read Aloud.

Caroline Feller Bauer. Bronx, NY: H. W. Wilson, 1987. 238 pp. Contains simple plays and poems to be read. For use with upper elementary students. [poetry; readers' theatre]

Putting On a Play.

Nick Pryor. New York: Thomson Learning, 1994. 48 pp. Describes how to direct and produce a play. Contains a useful bibliography. Good resource for elementary teachers.

Readers Theatre for Children: Scripts and Script Development.

Milfred Knight Laughlin and Kathy Howard Latrobe. Englewood, CO: Teacher Ideas Press, 1990. 138 pp. ISBN 0-87287-753-1. Ideas for readers' theatre. Suitable for use with upper elementary students. [readers' theatre]

Red Licorice: Monologues for Young People.

Carole Tippit. Rancho Mirage, CA: Dramaline Pub., 1994. 61 pp. ISBN 0-940669-28-5. Contains monologues for children. Appropriate for upper elementary students. [monologues]

Representing Children's Book Characters.

Mary E. Wilson. Metuchen, NJ: Scarecrow Press, 1989. 174 pp. ISBN 0-8108-2169-9. Contains information on making simple costumes. Suitable for use in all elementary grades. [costumes; picture books]

Shakespeare Stories.

Leon Garfield. New York: Schocken Books, 1985. 288 pp. ISBN 0-395-56397-6. Contains twelve Shakespearean plays that have been rewritten in narrative form. Suitable for students in grade 5 and up. [Shakespeare, William]

Showkits: Whole Language Activities: Patterns for Masks, Puppets, Costumes to Use With Picture Books.

Candy Jones and Lea McGee. Palo Alto, CA: Monday Morning Books, 1991. 64 pp. Contains many easy-to-follow patterns. Suitable for use in all elementary grades. [costumes; masks; picture books; puppets]

Show Time at the Polk Street School: Plays You Can Do Yourself Or In the Classroom.

Patricia Reilly Giff. New York: Delacorte, 1992. 101 pp. ISBN 0-385-30794-2. Contains three plays featuring the students in Ms. Rooney's class. Appropriate for grades 1–4. [plays]

The Skit Book: 101 Skits from Kids.

Margaret Read MacDonald. Hamden, CT: Shoe String Press, 1990. A collection of short skits written by young authors. Suitable for use with elementary students. [plays]

Social Studies Reader's Theatre for Children.

Mildred Laughlin. Englewood, CO: Teacher Ideas Press, 1991. ISBN 0-87287-865-1. Includes a good bibliographic reference. Suitable for use with upper elementary students. [readers' theatre]

Special Plays for Holidays.

Helen Louise Miller Gotwalt. Boston, MA: Plays, Inc., 1986. 187 pp. ISBN 0-8238-0275-2. Contains fifteen one-act holiday plays. Appropriate for use with elementary students, grades 1–6. [holiday plays; plays]

Stage Plays from the Classics: One-act Adaptations from Famous Short Stories, Novels, and Plays.

Joellen Bland. Boston, MA: Plays, Inc., 1987. 266 pp. ISBN 0-8238-0281-7. Contains adaptations of short stories and novels into plays. Suitable for students in grades 7–12. [one acts; plays]

Stories on Stage: Scripts for Reader's Theater.

Aaron Shepard. Bronx, NY: H. W. Wilson, 1993. 162 pp. ISBN 0-8242-0851-X. Collection of twenty-two plays from folk tales, myths, short stories, and novels suitable for middle grades. [folklore; readers' theatre]

Take a Walk in Their Shoes.

Glennette Tilley Turner. New York: Cobblehill, 1989. 174 pp. ISBN 0-525-65006-7. Contains short skits to act out about fourteen prominent Black leaders such as Rosa Parks and Martin Luther King. Suitable for grades 4–8. [African Americans; plays]

Take It from the Top: Monologues from the Multicultural Experience.

Kathleen Gaffney. El Paso, TX: Firestein Books, 1993. 81 pp. Contains monologues and includes a bibliography. Appropriate for upper elementary and middle school students. [monologues; multicultural]

Ten Out of Ten: Ten Winning Plays Selected from the Playwrights Festival, 1982-1991.

Wendy Lamb, ed. New York: Bantam Doubleday Dell, 1995. 296 pp. ISBN 0-440-21914-0. A collection of ten plays. Suitable for upper elementary and older students. [plays]

Theater.

Howard Loxton. Austin, TX: Steck-Vaughn, 1990. 48 pp. ISBN 0-8114-2359-X. Gives an over-view of theater with information about acting methods, staging plays, and all that's involved in putting on a play. Appropriate for grades 6–11. [acting; plays]

Theatre for the Young.

Alan England. New York: St. Martin's, 1990. 243 pp. ISBN 0-312-03459-8. Contains plays by modern dramatists. For upper elementary and older students. [plays]

Theatre for Youth: Twelve Plays With Mature Themes.

Coleman A. Jennings and Gretta Berghammer, eds. Austin, TX: University of Texas Press, 1986. 512 pp. ISBN 0-292-78081-8. ISBN 0-292-78085-0 (paper). Contains drama suitable for young adults. [plays]

Theatre Games for Young Performers: Improvisations and Exercises for Developing Acting Skills.

Maria C. Novelly. Colorado Springs, CO: Meriwether Pub., 1985. 147 pp. ISBN 0-916260-31-3. Contains ideas for introducing young actors to a variety of theatre games. Appropriate for grades 6–10. [acting]

Theater Magic: Behind the Scenes At a Children's Theatre.

Cheryl Walsh Bellville. Minneapolis, MN: Carolrhoda Books, 1986. 48 pp. ISBN 0-87614-278-1. Follows a children's theatre company and describes how a play is designed, cast, and presented. Appropriate for preschool to grade 5. [acting]

Three-Minute Bible Skits and Songs.

Compiled by Rebecca Daniel. Carthage, IL: Shining Star Publications, 1991. 96 pp. Simple Christian skits for children aged six to twelve. [Bible skits]

Where Do You Get Your Ideas? Helping Young Writers Begin.

Sandy Asher. New York: Walker & Co., 1987. 88 pp. ISBN 0-8027-6690-0. Contains tips from authors on finding ideas for plays, poems, and stories. Suitable for grade 5 and up. [creative writing; plays]

Why the Willow Weeps: A Story Told With Hands.

Marshall Izen. New York: Dell, 1992. 1v. unpaged. In this story, a willow weeps over the theft of a rose. It includes photos of hands acting out the story. Appropriate for all elementary grades. [storytelling]

WKID: Easy Radio Plays.

Carol Adorjan and Yuri Rasovsky. Niles, IL: A. Whitman, 1988. 79 pp. ISBN 0-8075-9155-6. Contains four radio plays with advice for music and sound effects. Appropriate for grades 3–8. [radio plays]

Writing Your Own Plays: Creating, Adapting, Improvising.

Carol Korty. New York: Scribner's, 1986. 116 pp. ISBN 0-684-18470-2. Identifies the different characteristics of a play and gives tips for developing ideas into a finished script. Suitable for grade 6 and up. [creative writing; plays]

Year-Round Programs for Young Players.

Aileen Fisher. Boston, MA: Plays, Inc., 1990. 334 pp. ISBN 0-8238-0266-3. Contains a collection of plays, poems and recitations for special occasions. Appropriate for grades 2–5. [plays; poetry]

Other resources

One magazine that will be valuable to a creative dramatics class is *Plays* which is published by Plays Inc. in Boston, MA. Described as the "drama magazine for young actors," it is published monthly, October through May.

Classroom Plays.

Crystal Lake, IL: Rigby. Sells several titles written by professional playwrights in packages of six for classroom use. Included are: *Anansi and the Old Tiger Riding Horse, The Emperor's New Clothes, The Fizzalot Commercial, The Night the Ghosts Got Haunted, The Kidnapping of Lady Filthyrich,* and *The Rice Pudding Riot.* Suitable for use in elementary grades. [plays]

Creating Character Voices.

Patrick Fraley. New Rochelle, NY: Spoken Arts, 1989. 2 sound cassettes. Teaches techniques and exercises for creating voices with taped workshop examples. Suitable for use with upper elementary students. [acting]

Dialect Monologues.

Roger Karshner. Toluca Lake, CA: Dramaline Pub., 1990. 1 sound cassette. Teaches thirteen dialects. Valuable teacher resource. [monologues]

Fingerplays and Footplays.

Rosemary Hallum and Henry Glass. Freeport, NY: Educational Activities, 1987. 1 sound disk, 1 booklet, AR 618. Simple plays for young children, preschool and primary grades. [finger plays; foot plays]

Hap Palmer Finger Plays and Foot Plays.

Fort Atkinson, WI: NASCO. Available on LP record, cassette, or CD. Entertaining finger and foot plays with music. For preschoolers and primary grade students. [finger plays; foot plays]

Kids' Playwriting.

Noerena Abookire. Produced by Linda Robiner. Lincoln, NE: Great Plains National Instructional Television Library, 1987. 5 videocassettes, 75 minutes, with teachers' guide. Motivates children, ages 8–12 to adapt stories into plays. [creative writing]

Marc Brown Does Play Rhymes.

Marc Brown. Westminster, MD: Random House Video/American School Publishers, 1989. 1 videocassette, 11 minutes. A collection of 12 play rhymes with illustrations to demonstrate finger plays or physical activities to go along with them. Includes music. Suitable for preschoolers and primary grade students. [finger plays]

The Reluctant Dragon.

Kenneth Grahame. Imagication, 1984. One sound cassette, 48 minutes. This story is performed in readers' theater form. Will be enjoyed by all elementary grades. [readers' theatre]

The Story of the Chicken Made of Rags.

Sound recording by Nina Serrano and Judith Binder. Oakland, CA: Redwood Records, 1991. 1 sound cassette. This is a musical play about a chicken on its way to a big fiesta. Suitable for elementary students. [chickens; plays]

5

Poetry

*E*xploring poetry can begin with the youngest child and continue for a life time. There are simple activities that can be done at home with toddlers, and there are challenging ones for upper elementary grade students. Teachers, librarians, parents, grandparents, and adult youth leaders can all take part in the fun of poetry.

There are many delightful finger plays and nursery rhymes that tiny tots love. Often these old favorites, half-forgotten, are stored away in the back of an adult's memory and can easily be refreshed by reading some of the resource books listed at the end of this chapter.

Around the campfire or at a scouting ceremony, students might be asked to read a spooky poem, a patriotic poem, a poem about friendship, or a poem in celebration of the beauties of nature.

In the elementary classroom, the enjoyment that comes from listening to or reading poems sometimes leads to a desire to write poetry. There is no "right" or "wrong" way to introduce poetry to a group of students, although the ideas which follow have proved successful with a wide variety of children.

Directions for Ideas That Work

LUNES: Writing lunes might be an excellent beginning in introducing students to different types of poetry. Lunes are an easy type of poem for many children to write. These poems are short and unrhymed, and unlike Haiku, do not require the counting of syllables.

Lunes are three-line poems, in any mood, and about any subject. They have three words in lines one and three, and five words in line two. For example:

Tiny raindrops fall,
On the dusty street, washing
It sparkling clean.

Another poetic form worth exploring is the Pantoum which is Malaysian in origin. Students who have not written much poetry may feel more comfortable at first if they are asked to work within a prescribed format such as the Lune or the Pantoum. The very structure of such poems provides a helpful skeleton around which students can shape their poems.

Directions for Ideas That Work

PANTOUM VARIATIONS: Each stanza of the Pantoum will be a single sentence written in four lines. The second line of each stanza becomes the opening line of the stanza that follows. This repetition of lines from one stanza to the next helps to knit the whole poem together. For example:

> *A sea bird, far from the ocean,*
> *Flies against the blue sky*
> *In a wide arc*
> *With wings moving easily.*
>
> *Flies against the blue sky*
> *Knowing exactly where it is going*
> *And why it has left the Pacific*
> *So far behind.*
>
> *Knowing exactly where it is going*
> *Without panic or concern*
> *Hovering and dipping above me,*
> *It continues on its solitary way.*
>
> *Without panic or concern*
> *I take a lesson from the sea bird,*
> *And make my own way forward*
> *Into unfamiliar territory.*

Shape poems might be another way to introduce students to poetry.

Directions for Ideas That Work

DIAMANTE: The "Diamante" or diamond-shaped poem has seven lines. The first and seventh line use contrasting nouns. The second line has two words that describe line one. The third line contains three words ending in "ing" which describe line one. The fourth line has four words, the first two relating to line one, and the last two connecting to line seven. Line five contains three "ing" words and line six contains two adjectives that describe line seven. For example:

> *Summer*
> *Hot, Relaxed*
> *Panting, Pulsing, Sweltering*
> *Pools, Vacations, Slopes, Snowmen*
> *Skiing, Sledding, Shoveling*
> *Cold, White*
> *Winter*

Special occasions often arise for sending cards or notes to relatives, classmates and friends. Few cards are appreciated more than home-made ones. An acrostic poem is one that can be fashioned as a verse for a get-well card or a birthday card.

Directions for Ideas That Work

ACROSTIC VERSE: To write an acrostic verse, have each student write one word, perhaps a person's name or the name of a holiday or special event, vertically on the inside of a piece of paper which has been folded in half to form a greeting card. (The cover of the card might later be decorated with an appropriate pattern or drawing using crayons, colored pencils, etc.)

After the word is written vertically, the student writes a line of poetry following each letter. The lines need not rhyme and they can be of any length. But they should have something to do with the subject of the poem. For example,

> **A** *lways ready to help others,*
>
> **L** *oves to play jokes and do magic tricks,*
>
> **B** *ats .500 in Little League play,*
>
> **E** *ats a ton of chocolate ice cream every year,*
>
> **R** *eally likes to sit and watch TV,*
>
> **T** *en today! Congratulations and Happy Birthday!*

Once students have met with success by following the requirements of a very specific form, they may be ready to try some poetry in which there is more freedom for them to choose the subject, shape, and number of lines. They may also enjoy including some rhymes.

From a collection of poetry, the teacher might read some poems and point out and discuss the rhymes and rhyming patterns. The selections might include some poems written in couplets, some in which lines one and three have matching end rhymes, and some in which lines two and four rhyme. Some of the poems might include internal rhyme.

Holidays provide a good spring-board to creative writing of stories and poetry. Since choice is always valued by students, you might make an assignment where students may respond to a holiday assignment by either writing a short story or a poem.

Directions for Ideas That Work

HALLOWEEN VERSE: Begin by brainstorming with students what they associate with Halloween. Don't interrupt the brain-storming process by stopping to have a student explain a word association, but simply list on the chalkboard all the words that students suggest. Your list might be something like this: black cat, pumpkin, scarecrow, full moon, tricks and treats, candy, apples, ghosts, haunted house, witch, broomstick, costumes, party, bats, spiders, brew, and jack-o'-lantern.

Now suggest that students use some of the words from this list as they write either a Halloween short story or poem. If they write poems, encourage them to use some end rhymes. An example might be:

Trick or treat! Trick or Treat!
Shout while you rush up and down the street.
Doors swing wide and people stare
At witches and pirates standing there.

Trick or treat! Trick or Treat!
Please give us something good to eat.
Candy bars, apples, and bubble gum.
Halloween! At last it's come.

Provide time after such an exercise for students to volunteer to share their stories and poems aloud. You might also post the results on a class bulletin board. As students read and hear more poetry in their class, they will become increasingly comfortable with it and more willing to try writing their own poems.

Rather than a unit of study on poetry, it may be more successful to incorporate poetry into various units throughout the school year and in areas other than language arts. Many of the resources included give examples of how poetry can be used to enhance social studies, science, health, and music.

There are collections of poems about horses, cats, dogs, and birds which will add a dimension to a unit of study on animals. And there are collections of poems about body parts, outer space, machines, famous people, and historical events. Weaving poetry into each unit of study will add an additional richness.

Poet Jack Collum, whose book *Moving Windows* is included among the resources, often uses an "I remember" poem on the opening day of one of his poetry workshops with students. An "I remember" poem can also be used as a special greeting card and might be especially appropriate to put in a memory book to honor a student or staff member who is leaving the school.

Directions for Ideas That Work

I REMEMBER POEM: Three or more lines are written in an "I remember" poem. All lines are on the same topic and each begins with the phrase "I remember." For example:

I remember that whenever it was my birthday, you always blew up pink balloons and hung them with streamers from the light above the dining room table.

I remember that you always baked for me my favorite chocolate cake with cherry pink icing on the top and added pink candles, too.

I remember how you turned out the lights after the candles were lit and how everyone sang happy birthday to me before I blew out the dancing flames.

I remember that it's your birthday today, Mom, and I'm wishing you pink balloons, cake, candles, and the happiest birthday ever!

Educators often ask children to "be original," but imitation has its place in a program of studies also. The art educator may show and discuss a number of prints done by a painter, such as Picasso, and ask students to create an original piece of art "in the style of" Picasso. The resulting works have elements of both imitation and of originality.

The same technique might be used with poetry. The teacher might select a poet with a distinctive style, read and discuss several poems, and suggest that the students write an original poem using that poet's style.

Directions for Ideas That Work

ANIMAL POEMS A LA OGDEN NASH: It should be easy for a teacher to get a collection of poetry which includes works by the humorous poet, Ogden Nash. Read a few of his poems to the class. Some of his short animal poems such as "The Duck" and "The Camel" would be good choices. These are short, simple, and funny.

Invite students to browse through a collection of old magazines, suitable for being cut up, that contain lots of pictures of animals. Ask students to locate and cut out a picture of an animal that they like. Then have the students write a very short poem "in the style of Ogden Nash" about the animal that they chose.

Follow up the writing by allowing students to volunteer to read their poems to the class. You might also want to share these on a bulletin board along with the cut-out pictures of the animals that inspired the poems. An example might be:

The Penguin
Have you heard
There's a bird
Black and white,
Quite a sight,
As it slides,
And it glides
On slippery ice.

Oooh! That's nice.

Poetry is so closely tied to rhythm that the resources included in the chapter on Music and Movement should also be consulted. And, since many poems are related to special holidays, the chapter on Holidays Around the World may also be of interest as you explore poetry with children.

Resource books

Abecedario de los Animales.

Alma Flor Ada. Madrid, Spain: Espasa-Calpe, 1990, 39 pp. This book is in Spanish and is an alphabet book of animal rhymes. Suitable for use in all elementary grades. [alphabet books; animals; Spanish language]

The Alphabet from Z to A: With Much Confusion On the Way.

Judith Viorst. New York: Atheneum, 1994. 30 pp. ISBN 0-689-31768-9. This book goes backward through the alphabet taking note of some anomalies in English spelling and grammar. For use with grades 2–5. [alphabet books]

Animal Poems.

Selected by Heather Amery. London: Usborne, 1990. 32 pp. ISBN 0-7560-0442-7. Poems about animals written mainly by modern poets. Suitable for grades 2–6. [animals]

Anna's Summer Songs.

Mary Q. Steele. New York: Greenwillow, 1988. 30 pp. ISBN 0-688-07180-5. Poems about summer plants such as the fern and the strawberry. Suitable for all primary grades. [plants]

Bam, Bam, Bam.

Eve Merriam. New York: Holt, 1995. 26 pp. ISBN 0-8050-3527-3. This is a "noisy" poem in which a wrecking ball demolishes an old house to make way for stores and a skyscraper. For use in all elementary grades. [construction]

Bird Watch: A Book of Poetry.

Jane Yolen. New York: Philomel, 1990. 36 pp. ISBN 0-399-21612-X. Contains a variety of poems about birds and their activities. Suitable for all elementary grades. [birds]

At Christmas Be Merry: Verses.

Selected by Patricia K. Roche. New York: Viking Kestrel, 1986. 32 pp. ISBN 0-14-050680-2. These verses describe activities from holiday preparation to Christmas Day. For use with preschoolers through grade 1. [Christmas]

Beasts by the Bunches.

A. Mifflin Lowe. Garden City, NY: Doubleday, 1987. 46 pp. An illustrated collection of animal poetry. Suitable for all elementary grades. [animals]

Believers in America: Poems About Americans of Asian and Pacific Islander Descent.

Steven Izuki. Chicago, IL: Children's Press, 1994. 48 pp. ISBN 0-516-05152-0. Poems about Asian-Americans. For use in grades 4–6. [Asian Americans]

Birds, Beasts, and Fishes: A Selection of Animal Poems.

Selected by Reg Cartwright. New York: Macmillan, 1991. 64 pp. ISBN 0-02-717776-9. An illustrated anthology of poems from around the world. For use in preschool and up. [animals; birds; fish]

Black Swan, White Crow: Haiku.

J. Patrick Lewis. New York: Atheneum, 1995. 32 pp. ISBN 0-689-31899-5. Nineteen poems on nature themes. Suitable for grades 2–4. [haiku]

Blast Off: Poems About Space.

Selected by Lee Bennett Hopkins. New York: HarperCollins, 1995. 48 pp. ISBN 0-06-444219-5. A collection of poems about topics such as astronauts, the moon, and stars. For use in preschool through grade 3. [astronauts; astronomy; space]

Breaking Free: An Anthology of Human Rights Poetry.

Selected by Robert Hull. New York: Thomson Learning, 1995. 64 pp. Poetry with a human rights focus. For upper elementary students. [human rights]

Cat Poems.

Selected by Myra Cohn Livingston. New York: Holiday House, 1987. 32 pp. ISBN 0-8234-0631-8. A collection of poems about cats written by a variety of poets. For use in preschool through grade 3. [cats]

Cat Purrs.

Phyllis Halloran. St. Louis, MO: Milliken Pub. Co., 1987. 30 pp. Brief poems about cats. For use in all elementary grades. [cats]

A Celebration of Bees: Helping Children Write Poetry.

Barbara Juster Esbensen. New York: Holt, 1995. 275 pp. A guide for adults helping children to approach the writing of poetry. (First printed in 1975). [bees; creative writing]

City Night.

Eve Rice. New York: Greenwillow, 1987. 24 pp. ISBN 0-688-06856-1. A book of illustrated poems showing the beauty and diversity of the city. For use in preschool through grade 1. [cities]

Click, Rumble, Roar: Poems About Machines.

Selected by Lee Bennett Hopkins. New York: T. Y. Crowell, 1987. 40 pp. ISBN 0-690-04589-1. A collection of eighteen poems about machines written by a variety of poets. For use in grades 2–6. [machines]

Come On Into My Tropical Garden: Poems for Children.

Grace Nichols. New York: Lippincott, 1990. 38 pp. ISBN 0-397-32349-2. A collection of poems about the Caribbean and its people. For use in grades 2–6. [Caribbean]

Consider the Lemming.

Jeanne Steig. New York: Farrar, Straus & Giroux, 1988. 48 pp. ISBN 0-374-31536-1. A collection of humorous poems. For use in all primary grades. [humor]

Dancing Teepees: Poems of American Indian Youth.

Selected by Virginia Driving Hawk Sneve. New York: Holiday House, 1990. 32 pp. ISBN 0-8234-0724-1. An illustrated collection of poems from the oral tradition of Native Americans. Suitable preschool through grade 4. [Indians of North America]

Dinosaur Dances.

Jane Yolen. New York: Putnam, 1990. 39 pp. ISBN 0-399-21629-4. Contain seventeen whimsical poems about stegosaurus and other dinosaurs. Suitable for all elementary grades. [animals; dinosaurs]

Dinosaurs: Poems.

Selected by Lee Bennett Hopkins. San Diego, CA: Harcourt Brace Jovanovich, 1987. 46 pp. ISBN 0-15-223495-0. A collection of eighteen poems about dinosaurs by different poets. For grade 1 and up. [dinosaurs]

Dog Poems.

Selected by Myra Cohn Livingston. New York: Holiday House, 1990. 32 pp. ISBN 0-8234-0776-4. Contains poems by a variety of authors about dogs and puppies. Suitable for preschool through grade 3. [dogs]

Don't Read This Book Whatever You Do: More Poems About School.

Kalli Dakos. New York: Four Winds Press, 1993. 64 pp. ISBN 0-02-725582-4. These poems are about lively classroom activities. Suitable for grades 2–6. [school]

The Dragons Are Singing Tonight.

Jack Prelutsky. New York: Greenwillow, 1993. 39 pp. ISBN 0-8072-0220-7. Poetry about dragons. For use in all elementary grades. [dragons]

Dreams of Glory, Poems Starring Girls.

Selected by Isabel Joshlin Glaser. New York: Atheneum, 1995. 47 pp. ISBN 0-689-31891-X. Girls are featured in these poems. With particular appeal to girls in grade 3 and up. [girls]

Early in the Morning: A Collection of New Poems.

Charles Causley. New York: Viking Kestrel, 1986. 62 pp. This collection of poems contains music and illustrations. Appropriate for all elementary grades. [music]

The Earth Is Painted Green: A Garden of Poems About Our Planet.

Barbara Brenner, ed. New York: Scholastic, 1994. 81 pp. ISBN 0-590-45134-0. Poems about the planet Earth from around the world. Appropriate for upper elementary students. [Earth]

Earth Lines: Poems for the Green Age.

Pat Moon. New York: Greenwillow, 1993. 63 pp. ISBN 0-688-11853-4. This poet voices concerns about the survival of the planet. Appropriate for grade 5 and up. [Earth]

Earth Songs.

Myra Cohn Livingston. New York: Holiday House, 1986. 32 pp. These poems make a poetic tribute to the planet Earth. Appropriate for upper elementary students. [Earth]

Eric Carle's Dragons, Dragons & Other Creatures That Never Were.

Compiled by Laura Whipple. New York: Philomel, 1991. 68 pp. An Illustrated collection of poems about dragons and other creatures by a variety of authors. With particular appeal to primary grade students. [dragons]

Families—Poems Celebrating the African American Experience.

Selected by Dorothy S. Strickland and Michael R. Strickland. Honesdale, PA: Boyds Mills Press, 1994. 31 pp. ISBN 1-56397-560-2. An anthology of family-related poetry including poems by Gwendolyn Brooks and Langston

Hughes. For use in preschool through grade 3. [African Americans; families]

Fast Freddy Frog and Other Tongue-Twister Rhymes.

Ennis Rees. Honesdale, PA: Boyds Mills Press, 1993. 32 pp. ISBN 1-56397-038-4. Filled with tongue-twisters. With particular appeal to preschool through grade 3. [tongue twisters]

Followers of the North Star: Rhymes About African American Heroes, Heroines, and Historical Times.

Susan R. Altman and Susan Lechner. Chicago: Children's Press, 1993. 48 pp. ISBN 0-516-05151-2. Includes poetry about people including Benjamin Banneker, Rosa Parks, and Leontyne Price. For use with preschoolers through grade 4. [African Americans]

Freckly Feet and Itchy Knees.

Michael Rosen. New York: Doubleday, 1990. 32 pp. ISBN 0-385-41251-7. Contains humorous poems about body parts. With particular appeal to upper elementary students. [body, human]

Ghosts and Goosebumps: Poems to Chill Your Bones.

Selected by Bobbi Katz. New York: Random House, 1991. 32 pp. ISBN 0-679-80372-6. Contains scary poems written by a variety of notable poets. With particular appeal to preschoolers through grade 3. [ghosts]

Good Books, Good Times!

Selected by Lee Bennett Hopkins. New York: Harper & Row, 1990. 30 pp. ISBN 0-06-022527-0. An anthology of poetry about the joys of reading books. Suitable for preschool through grade 3. [reading]

Goosebumps & Butterflies.

Yolanda Nave. New York: Orchard Books, 1990. 31 pp. These poems are about childhood fears and anxieties. Suitable for all elementary grades. [fear]

Granny, Will Your Dog Bite, and Other Mountain Rhymes.

Gerald Milnes. New York: Knopf, 1990. 45 pp. ISBN 0-394-85363-6. This collection of poems describes a variety of aspects of mountain life. Appropriate for upper elementary students. [mountains]

A Grass Green Gallop: Poems.

Patricia Hubbell. New York: Atheneum, 1990. 48 pp. A collection of poems about horses. For use in all elementary grades. [horses]

Hailstones and Halibut Bones: Adventures in Color.

Mary LeDuc O'Neill. New York: Doubleday, 1989. 62 pp. ISBN 0-385-24484-3. Contains a dozen poems about colors. For use in all elementary grades. [color]

Halloween A B C, Poems by Eve Merriam.
Eve Merriam. New York: Macmillan, 1987. 28 pp. ISBN 0-02-766870-3. There is a Halloween-related poem for each letter of the alphabet. Suitable for all elementary grades. [Halloween; alphabet books]

Hand in Hand: American History Through Poetry.
Selected by Lee Bennett Hopkins. New York: Simon & Schuster Books for Young Readers, 1994. 144 pp. Poems about American history from colonial times to the present. Suitable for upper elementary students. [history]

A Hippopotamusn't and Other Animal Verses.
Patrick J. Lewis. New York: Dial Books, 1990. 40 pp. Contains more than 40 humorous poems. Suitable for all elementary grades. [animals]

How Beastly!: A Menagerie of Nonsense Poems.
Jane Yolen. Honesdale, PA: Boyds Mills Press, 1994. 46 pp. ISBN 1-56397-086-4. A collection of funny and nonsense poems. Suitable for grades 2–6. [nonsense poems]

How to Read and Write Poems.
Margaret Ryan. New York: Franklin Watts, 1991. 63 pp. ISBN 0-531-20043-4. Introduces components of poetry such as rhythm, meter, imagery, and rhyme. Contains bibliographic references. Good teacher resource. For use in grade 5–8. [creative writing]

If the Owl Calls Again: A Collection of Owl Poems.
Selected by Myra Cohn Livingston. New York: Margaret K. McElderry Books, 1990. 114 pp. ISBN 0-689-50501-9. Contains poems about owls written by a variety of poets. For use in grade 5 and up. [owls]

January Brings the Snow.
Sara Coleridge. New York: Simon & Schuster, 1987. 26 pp. ISBN 0-671-72338-3. Contains rhymes and poems about months of the year. Suitable for all elementary grades. [months]

Joyful Noise: Poems for Two Voices.
Paul Fleischman. New York: Harper & Row, 1988. 44 pp. ISBN 0-06-021852-5. A collection of poems about the activities and characteristics of insects. For use with grades 3–8. [insects]

If You're Not Here, Please Raise Your Hand: Poems About School.
Kalli Dakos. New York: Four Winds Press, 1990. 60 pp. ISBN 0-02-725581-6. An illustrated collection of poems about school. With particular appeal to students in grades 2–6. [school]

I Like You, If You Like Me: Poems of Friendship.
Selected by Myra Cohn Livingston. New York: Margaret K. McElderry Books, 1987. 144 pp. ISBN 0-689-50408-X. This is a collection of 90 poems

divided into nine sections written by contemporary and traditional poets. Suitable for grade 5 and up. [friendship]

I Thought I'd Take My Rat to School: Poems for September to June.

Selected by Dorothy M. Kennedy. Boston, MA: Little, Brown, 1993. 63 pp. ISBN 0-316-48893-3. Various authors are included in this anthology of poems which describes the good and bad sides of going to school. Suitable for all elementary grades. [school; seasons]

It's Hard to Read a Map With a Beagle On Your Lap.

Marilyn Singer. New York: Holt, 1995. 30 pp. ISBN 0-8050-2201-5. Contains playful poems about dogs. For use in grades 1–4. [dogs]

Land, Sea & Sky: Poems to Celebrate the Earth.

Selected by Catherine Paladino. Boston, MA: Little, Brown, 1993. 32 pp. ISBN 0-316-68892-4. Illustrated with photos, this book contains poems celebrating nature by various authors. For use in preschool through grade 3. [nature]

Latino Rainbow: Poems About Latin Americans.

Carlos Cumpian. Chicago: Children's Press, 1994. 47 pp. ISBN 0-516-05153-9. Poems about people, including Caesar Chaves, Linda Ronstadt, and Henry Cisneros. Suitable for students in grades 3–6. [Latin Americans]

Let Freedom Ring: A Ballad of Martin Luther King.

Myra Cohn Livingston. New York: Holiday House, 1992. 32 pp. ISBN 0-8234-0957-0. Celebrates the life of Martin Luther King. For students in preschool through grade 3. [King, Martin Luther, Jr.]

Listen to the Desert.

Pat Mora. New York: Clarion, 1994. 25 pp. ISBN 0-395-67292-9. This bilingual text describes the sounds and nature of the desert. For use in preschool through grade 2. [deserts]

Make a Joyful Sound: Poems for Children by African-American Poets.

Illustrated by Cornelius Van Wright and Ying-Hwa Hu. New York: Checkerboard Press, 1991. 97 pp. ISBN 1-56288-000-4. These poems are written by African-American poets. For use in all elementary grades. [African Americans]

A Moment in Rhyme.

Colin West and Julie Banyard. New York: Dial Books, 1987. 30 pp. This is an illustrated collection of twenty-four poems on a variety of subjects. For use in all elementary grades.

Moving Windows: Evaluating the Poetry Children Write.

Jack Collom. New York: Teachers and Writers Collaborative, 1985. 180 pp. ISBN 0-915924-55-2. An in-depth guide to evaluating student poetry based

on an examination of over three hundred student poems. Good adult
resource. [evaluation]

Mrs. Cole On an Onion Roll, and Other School Poems.
Kalli Dakos. New York: Simon & Schuster Books for Young Readers, 1995.
40 pp. ISBN 0-02-725583-2. Contains 32 school-related poems. For students
in grade 3 and up. [school]

Music of Their Hooves: Poems About Horses.
Nancy Springer. Honesdale, PA: Boyds Mills Press, 1994. 32 pp. ISBN 1-
56397-182-8. Poems about horses and the feel of riding. Suitable for grades
3–7. [horses]

My First Fourth of July Book.
Harriet W. Hodgson. Chicago: Children's Press, 1987. 31 pp. ISBN 0-516-
42907-8. A collection of holiday poems about parades, picnics, and fireworks. Suitable for preschool through grade 2. [Fourth of July]

New Year's Poems.
Selected by Myra Cohn Livingston. New York: Holiday House, 1987. 32 pp.
ISBN 0-8234-0641-5. A series of poems about the new year written by
various authors. For preschool through grade 3. [New Year's]

Oigan, Ninos = Listen Children: A Unique Collection of Mother Goose Rhymes,
Song, Jingles & Riddles in Spanish & English.
Compiled by Grace Barrington Hofer and Rachel Pressly Day.
Austin, TX: Eakin Press, 1992. 79 pp. A bilingual introduction to Mother
Goose. Of particular appeal to primary grade students. [Mother Goose
(Spanish); Spanish language]

Once Inside the Library.
Barbara A. Huff. Boston, MA: Little, Brown, 1990. 32 pp. ISBN 0-316-
37967-0. These poems describe the joys of books and reading. Appropriate
for preschool through grade 4. [libraries]

1001 Rhymes & Fingerplays for Working With Young Children.
Compiled by Totline Staff. Everett, WA: Warren Publishing, 1994, 307 pp.
Good source of rhymes and fingerplays. For preschoolers and primary
students. [finger plays]

1-2-3 Rhymes, Stories & Songs: Open-Ended Language Experience for Young
Children.
Jean Warren. Everett, WA: Warren Publishing, 1992. 78 pp. ISBN 0-911019-
50-2. An interdisciplinary approach to language experience with children.
For preschoolers. [music]

Our Village: Poems.
John Yeoman. New York: Atheneum, 1988. 41 pp. A collection of poems
introducing members of the village, such as the baker. Of particular appeal
to primary children. [occupations]

Pass It On: African-American Poetry for Children.

New York: Scholastic. 1993. 28 pp. An illustrated collection of poems by Afro-American poets. For all elementary grades. [African Americans]

A Paper Zoo: A Collection of Animal Poems by Modern American Poets.

Selected by Renee Karol Weiss. New York: Macmillan, 1987. 38 pp. An illustrated collection of poems about pets and wild animals. Suitable for all elementary grades. [animals; pets]

The Place My Words Are Looking For: What Poets Say About and Through Their Work.

Selected by Paul B. Janeczko. New York: Bradbury. 1990. 150 pp. ISBN 0-02-747671-5. Thirty-nine U.S. poets share their thoughts and inspirations. Good adult reference book. For use with students in grades 4–8. [poets]

Puddle Wonderful: Poems to Welcome Spring.

Selected by Bobbi Katz. New York: Random House, 1992. 30 pp. ISBN 0-679-81493-0. These poems about spring are written by a variety of poets. Suitable for preschool through grade 1. [spring]

Pussycat Ate the Dumplings: Cat Rhymes from Mother Goose.

Compiled by Robin Michal Koontz. New York: Dodd Mead, 1987. 47 pp. Many poems involving cats. With particular appeal to primary grade students. [cats]

Red Dragonfly On My Shoulder: Haiku.

Translated by Sylvia Cassedy and Kunichiro Suetake. New York: HarperCollins, 1992. 30 pp. ISBN 0-06-022624-2. Contains thirteen haiku on animal subjects. Illustrated with collage. Suitable for all elementary grades. [animals; haiku]

Roll Along: Poems About Wheels.

Selected by Myra Cohn Livingston. New York: Margaret K. McElderry Books, 1993. 72 pp. ISBN 0-689-50585-X. An anthology of contemporary poems by a variety of poets about wheels and vehicles that roll. For grade 4 and up. [vehicles; wheels]

Sad Underwear and Other Complications: More Poems for Children and Their Parents.

Judith Viorst. New York: Atheneum, 1995. 78 pp. ISBN 0-689-31929-0. Contains humorous poems on feelings and experiences from a child's point of view. For all elementary grades. [humor]

The Sea Is Calling Me: Poems.

Selected by Lee Bennett Hopkins. San Diego, CA: Harcourt Brace Jovanovich, 1986. 32 pp. ISBN 0-15-271155-4. This is a collection of poems by various authors about the seashore, the ocean, sand castles, etc. Suitable for grades 3–7. [marine life; ocean; seashore]

Seasons.

Warabe Aska. New York: Doubleday, 1990. 44 pp. ISBN 0-385-25265-X. The four seasons are shown around the world in paintings and in poetry. Suitable for all elementary grades. [seasons]

Shadow Play: Night Haiku.

Penny Harter. New York: Simon & Schuster Books for Young Readers, 1994. 32 pp. ISBN 0-671-88396-8. Good examples of the haiku poetic form. For all elementary grades. [haiku]

Sign Language Talk.

Laura Greene and Eva Barash. New York: Franklin Watts, 1989. 95 pp. Explains American Sign Language with instructions for using sign language for playing games, signing songs, and reading poetry. Suitable for all elementary grades. [sign language]

Sky Words.

Marilyn Singer. New York: Macmillan, 1994. 32 pp. ISBN 0-02-782882-4. Poems about subjects such as the sky, clouds, and storms. Suitable for preschool through grade 3. [sky; weather]

Snow Toward Evening: A Year in a River Valley: Nature Poems.

Selected by Josette Frank. Paintings by Thomas Locker. New York: Dial Books, 1990. 32 pp. ISBN 0-8037-0810-6. A poem for each month of the year with beautiful matching paintings. For all elementary grades. [months]

Somebody Catch My Homework: Poems.

David L. Harrison. Honesdale, PA: Boyds Mills Press, 1993. 30 pp. These poems describe school experiences. With particular appeal to upper elementary students. [school]

Songs of Our Ancestors: Poems About Native Americans.

Mark Turcotte. Chicago: Children's Press, 1995. 45 pp. ISBN 0-516-05154-7. Contains more than twenty poems about North American Indians and special events. For use with upper students in grade 3 and up. [Indians of North America]

Space Songs.

Myra Cohn Livingston. New York: Holiday House, 1988. 32 pp. ISBN 0-8234-0675-X. An illustrated collection of outer space related poems. For preschoolers through grade 3. [space]

Spin a Soft Black Song: Poems for Children.

Nikki Giovanni. New York: Hill and Wang, 1985. 57 pp. ISBN 0-8090-8796-0. Recounts the feelings of Afro-American children about themselves and their neighborhoods. For students in grade 2 and up. [African Americans]

The Spook Matinee: And Other Scary Poems for Kids.

George Ulrich. New York: Delacorte Press, 1992. 30 pp. ISBN 0-440-40956-X. This is a collection of poems about ghosts, vampires, and spiders. For upper elementary students. [ghosts; scary poems]

Still As a Star.

Selected by Lee Bennett Hopkins. Boston, MA: Little, Brown, 1989. 31 pp. ISBN 0-316-37272-2. Contains fifteen nighttime poems written by well-known poets. For use in preschool through grade 3. [night]

Street Music: City Poems.

Arnold Adoff. New York: HarperCollins, 1995. 32 pp. ISBN 0-06-021522-4. Fifteen poems about the sights and sounds of the city for children aged five to nine. [cities]

Talkaty Talker: Limericks.

Molly Manley. Honesdale, PA: Boyds Mills Press. 1994. 24 pp. ISBN 1-56397-195-X. A collection of humorous limericks. For use in preschool through grade 1. [humor; limericks]

There's an Awful Lot of Weirdos in Our Neighborhood: & Other Wickedly Funny Verse.

Colin McNaughton. New York: Simon & Schuster, 1987. 93 pp. A collection of humorous poems about eccentric characters. For upper elementary students. [humor]

Thirteen Moons On Turtle's Back: A Native American Year of Moons.

Joseph Bruchac and Jonathan London. New York: Philomel, 1992. 32 pp. ISBN 0-399-22141-7. These poems which celebrate the seasons come from legends of the Cherokee, Cree, and Sioux. For preschool through grade 8. [Cherokee; Cree; Indians of North America; Sioux; seasons]

This Land Is Our Land: A Guide to Multicultural Literature for Children and Young Adults.

Alethea K. Helbig and Agnes Regan Perkins. Westport, CT: Greenwood Press, 1994. 401 pp. ISBN 0-313-28742-2. A guide to children's multicultural literature with a good bibliography. A good teacher resource. [multicultural literature]

The Tigers Brought Pink Lemonade.

Patricia Hubbell. New York: Atheneum, 1988. 32 pp. Poems, both fantastic and humorous, about animals. Suitable for all elementary grades. [fantasy; humor]

Time Is the Longest Distance: An Anthology of Poems.

Selected by Ruth Gordon. New York: HarperCollins, 1991. 74 pp. ISBN 0-06-022297-2. This is an international anthology of poetry. For use in grade 6 and up. [multicultural poems]

Time of Rhyme: A Rhyming Dictionary.
Marvin Terban. Honesdale, PA: Boyds Mills Press, 1994. 96 pp. ISBN 1-56397-128-3. Gives examples for poems and includes a list of words that rhyme. For use in grades 2–4. [rhyming dictionaries]

Tyrannosaurus Was a Beast: Dinosaur Poems.
Jack Prelutsky. New York: Greenwillow Books, 1988. 31 pp. ISBN 0-688-06442-6. A collection of humorous dinosaur poems. For all elementary grades. [dinosaurs; humor]

Under the Sunday Tree: Poems.
Eloise Greenfield. New York: Harper & Row, 1988. 38 pp. ISBN 0-06-022257-3. A collection of poems and illustrations showing life in the Bahamas. For use in preschool through grade 1. [Bahamas]

Under Your Feet.
Joanne Ryder. New York: Four Winds Press, 1990. 42 pp. ISBN 0-02-777955-6. A collection of poems about nature, wildlife, and the seasons. Appropriate for preschool through grade 3. [nature; seasons]

Up in the Air.
Myra Cohn Livingston. New York: Holiday House, 1989. 32 pp. ISBN 0-8234-0736-5. These poems capture the sights and sensations of flying in an airplane. For use in preschool through grade 3. [airplanes]

Valentine Poems.
Selected by Myra Cohn Livingston. New York: Holiday House, 1987. 32 pp. ISBN 0-8234-0587-7. This is a collection of twenty poems about Valentine's Day. Appropriate for preschool through grade 3. [Valentine's Day]

Voices On the Wind: Poems for All Seasons.
Selected by David Booth. New York: Morrow Junior Books, 1990. 40 pp. ISBN 0-688-09554-2. An anthology of poetry about the four seasons. For all elementary grades. [seasons]

The Way I Feel—Sometimes.
Beatrice Schenk De Regniers. New York: Clarion, 1988. 48 pp. ISBN 0-89919-647-0. A collection of poems about emotions. Appropriate for grades 1–4. [emotions]

Weather, Poems.
Selected by Lee Bennett Hopkins. New York: HarperCollins, 1994. 63 pp. ISBN 0-06-444191-1. This anthology about weather has poems from several authors, and is appropriate for use in preschool through grade 3. [weather]

Weather Report: Poems.

Selected by Jane Yolen. Honesdale, PA: Boyds Mills Press, 1993. 64 pp. ISBN 1-56397-101-1. Contains poetry about all types of weather. For all elementary grades. [weather]

Wherever Home Begins: 100 Contemporary Poems.

Selected by Paul B. Janeczko. New York: Orchard Books, 1995. 114 pp. ISBN 0-531-09481-2. Contains poetry about the home. Appropriate for grade 6 and up. [homes]

Whiskers and Paws.

Fiona Waters, ed. New York: Interlink Pub., 1990. 29 pp. ISBN 0-940793-51-2. Traditional and original rhymes about animals. For use in all elementary grades. [animals]

Wind in the Long Grass: A Collection of Haiku.

William J. Higginson, ed. New York: Simon & Schuster Books for Young Readers, 1991. 48 pp. ISBN 0-671-67978-3. This is an illustrated collection of haiku arranged by season. Appropriate for use in grades 2–5. [haiku; seasons]

Without Words/Poems by Joanne Ryder.

Joanne Ryder. San Francisco, CA: Sierra Club Books for Children, 1995. 32 pp. ISBN 0-87156-580-3. These poems involve the nonverbal communication between humans and animals. Suitable for use in the elementary grades. [animals; communication]

Zoomerang a Boomerang: Poems to Make Your Belly Laugh.

Compiled by Caroline Parry. New York: Puffin, 1993. 32 pp. ISBN 0-14-054869-6. Contains humorous poetry suitable for use in preschool through grade 3. [humor]

Other resources

Amazing Writing Machine.

Broderbund Series. Liberty Lake, WA: Egghead. Win. # 312801, CD-ROM ed. This computer program for ages six to twelve encourages students to write and illustrate books and poems with over 2,000 clip art images and nine exciting writing environments. [clip art; creative writing]

American History in Verse.

Donald Thompson. University City, CA: MCA Home Videos, 1986. 3 videocassettes (90 minutes.) Tells stories and legends of America in verse. Suitable for upper elementary students. [history]

The Body Machine.

Radford Stone Newall. Stamford, CT: Capital Cities/ABC Video Pub., 1995. 1 videocassette, 26 minutes. Contains short, musical rhymes that explain for children the various systems of the body. Appropriate for grade 3 and up. [body, human]

Christmas Poems for You and Me.
  Richard Laurent. Chicago: Encyclopedia Britannica Ed. Corp., 1988.
  1 videocassette, 5 min., with booklet. Contains some presentations with live
  action and some that are animated. Appropriate for use with preschoolers
  and primary-aged students. [Christmas]

Hiawatha.
  Henry Wadsworth Longfellow. Milwaukee, WI: Raintree Children's Books,
  1984. 1 sound cassette. Presents an abridgement of this epic poem. For
  students in grade 3 and up. [Hiawatha]

Holiday Poems for December.
  Richard Laurent. Chicago: Encyclopedia Britannica Ed. Corp., 1988.
  1 videocassette, 6 min. Eight short presentations about Christmas,
  Hanukkah, and Kwanzaa. Suitable for use in all elementary grades.
  [Christmas; Hanukkah; Kwanzaa]

Exciting Writing, Successful Speaking.
  Martin Kimeldorf. Waco, TX: Prufrock Press, available in student and
  teacher editions for grades 4–9. A complete program with hands-on activities including writing poems that are built by rolling dice. [creative writing]

Martha's Attic: Using My Imagination.
  Martha Lambert and James Bryce. Framework Two Production in association with Crystal Clear Imagining. Distributed by Listening Library, Inc.
  1986. 1 videocassette, 60 min. Discusses imagination, using stories and
  poems. For use in all elementary grades. [imagination]

Starlight, Star Bright: Whole-Language Activities With Nursery Rhymes.
  Beth Rose Neiderman and Jean Naples Kuhn. Palo Alto, CA: Dale Seymour
  Publications. 142 pp. For grades K–3. Includes familiar verses and cross-
  curricular activities. Includes easy-to-use lessons and blackline masters.
  [nursery rhymes]

Wiggles and Giggles.
  Selected by Debbie Powell. Crystal Lake, IL: Rigby. Available as a Big Book,
  6 Small Books, and on cassette. These are humorous poems and rhymes.
  For grades K–3. [humor]

6

Folktales, Fables, Myths, and Legends

*I*t might seem that folktales, fables, myths, and legends could easily be incorporated into the earlier chapters on storytelling and puppetry or creative drama. While that would be possible, there is such a wealth of worthy material on these traditional stories that this chapter seemed to be essential to even begin to give adequate treatment to the richness of resources available to those who are working in the field of elementary language arts.

What binds folktales, fables, myths, and legends together is the fact that they are born out of the oral tradition. Folktales and fables are stories about people and talking animals who often live in a world filled with magical qualities. Myths usually deal with Gods and the origins of things, while legends recount the stories of heroes and their deeds.

Since these stories are from the oral tradition, they tend to be fairly short (except for epics) and have fast-moving plots. Often they are humorous, and usually, they end happily. Wishes may come true and justice usually wins out in the end. These factors make such tales particularly appealing to children who often have a strong sense of right and wrong and who sometimes feel themselves to be totally without power.

One type of folktale is the cumulative tale. "The Gingerbread Boy" is a good example of this form. There is repetition as the run-away meets one character after another and challenges each one to "Catch me if you can." Another type of common folktale is the "why" story in which there is an explanation of why something is the way it is. The Native American tale of "The Theft of Dawn," for example, explains why the sun disappeared.

There are many other types of folktales that students may wish to explore. In "noodlehead stories" there is a foolish person who follows the right advice at the wrong time. There are fairy tales with elves and giants. Many of these stories include a long sleep or enchantment, magical powers or objects, trickery and the granting of wishes.

After reading a number of folktales to students, they may wish to try their hand at writing one.

Directions for Ideas That Work

WHY STORIES: After reading some old folktales that explain why something is the way it is, read aloud to the students one or two of Rudyard Kipling's Just So stories. Then have students generate a list of animals and their prominent feature which you will write on the chalkboard. The list might include: elephant/trunk; zebra/stripes; lion/mane; kangaroo/pocket; alligator/armor; butterfly/wing; beaver/teeth; rat/tail; turtle/shell; and bird/beak.

Then encourage students to write an original folktale in which they explain that there once was a time when elephants didn't have trunks or when zebras didn't have stripes, until something strange and unusual happened to cause a change in them.

After the students have finished their "why" folktales, allow time for those who wish to do so to share them with the class.

The best-known fables are those of Aesop. In a fable, usually animals speak as human beings, there are only two or three animals in the story, the characters do not have names but are simply called "rabbit" or "fox," and there is a single incident. The purpose of the fable is to instruct, and there is an implied or stated moral. A typical fable would be the race between the hare and the tortoise.

Directions for Ideas That Work

WRITING A FABLE: First share with the class some fables. Take time to discuss the implied or stated moral. When students are comfortable with under-standing fables and morals, give them the opportunity to try to write some.

Ahead of time, write down the names of a variety of birds and animals on slips of paper and put these names into an empty coffee tin. You might include eagle, crow, skunk, tortoise, bear, fox, coyote, snake, porcupine, etc.

Have the students divide themselves into teams of three. Each student will then reach into the coffee tin and pull out one of the slips of paper with a creature's name on it.

The students are now challenged to write a very brief fable, with a moral, using at least two, and no more than the three, of the characters that they have drawn. This will require some "think time." When the fables are complete, allow a time for sharing and discussion.

Myths are explanations of such things as how the world began, why there are seasons of the year, and stories of gods, goddesses, heroes, and monsters. For a fuller understanding, it will be important for students to know the names of the various gods and their titles.

Directions for Ideas That Work

CHARTING THE GODS: During a unit of study on mythology, you might list the titles of the gods on the chalkboard (God of war, Sun God, etc.) and then have students select one of the titles and then work in pairs to learn a little about the god they chose, and the name of the Greek God and the Roman God. This information could be used to fill in the following chart.

The Greek and Roman Gods

Greek	Roman	Title
Ares	Mars	God of war
Aphrodite	Venus	Goddess of love and beauty.
Apollo	Apollo	God of truth, Sun god
Artemis	Diana	Goddess of the moon and hunt.
Athena	Minerva	Goddess of wisdom
Demeter	Ceres	Goddess of corn.
Dionysus	Bacchus	God of wine.
Eros	Cupid	God of love.
Hades/Pluto	Dis	God of the underworld.
Hera	Juno	Goddess of women and marriage.
Hestia	Vesta	Goddess of home and hearth.
Hephaestus	Vulcan	God of fire.
Hermes	Mercury	Messenger of the gods.
Persephone	Proserpine	Maiden of Spring.
Poseidon	Neptune	God of the sea.
Zeus	Jupiter/Jove	Supreme ruler, Lord of sky.

Have the pairs of students share with their classmates any information that they learned. Once it is complete, post this chart somewhere in the classroom. Having this chart available will make it easier for students as they read, discuss, and perhaps write their own myths.

Students may read humorous legends of American heroes or they may read epic stories. These usually involve "superheroes." Among the familiar heroes are John Henry, a railroad man; Mike Fink, a keelboatman; Davy Crockett, a frontiersman; Paul Bunyan, a lumberman; Pecos Bill, a cowboy, and Johnny Appleseed, a wanderer and planter of trees.

Directions for Ideas That Work

THE NEW ADVENTURES OF PECOS BILL: First be certain that students have had a chance to read some of the legends of American heroes and understand how exaggeration is a big part in the development of humor in these stories.

Choose one of the favorite heroes of the class and list on the chalkboard some information about the hero's characteristics and early childhood experiences.

Pecos Bill, for example, was one of 18 children. He was lost by his parents as an infant and raised by a pack of coyotes.

As a baby, he drank mountain lion's milk. Pecos Bill was of average size but he had great strength and daring. He could ride a cyclone the way another man might ride a horse. He could hug a bear to death. He was very clever at inventing things such as the lasso and the six-shooter. He rode a white mustang named Widow-Maker.

Gather the class in a circle to tell the new adventures of Pecos Bill. One student or the teacher begins the story. Explain that the story starter will hold a potato in his/ her hands. When that person who begins the story has said enough, the "hot potato" is passed to the next person in the circle who immediately goes on with the story. The adventures may be wild and fanciful but should be in keeping with what is listed as Pecos Bill's upbringing and characteristics. The teacher might run a tape recorder to catch this oral storytelling on tape.

There are many versions and collections of folktales, fables, myths, and legends. Sometimes it is interesting to speculate on how so many cultures, widely separated by time and distance, have come up with stories that in many ways are so similar. The resource list, for example, contains many different versions of the basic Cinderella story. Many of these collections are beautifully illustrated.

This traditional literature is an important component of elementary language arts and will be exciting to explore with students. It is an area that lends itself well to a cross-curricular approach. Students studying the gods might want to do an artistic mural displaying some of the more famous beasts. A folktale, fable, or legend might lend itself to a puppetry production. A social studies project where students are involved in studying another culture will be richer for having a component that includes the folktales and legends that evolved from that culture.

Other related chapters in this book on Music and Movement; Storytelling and Puppetry; Creative Dramatics; Holidays Around the World; and Poetry might also supply additional ideas and resources as you explore Folktales, Fables, Myths, and Legends.

Resource Books

American Tall Tales.
Mary Pope Osborne. New York: Knopf, 1991. 115 pp. ISBN 0-679-80089-1. Includes tales of folk heroes such as John Henry, Pecos Bill and Paul Bunyan. Suitable for use in grade 1 and up. [heroes]

Anansi.
Brian Gleeson. Saxsonville, MA: Picture Books Studio, 1991. 36 pp. ISBN 0-88708-230-0. Two Jamaican folktales about Anansi the spider and his trickery. Appropriate for preschool and up. [Jamaica; tricksters]

Anansi Finds a Fool: An Ashanti Tale.
Retold by Verna Aardema. New York: Dial Books, 1992. 32 pp. ISBN 0-8037-1164-6. A retelling in which lazy Anansi tries to trick someone but is fooled himself. Appropriate for preschool through grade 3. [tricksters]

Angels, Prophets, Rabbis, and Kings from the Stories of the Jewish People.

Jose Patterson. New York: P. Bedrick Books, 1991. 144 pp. ISBN 0-87226-912-4. A collection of traditional Jewish legends and tales. For grade 6 and up. [Jews]

Animal Lore and Legends – Buffalo: American Indian Legends.

Retold by Tiffany Midge. New York: Scholastic, 1995. 32 pp. ISBN 0-590-22489-1. Contains factual information as well as legends. Suitable for preschool through grade 3. [Indians of North America]

Atlanta's Race: A Greek Myth.

Retold by Shirley Climo. New York: Clarion, 1995. 31 pp. ISBN 0-395-67322-4. This story tells how a Greek princess is rejected by her father, raised by bears, won in marriage in a race, and turned into a lioness by Aphrodite. For upper elementary grades. [mythology]

Bearhead: A Russian Folktale.

Adapted by Eric A. Kimmel. New York: Holiday House, 1991. 32 pp. ISBN 0-8234-0902-3. In this Russian story, Bearhead outwits both a witch and a frog-headed goblin. Appropriate for preschool through grade 3. [Russia]

Big Trouble for Tricky Rabbit.

Retold by Gretchen Mayo. New York: Walker & Co., 1994. 37 pp. ISBN 0-8027-8275-2. This is a Native American trickster tale. Suitable for grades 2–3. [tricksters; Indians of North America]

The Bird, the Frog, and the Light: A Fable.

Avi. New York: Orchard Books, 1994. 28 pp. ISBN 0-531-06808-0. A frog learns from a bird that has a simple song. Suitable for preschool through grade 2. [birds; fables; frogs]

The Blind Men and the Elephant.

Retold by Karen Blackstein. New York: Scholastic, 1992. 48 pp. In this fable from India, six blind men get a limited understanding of an elephant because each feels only one part of the elephant. For all elementary grades. [fables; India]

Boots and His Brothers: A Norwegian Tale.

Retold by Eric A. Kimmel. New York: Holiday House, 1992. 32 pp. ISBN 0-8234-0886-8. A young man's kindness to a beggar woman earns him his weight in gold and half of a kingdom. Suitable for preschool through grade 3. [Norway]

The Boy and the Giants.

Fiona Moodie. New York: Farrar, Straus & Giroux, 1993. 32 pp. ISBN 0-374-30927-2. Thomas, a fisherboy, tries to rescue a girl from the giants. For preschool through grade 3. [giants]

The Boy Who Could Do Anything & Other Mexican Folk Tales.

Retold by Anita Brenner. Hamden, CT: Linnet Books, 1992. 133 pp. ISBN 0-208-02353-4. Contains twenty-four Mexican folktales including the legendary character Tepozton. For use in grades 3–7. [Mexico]

The Boy Who Lived With the Seals.

Rafe Martin. New York: Putnam, 1993. 32 pp. ISBN 0-399-22413-0. In this Chinook Indian legend a boy grows up with seals and returns home changed. For preschool through grade 3. [Indians of North America; legends; seals]

Buffalo Dance: A Blackfoot Legend.

Retold by Nancy Laan. Boston, MA: Joy Street Books, 1993. 30 pp. ISBN 0-316-89728-0. Describes the rituals before starting the buffalo hunt. For grade 3 and up. [buffalo; Indians of North America]

Buried Moon.

Retold by Margaret Hodges. Boston, MA: Little, Brown, 1990. 32 pp. ISBN 0-316-36793-1. This is an English folktale about rescuing the moon after she is buried in a dark pool. For use in preschool through grade 3. [Great Britain; moon]

Children of the Morning Light: Wampanoag Tales As Told by Manitonquat.

Medicine Story. New York: Macmillan, 1994. 72 pp. ISBN 0-02-765905-4. This is a collection of traditional stories. For use in grade 1 and up. [Africa; Wampanoag]

Children of Wax: African Folk Tales.

Alexander McCall Smith. New York: Interlink Pub., 1991. 119 pp. ISBN 0-940793-73-3. This book of African folktales was originally published in Edinburgh. For grade 2 and up. [Africa]

Children of Yayoute: Folk Tales of Haiti.

Turenne des Pres. New York: Universe Pub., 1994. 96 pp. ISBN 0-87663-791-8. A collection of Haitian folktales featuring magical human and animal characters. For grade 2 and up. [Haiti]

Classic American Folk Tales.

Retold by Steven Zorn. Philadelphia, PA: Running Press, 1992. 55 pp. ISBN 1-56138-062-8. Contains stories such as "Johnny Appleseed," "The Story of Bobcat & Coyote," and "How Brer Rabbit Tricked Brer Fox." Appropriate for all elementary grades. [North America]

The Cook and the King.

Maria Cristina Brusca. New York: Holt, 1993. 32 pp. ISBN 0-8050-2355-0. This South American tale tells how a wise cook teaches a bossy king how to rule his people wisely. For grades 1-4. grades. [South America]

Coyote Makes Man.

James Sage. New York: Simon & Schuster Books for Young Readers, 1995. 28 pp. ISBN 0-689-80011-8. A Native American creation myth. For preschool through grade 3. [creation myths; Indians of North America]

Dictionary of World Myth.

Peter Bentley, ed. New York: Facts On File, 1996. 240 pp. ISBN 0-614-97820-3. A generously illustrated book on gods, goddesses, heroes, heroines, supernatural creatures, sacred cities, and temples. For upper elementary grades and a teacher resource. [mythology–dictionaries]

Dragons: Truth, Myth, and Legend.

David Passes. New York: Western Publishing, 1993. 41 pp. ISBN 0-307-17500-6. Discusses dragon lore from around the world. For preschool through grade 3. [dragons; legends]

Dreamtime: Aboriginal Stories.

Oodgeroo Nunukul. New York: Lothrop, Lee & Shepard, 1994. 95 pp. ISBN 0-688-13296-0. Contains Australian aboriginal folklore. For grade 3 and up. [Australian Aborigines]

Earth Maker's Lodge: Native American Folklore, Activities, and Foods.

E. Barrie Kavasch, ed. Peterborough, NH: Cobblestone, 1994. 158 pp. ISBN 0-942389-09-3. A collection of stories, legends, and poems as well as projects, activities, games and recipes of Native Americans. For preschool through grade 4. [Indians of North America]

East O' the Sun and West O' the Moon.

Translated by Sir George Webbe Dasent. Cambridge, MA: Candlewick Press, 1992. 41 pp. ISBN 1-56402-437-7. A collection of Norwegian fairy tales. For use in preschool through grade 3. [Norway]

The Elephant-Headed God and Other Hindu Tales.

Retold by Debjani Chatterjee. New York: Oxford University Press, 1992. 88 pp. ISBN 0-19-508112-9. A collection of Hindu myths. For use in upper elementary grades. [Hindu]

Fables Aesop Never Wrote/But Robert Kraus Did.

Robert Kraus. New York: Viking, 1994. 32 pp. 0-670-85630-4. Contains fifteen original fables. For use in all elementary grades. [fables]

The Fables of Aesop.

Retold by Frances Barnes-Murphy. New York: Lothrop, Lee & Shepard, 1994. 93 pp. ISBN 0-688-07051-5. A collection of fables. For use in all elementary grades. [Aesop; fables]

Fairy Tales, Fables, Legends, and Myths: Using Folk Literature in Your Classroom.

> Bette Bosma. New York: Teachers College Press, 1992. 190 pp. ISBN 0-8077-3134-X. Explains the use of folktales in the classroom and contains a bibliography. Useful resource for adults. [fables; fairy tales]

The Fifth and Final Sun: An Ancient Aztec Myth of the Sun's Origin.

> Retold by C. Shana Greger. Boston, MA: Houghton Mifflin, 1994. 32 pp. ISBN 0-395-67438-7. In this myth, Nanautzin takes on the permanent job of being the sun. For preschool through grade 6. [Aztecs; mythology]

Fire Race: A Karuk Coyote Tale About How Fire Came to the People.

> Retold by Jonathan London with Lanny Pinola. San Francisco, CA: Chronicle Books, 1993. 32 pp. ISBN 0-8118-0241-8. In this tale, Wise Old Coyote acquires fire from the wicked Yellow Jacket Sisters. For all elementary grades. [Karuk]

First Houses: Native American Homes and Sacred Structures.

> Jean Guard Monroe and Ray A. Williamson. Boston, MA: Houghton Mifflin, 1993. 147 pp. ISBN 0-395-51081-3. Contains a variety of North American Indian creation myths. For grade 3 and up. [creation myths; Indians of North America]

Folk Stories of the Hmong: People of Laos, Thailand, and Vietnam.

> Compiled by Norma J. Livo and Dia Cha. Englewood, CO: Libraries Unlimited, 1991. 135 pp. ISBN 0-87287-854-6. Contains stories that give details of folklore, life and customs. Includes a bibliography. For use with upper elementary students. [Hmong]

Folk Tales & Fables of Asia & Australia.

> Robert Ingpen and Barbara Hayes. New York: Chelsea House, 1994. 92 pp. ISBN 0-7910-2755-4. Traditional tales from Asia and Australia. For grade 5 and up. [Asia; Australia]

Folk Tales & Fables of Europe.

> Robert Ingpen and Barbara Hayes. New York: Chelsea House, 1994. 92 pp. ISBN 0-7910-2756-2. Traditional tales from Europe. For use with grade 5 and up. [Europe]

Folk Tales & Fables of the Americas and the Pacific.

> Robert Ingpen and Barbara Hayes. New York: Chelsea House, 1994. 93 pp. ISBN 0-7910-2759-7. Contains folklore of the Indians of North and South America and Polynesia. For use in grade 5 and up. [Indians of North America; Indians of South America; Pacific Islanders]

The Four Gallant Sisters, Adapted from the Brothers Grimm.

> Adapted by Eric A. Kimmel. New York: Holt, 1992. 32 pp. ISBN 0-8050-1901-4. In this German tale, four orphaned sisters disguise themselves and go out to try to learn a trade. For grades 1–4. [Grimm]

From Sea to Shining Sea.

Selected by Amy Cohn. New York: Scholastic, 1993. 399 pp. ISBN 0-590-42868-3. An illustrated compilation of 140 folk songs, tales, poems and stories telling the history of America. For use with upper elementary students. Good teacher resource. [poetry; history]

Ghosts!: Ghostly Tales from Folklore.

Retold by Alvin Schwartz. New York: HarperCollins, 1991. 63 pp. ISBN 0-06-021796-0. Contains seven easy-to-read folktales and legends from various countries. For use with preschool through grade 3. [ghosts]

The Greatest of All: A Japanese Folktale.

Retold by Eric A. Kimmel. New York: Holiday House, 1991. 32 pp. ISBN 0-8234-0885-X. A mouse father goes in search of a husband for his daughter. For students in preschool through grade 3. [Japan; mice]

Greek Myths.

Retold by Geraldine McCaughrean. New York: Margaret K. McElderry Books, 1993. 96 pp. ISBN 0-689-50583-3. Retellings of some of the more famous Greek myths with illustrations by Emma Chichester Clark. Suitable for grade 4 and up. [mythology–Greek; Greece]

Greek Myths for Young Children.

Marcia Williams. Cambridge, MA: Candlewick Press, 1992. 36 pp. ISBN 1-56402-440-7. Retellings of eight Greek myths in comic strip format. Appropriate for preschool through grade 3. [cartoons; mythology–Greek; Greece]

Here Comes Tricky Rabbit.

Retold by Gretchen Will Mayo. New York: Walker & Co., 1994. 38 pp. ISBN 0-8027-8273-6. A traditional trickster tale. For use in grades 2–3. [tricksters]

How Music Came Into the World: An Ancient Mexican Myth.

Retold by Hal Ober. Boston, MA: Houghton Mifflin, 1994. 32 pp. ISBN 0-395-67523-5. This Aztec legend tells how the Sky God and the Wind God bring music from the Sun's house to Earth. Appropriate for all elementary grades. [Mexico; mythology]

How the Seasons Came: A North American Indian Folk Tale.

Retold by Joanna Troughton. New York: Bedrick/Blackie Books, 1992. 26 pp. An Algonquin Indian tale. Suitable for all elementary grades. [Algonquin; seasons]

How the Stars Fell Into the Sky: A Navajo Legend.

Jerrie Oughton. Boston, MA: Houghton Mifflin, 1992. 28 pp. ISBN 0-395-58798-0. This Navajo legend explains how patterns were formed among the stars. For use in preschool through grade 3. [Navajo; stars]

How Turtle's Back Was Cracked: A Traditional Cherokee Tale.
Retold by Gayle Ross. New York: Dial Books, 1995. 32 pp. ISBN 0-8037-1728-8. This story tells how wolves plot to stop turtle's boasting. For use in preschool through grade 3. [Cherokee; wolves]

How We Saw the World: Nine Native Stories of the Way Things Began.
Carrie J. Taylor. Plattsburg, NY: Tundra Books, 1993. 32 pp. ISBN 0-88776-302-2. Contains stories from many Indian tribes including the Algonquin, Blackfoot, Cheyenne, Kiowa, and Mohawk. For grades 1–5. [Indians of North America]

Iktomi and the Buffalo Skull: A Plains Indian Story.
Paul Goble. New York: Orchard Books, 1991. 32 pp. ISBN 0-531-05911-1. In this story, a trickster interrupts the Mouse People and gets his head stuck in a buffalo skull. For preschool through grade 2. [tricksters]

The Illustrated Book of Myths: Tales and Legends of the World.
Neil Phillip. New York: Dorling Kindersley, 1995. 192 pp. This collection of tales comes from many cultures. Good teacher resource. For use with upper elementary students. [legends; multicultural stories]

Ishi's Tale of Lizard.
Translated by Leanne Hinton. New York: Farrar, Straus & Giroux, 1992. 32 pp. ISBN 0-374-43625-8. This is a Yana Indian legend about lizard's work making arrows. For use with students in grade 2 and up. [lizards; Yana]

Jamie O'Rourke and the Big Potato: An Irish Folktale.
Retold by Tomie dePaola. New York: Putnam, 1992. 30 pp. ISBN 0-399-22257-X. When the laziest man in Ireland catches a leprechaun, he is offered a potato seed instead of a pot of gold. For preschool through grade 3. [Ireland; leprechauns]

John Henry.
Julius Lester. New York: Dial Books, 1994. 36 pp. ISBN 0-8037-1606-0. Tells the story of the legendary African American who races against a steam drill. For students preschool through grade 3. [African Americans]

King Arthur & the Legends of Camelot.
Molly Perham. New York: Viking, 1993. 171 pp. ISBN 0-670-84990-1. The Arthurian romances. For grade 1 and up. [Arthurian romances]

The King Who Tried to Fry an Egg On His Head.
Mirra Ginsburg. New York: Macmillan, 1994. 32 pp. ISBN 0-02-736242-6. This story is based on a Russian folktale about a foolish king. For preschool through grade 3. [kings; Russia]

Korean Folk-Tales.

Retold by James Riordan. New York: Oxford University Press, 1994. 133 pp. ISBN 0-19-274160-8. Contains myths and legends from Korea. For students in grade 2 and up. [Korea]

The Legend of El Dorado: A Latin American Tale.

Adapted by Nancy Van Laan. New York: Knopf, 1991. 38 pp. ISBN 0-679-80136-7. A retelling of the Chibcha Indian legend about the treasure of El Dorado. For preschool through grade 4. [Chibcha]

The Legend of Pecos Bill.

Retold by Terry Small. New York: Bantam, 1992. 30 pp. Retells in verse the story of this extraordinary cowboy. For grade 3 and up. [cowboys]

The Legend of Slappy Hooper: An American Tall Tale.

Retold by Aaron Shepard. New York: Scribner's, 1993. 28 pp. ISBN 0-684-19535-6. A sign painter gets into trouble because of his realistic signs. For grades 1–3. [tall tales]

Lilith's Cave: Jewish Tales for the Supernatural.

Selected by Howard Schwartz. New York: Oxford University Press, 1991. 274 pp. ISBN 0-19-506726-6. Jewish folklore with bibliographic references. For upper elementary students. [Jews]

The Little House: A Jewish Folk Tale from Eastern Europe.

Retold by Erica Gordon. New York: Bedrick/Blackie Books, 1991. 30 pp. In this tale, a poor man seeks advice from the Rabbi. For grade 2 and up. [Jews]

Ma'ii and Cousin Horned Toad: A Traditional Navajo Story.

Retold by Shonto Begay. New York: Scholastic, 1992. 32 pp. ISBN 0-590-45391-2. A lazy coyote is taught a lesson by a horned toad. For preschool through grade 2. [coyotes; Navajo]

Make Believe Tales: A Folk Tale from Burma.

Retold by Joanna Troughton. New York: Bedrick/Blackie Books, 1991. 26 pp. ISBN 0-87226-451-3. Four animals challenge a traveller to a tale-telling contest. For preschool through grade 3. [Burma]

Maruska's Egg.

Elsa Okon Rael. New York: Four Winds Press, 1993. 40 pp. In this Russian tale, nine-year-old Marushka is sucked into a magic egg and is housekeeper to a witch. For grade 3 and up. [Russia]

Merry-Go-Round: Four Stories.

Mirra Ginsburg. New York: Greenwillow, 1992. 48 pp. ISBN 0-688-09256-X. A collection of four fables with pictures by Jose Aruego and Ariane Dewey. For use in all elementary grades. [fables]

Midwestern Folk Humor.

James P. Leary, ed. Little Rock, AR: August House, 1991. 268 pp. ISBN 0-87483-108-3. ISBN 0-87483-107-5 paper. This is part of a folklore series, and it contains a bibliography. Good teacher resource. For use with upper elementary students. [humor; Midwest (U.S.)]

The Moles and the Mireuk: A Korean Folktale.

Retold by Holly H. Kwon. Boston, MA: Houghton Mifflin, 1993. 32 pp. ISBN 0-395-64347-3. In this tale, a mole goes everywhere trying to find a powerful husband for his daughter. For preschool through grade 3. [Korea; moles]

The Monkey and the Panda.

Antonia Barber. New York: Macmillan Books for Young Readers, 1995. 26 pp. ISBN 0-02-708382-9. This tale is about a monkey who is jealous of a panda beloved by children. For all elementary grades. [monkeys; pandas]

Monster Myths: The Truth About Water Monsters.

Staton Rabin. New York: Franklin Watts, 1992. Information about sharks, octopuses, etc. and some of the myths that surround sea creatures. For upper elementary students. [marine life; monsters]

Moontellers: Myths of the Moon from Around the World.

Lynn Moroney. Flagstaff, AZ: Northland, 1995. 32 pp. ISBN 0-87358-601-8. Contains moon folklore and mythology. For preschool and up. [moon; mythology]

Moon Was Tired of Walking on Air: Origin Myths of South American Indians.

Compiled by Natalia M. Belting. Boston, MA: Houghton Mifflin, 1992. 46 pp. ISBN 0-395-53806-8. A collection of myths from various tribes explaining the natural world. For grades 4–7. [moon; Indians of South America]

Myths and Legends from Ghana.

Retold by Rute Larungu. Mogodore, OH: Telcraft Books, 1992. 94 pp. ISBN 1-878893-21-1. ISBN 1-878893-20-3 paper. A collection of Ashanti legends. For grade 3 and up. [Ashanti; Ghana; legends]

Myth's & Legends of the Indians of the Southwest.

Bertha Dutton and Caroline Olin. Santa Barbara, CA: Bellerophon Books, 1994. 48 pp. ISBN 0-88388-062-8. Includes myths from various tribes. For use in grades 1–9. [Indians of North America]

Nathaniel Willy, Scared Silly.

Retold by Judith Mathews and Fay Robinson. New York: Bradbury, 1994. 32 pp. ISBN 0-02-765285-8. A squeak in the door scares Nathaniel so badly that Gramma puts farm animals in bed with him for company. Appropriate for preschool through grade 3. [ghost stories]

Night Visitors.

Retold by Ed Young. New York: Philomel, 1995. 32 pp. ISBN 0-399-22731-8. This Chinese folktale tells of a scholar who learns respect for all forms of life. For preschool through grade 3. [China]

Our Folk Heroes.

Karen Bornemann Spies. Brookfield, CT: Millbrook Press, 1994. 48 pp. ISBN 1-56294-440-1. Tales of American heroes. For grades 2-4. [heroes]

Over Nine Waves: A Book of Irish Legends.

Marie Heaney, ed. Boston, MA: Faber & Faber, 1994. 254 pp. ISBN 0-571-14231-1. Contains Irish stories and has bibliographic references. For upper elementary grades. [Ireland]

Peach Boy.

William H. Hooks. New York: Bantam, 1992. 48 pp. ISBN 0-553-07621-3. In this Japanese folktale, Momotaro is found inside a peach floating on a river by an old couple. Momotaro grows up and fights the village demons. For preschool through grade 3. [Japan]

Persephone.

Retold by Warwick Hutton. New York: Margaret K. McElderry Books, 1994. 30 pp. ISBN 0-689-50600-7. Tells the Greek myth of Persephone who spends six months of every year in Hades. For grade 2 and up. [mythology--Greek; Greece]

Prince Ivan and the Firebird: A Russian Folk Tale.

Retold by Bernard Lodge. Boston: Whispering Coyote Press, 1993. 32 pp. ISBN 1-879085-63-1. The youngest son of the king sets out to find the firebird which has been stealing golden apples from his father's tree. For all elementary grades. [Russia]

The Rabbit's Escape.

Suzanne Crowder Han. New York: Holt, 1995. 32 pp. ISBN 0-8050-2675-4. In this Korean folktale, a clever rabbit escapes after being tricked into visiting an underwater kingdom. For preschool through grade 3. [Korea; rabbits; tricksters]

Rachel the Clever and Other Jewish Folktales.

Selected by Josepha Sherman. Little Rock, AR: August House, 1993. 171 pp. ISBN 0-87483-306-X. ISBN 0-87483-307-8 paper. A collection of Jewish folk literature. For upper elementary grades. [Jews]

The Rainbow Bridge: A Chumash Legend.

Adapted by Kerry Nichodom. Los Osos, CA: Sand River Press, 1992. 29 pp. ISBN 0-944627-36-6. A Chumash boy hears his grandfather share legends about fire and dolphins. For preschool through grade 3. [Chumash; legends]

Raven's Light: A Myth from the People of the Northwest Coast.

Retold by Susan Hand Shetterly. New York: Atheneum, 1991. 32 pp. ISBN 0-689-31629-1. Explains how Raven made the Earth and the moon and sun. For grades 1–5. [creation myths; Indians of North America]

Realms of Gold: Myths & Legends from Around the World.

Ann Pilling. New York: Kingfisher Books, 1993. 91 pp. ISBN 1-85697-913-X. A collection of fourteen myths and legends from Greece, West Africa, Russia, etc. For upper elementary students. [Greece; myths; Russia; West Africa]

Reynard, the Fox.

Retold by Selina Hastings. New York: Tambourine Books, 1991. 76 pp. ISBN 0-688-09949-1. Deals with the schemes of the tricky fox, Reynard. For grades 2–4. [foxes; tricksters]

To Ride a Butterfly: Original Pictures, Stories, Poems, and Songs for Children.

Nancy Larrick and Wendy Lamb, eds. New York: Bantam Doubleday Dell, 1991. 96 pp. ISBN 0-440-50402-3. An illustrated collection of fables, folktales, stories, poems, and songs by various authors. For preschool through grade 3. [fables; poetry]

The Rhine.

Mark Smalley. Austin, TX: Raintree Steck-Vaughn, 1994. 48 pp. ISBN 0-8114-3102-9. Provides an overview of the Rhine River including the myths and legends associated with it. For grades 5–6. [myths; Rhine River]

The Robber Baby: Stories from the Greek Myths.

Anne F. Rockwell. New York: Greenwillow, 1994. 79 pp. Retellings of fifteen tales from Greek myths. For upper elementary grades. [Greece; mythology--Greek]

The Rough-Face Girl.

Rafe Martin. New York: Putnam, 1992. 32 pp. ISBN 0-399-21859-9. This is an Algonquin Indian version of the old Cinderella story. For preschool through grade 3. [Algonquin]

St. Jerome and the Lion.

Retold by Margaret Hodges. New York: Orchard Books, 1991. 30 pp. An illustrated retelling of the legend of St. Jerome and how he sheltered a lion in his monastery. For grade 3 and up. [legends; lions]

Salt: A Russian Folktale.

Retold by Jane Langton. New York: Hyperion Books for Children, 1992. 40 pp. ISBN 1-56282-681-6. A merchant's son barters the cargo of a ship for a princess and a fortune. For preschool through grade 3. [Russia]

Scheherazade's Cat and Other Fables from Around the World.

Retold by Amy Zerner. Boston, MA: Charles E. Tuttle, 1993, 115 pp. ISBN 0-8048-1807-X. An illustrated collection of nine stories from several different countries. Good teacher resource. [fables; multicultural stories]

The Seventh Sister: A Chinese Legend.

Cindy Chang. Mahwah, NJ: Troll, 1994. 32 pp. ISBN 0-8167-3411-9. A maid and her sisters weave the tapestry of the night sky. For grades 2–5. [China]

A Sip of Aesop.

Adapted by Jane Yolen. New York: Blue Sky Press, 1995. 32 pp. ISBN 0-590-47895-8. This book retells in verse thirteen fables. For all elementary grades. [Aesop; fables]

A Song of Stars: An Asian Legend.

Adapted by Tom Birdseye. New York: Holiday House, 1990. 27 pp. ISBN 0-8234-0790-X. Although they are banished to opposite sides of the Milky Way, the princess and the herdsman reunite each year on the seventh day of the seventh month. Appropriate for grades 4–8. [Asia; legends]

Sootface: An Ojibwa Cinderella Story.

Retold by Robert D. San Souci. New York, Doubleday Books for Young Readers, 1994. 30 pp. ISBN 0-385-31202-4. In this story a young maiden, scorned by her two sisters, wins a warrior. For all elementary grades. [Ojibwa]

Stone Soup.

Retold by John Warren Stewig. New York: Holiday House, 1991. 32 pp. A hungry and clever girl tricks villagers into adding to a meal started with a magic stone. For all elementary grades.

Strudel, Strudel, Strudel.

Steve Sanfield. New York: Orchard Books, 1995. 32 pp. ISBN 0-531-06879-X. This Polish folktale explains why teachers in Chelm can't live on top of a hill or eat apple strudel. For preschool through grade 2. [Poland]

Tales from the Bamboo Grove.

Yoko Kawashima Watkins. New York: Bradbury, 1992. 49 pp. ISBN 0-02-792525-0. A collection of Japanese folktales. For grades 4–11. [Japan]

The Thunder King: A Peruvian Folk Tale.

Amanda Loverseed. New York: Bedrick/Blackie Books, 1991. 28 pp. The condor helps Illanti rescue his twin brother in this tale. For all elementary grades. [condors; Peru]

Town Mouse, Country Mouse.

Retold by Carol Jones. Boston, MA: Houghton Mifflin, 1995. 32 pp. ISBN 0-395-71129-0. This is Aesop's fable about two mice who exchange visits and learn each is suited to its own home. For preschool through grade 3. [Aesop; fables; mice]

The Tree That Rains: The Flood Myth of the Huichol Indians of Mexico.

Retold by Emery Bernhard. New York: Holiday House, 1994. 32 pp. In this tale, Watakame survives a great flood. For all elementary grades. [floods; Huichol; Mexico]

Two Mice in Three Fables.

Lynn Reiser. New York: Greenwillow, 1995. 30 pp. ISBN 0-688-13389-4. Simple lessons are taught in these three stories featuring animals. For preschool and up. [animals; mice]

Watch Out for Clever Women = Cuidad Con Las Mujeres Astutas!: Hispanic Folktales.

Retold by Joe Hayes. El Paso, TX: Cinco Puntas Press, 1994. 77 pp. ISBN 0-938317-21-0. ISBN 0-938317-20-2 paper. A retelling in parallel English and Spanish text of traditional Hispanic folklore. For grades 3–7. [Hispanic folklore; Spanish language]

Watermelons, Walnuts, and the Wisdom of Allah: And Other Tales of the Hoca.

Barbara K. Walker. Lubbock, TX: Texas Tech University Press, 1991. 71 pp. ISBN 0-89672-254-6. A collection of tales from Turkey. For grade 3 and up. [Hoca; Turkey]

Whale's Canoe: A Folk Tale from Australia.

Retold by Joanna Troughton. New York: Bedrick/Blackie Books, 1993. 26 pp. ISBN 0-87226-509-9. This is a traditional Aboriginal tale. For preschool through grade 3. [Australian Aborigines]

White Wolf Woman: Native American Transformation Myths.

Retold by Teresa Pijoan. Little Rock, AR: August House, 1992. 167 pp. ISBN 0-87483-201-2. ISBN 0-87483-200-4 paper. A collection of 37 tribal myths showing the power of certain animals as they move between human and nonhuman worlds. For upper elementary grades. [animals; Indians of North America; transformation myths]

William Tell.

Retold by Margaret Early. New York: Harry Abrams, 1991. 29 pp. ISBN 0-8109-3854-5. This Swiss legend tells of a struggle for freedom. For grade 3 and up. [Switzerland]

Wishbones: A Folk Tale from China.

Retold by Barbara Ker Wilson. New York: Bradbury, 1993. 26 pp. ISBN 0-02-793125-0. This is the Chinese version of the Cinderella tale. For preschool through grade 2. [China]

The Woman Who Fell from the Sky: The Iroquois Story of Creation.

Retold by John Bierhorst. New York: Morrow, 1993. 30 pp. ISBN 0-688-10680-3. This story explains that the creation of the Earth started with a woman who fell from the sky country and then was finished by her two sons. For all elementary grades. [Iroquois]

The Wonderful Bag: An Arabian Tale from the Thousand & One Nights.
Retold by Gini Wade. New York: Bedrick/Blackie Books, 1993. 26 pp. ISBN 0-87226-508-0. A small boy and two gentlemen fight over a bag which supposedly has wonderful contents. For preschool through grade 3. [Arabs]

World Folktales: An Anthology of Multicultural Folk Literature.
Anita Stern. Lincolnwood, IL: National Textbook Co., 1994, 156 pp. ISBN 0-8442-0781-0. Includes folk literature and discussion of how to use it in an interdisciplinary approach. An adult reference book. [multicultural stories]

Other resources

Anansi.
Told by Denzel Washington. Westport, CT: Rabbit Ears Productions, 1991. 1 videocassette, 30 minutes. For ages 5 and up. Includes folktales and musical background. [tricksters]

The Boy Who Drew Cats.
David Johnson. Westport, CT: Rabbit Ears Productions, 1991. 1 videocassette, 30 minutes. For ages 5 and up. This is a Japanese folktale told by William Hurt. [cats; Japan]

Brer Rabbit and Boss Lion.
Westport, CT: Rabbit Ears Productions, 1992. 1 videocassette, 30 minutes. Told by Danny Glover. For ages 5 and up. In this tale, Brer Rabbit sets out to teach Boss Lion a lesson. [tricksters]

Davy Crockett.
Westport, CT: Rabbit Ears Productions, 1992. 1 videocassette, 30 minutes. Told by Nicolas Cage. This is the story of a frontier hero. For grade 2 and up. [heroes]

The Fool and the Flying Ship.
Westport, CT: Rabbit Ears Productions, 1991. 1 videorecording, 30 minutes. Told by Robin Williams. For ages 5 and up. A famous Russian folktale. [Russia]

Keepers of the Earth.
Golden, CO: Fulcrum, 1991. 2 sound cassettes, 133 minutes. Told by Joseph Bruchac. These are traditional tales of various Indian peoples with instruction for related activities involving the environment. For grade 2 and up. [Indians of North America]

King Midas and the Golden Touch.
Westport, CT: Rabbit Ears Productions, 1991. 1 videocassette, 30 minutes. For ages 5 and up. The folktale classic of a king who learns that some things

are more precious than gold is told by Michael Caine against a musical background.

Puss in Boots.

Hollywood, CA: Hanna Barbera Home Video, 1991. 1 videocassette, 30 minutes. An animated adaptation of Charles Perrault's tale of a clever cat that helps his master. For primary grades. [cats]

Rumpelstiltskin.

Retold by Paul Galdone. Boston, MA: Houghton Mifflin, 1994. 1 book of 30 pp. and 1 sound cassette, 13 minutes. This is the favorite tale of a strange little man who helps the miller's daughter spinning straw into gold and then claims her baby. For primary grades. [folklore]

The Steadfast Tin Soldier.

Hollywood, CA: Hanna Barbera Home Video, 1991. 1 videocassette, 30 minutes. This is an animated adaptation of the famous story in which the tin soldier is brave for his beloved ballerina. For primary grades. [ballet]

Stories Near, Stories Far.

Pam Faro. Lafayette, CO: Pam Faro, 1994. 1 sound cassette. Read and performed with background by alto recorder, guitar, and kalimba. For elementary grades. [music]

The Tiger and the Brahmin.

Westport, CT: Rabbit Ears Productions, 1991. 1 videocassette, 30 minutes. Told by Ben Kingsley. This is a traditional Indian folktale about a Brahmin who frees a tiger from its cage. For elementary grades. [India]

Why the Coyote Howls.

Derry, NH: Chip Taylor Communications, 1991. Finley Stewart, storyteller. 1 videocassette, 12 minutes. Explains where all the constellations in the sky came from and what they have to do with coyotes howling. For all elementary grades. [coyotes]

The World of Mythology: Gods and Heroes.

Gerald McDermott. Grades 4–12. Palo Alto, CA: Dale Seymour Publications, E53814. A set includes six posters and a 36-page study guide with stories and information. Provides cultural background with myths from India, China, and other countries. [mythology]

7

Music and Movement

*T*here are many ways to incorporate music and movement into learning activities in the elementary language arts classroom. Some of these can be done in conjunction with other educators in the school integrating learning, music, movement and fun.

◆ Students enjoy learning special seasonal songs in vocal music class. This can be followed up in the language arts classroom by encouraging students to write an original verse to sing to a familiar melody. The original verses could be duplicated and used as song sheets.

◆ When studying a particular culture and part of the world, the physical educator might be willing to work with the classroom teacher to teach one or more folk dances from that country. Or, during a unit on the western expansion, these same educators might combine their efforts at cross-curricular activities by teaching students a square dance that might have been popular with early pioneers. If there is a square-dance group in town, a caller or a small group of the dancers might be available to come to school and demonstrate some dances.

◆ Members of the community who are musicians might be willing to come to school and perform for the class. Students may have questions which the guest could answer including the ways in which different instruments produce different sounds. This could be an excellent introduction to a science unit on sound waves and acoustics. Students would have the opportunity to do research, take notes, and write science papers on specific topics. And this could be followed up by an activity in which simple instruments are made and played.

◆ Some students in the class may take private dance, voice, or instrumental music lessons and might be willing to perform for their classmates in a sort of "Show and Tell" performance. Since there appears to be no shortage of critics in this world, perhaps this school audience could concentrate on being a supportive group that shares admiration for successful sections performed rather than dwelling on mistakes.

◆   Poetry offers another avenue in which music and movement can be incorporated into the elementary language arts classroom. Students will quickly hear that the rhythm of rhymes and poetry is very similar to the rhythm of music. A poem can become the lyrics for a song.

◆   Music and sound effects can be an integral part of a puppet presentation or serve as background to the telling of a story. Music can be used to help set a mood before a play begins or as an interlude between acts as costume changes are made and scenery is being set up.

◆   Language arts teachers need to teach students how to carry out independent library research. Popular topics used in teaching reference and report-writing skills are presidents, inventors, leaders of social movements, countries, and their resources. But musical performers, composers, or rare musical instruments could also serve as excellent topics for such assignments. Similarly, the student who is preparing a paper to accompany a Science Fair project in acoustics, can learn about the science of sound waves while also utilizing research, reading, note taking, footnoting, and writing skills.

◆   Career possibilities are often studied throughout the elementary school years. Encouraging interested students to read and learn more about what opportunities exist and what studies are required to pursue a career as a ballet dancer or an orchestra member, etc. provide many opportunities for reading, writing and research in a cross-curricular context.

◆   Students who have had fun presenting puppet shows and plays may be intrigued in working with the language arts teacher and the music specialist in producing a short and simple musical.

Directions for Ideas That Work

A SHAKER: Even very young children may get excited about making and using simple rhythm instruments. They may use these as an accompaniment to a variety of class activities.

One of the easiest rhythm instruments to make is a shaker. This will require two Styrofoam cups, a handful or rice, some magic markers, and a piece of masking or packing tape.

Students can decorate their two Styrofoam cups by coloring simple designs with magic markers. Next, they put a handful or rice into one of the decorated cups, put the other cup on top, and securely tape the two cups together with masking tape or packing tape.

Now they are ready to shake away!

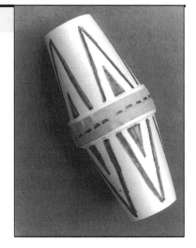

Illus. 7.1. Shaker: This shaker consists of two Styrofoam drinking cups, decorated with magic markers, and taped together. Inside are grains of rice.

Directions for Ideas That Work

A SIMPLE DRUM: This simple instrument can be used as the child keeps the beat while listening to a record or tape. It might also be a special sound effect used in taping an original story.

To make a simple drum, the teacher should send home a note to parents well in advance requesting that they send to class empty coffee cans with their plastic lids. When there is a sufficient collection of these, an adult uses a can opener to remove the bottoms of the coffee cans.

Contact paper, in whatever color or design seems most appropriate, can be cut to the height and circumference of an empty coffee can. This is simple for students to apply to the outside of the cans. Then they put a plastic lid on both ends of the empty coffee can, and the drum is complete.

Depending on the effect desired, students may drum with their hands or with pieces of doweling that are cut to the size of drumsticks.

When presenting an oral telling of one of the many Native American myths which are included in the resources in the chapter on Folktales, Fables, Myths and Legends, a drumming accompaniment can be very effective.

Sharing the music

Students may have the opportunity to take part in an all-school talent show, to be part of a class celebration where choral readings and musical solos are blended, or to take part in school district music events. Local service clubs, such as Kiwanis, may sponsor community activities such as "Stars of Tomorrow," where students may find an audience for their budding talents. Classroom teachers may share information about musical events with students, and might even join a young musician in a duet or accompany on the piano a vocal number or dance routine. This sharing of the musical experience increases the joy and pleasure involved.

◆ In classrooms where teachers are not musicians, music can still be an important ingredient. A record, CD, or tape may be played in the background during a kindergarten rest time. Music may be played as older elementary students work at a class interest center or during an arts and crafts activity.

◆ Listening skills can be sharpened as students hear a classic such as "Peter and the Wolf" and learn to recognize the instruments that are involved. If a teacher has a limited collection of recorded music, many libraries now check out CDs, records and tapes to supplement the collection.

◆ Other teachers, the music specialist, and parents may have recordings of a particular type of music that they might be willing to loan for a unit of study. Western music, for example, might be shared during a class unit of study that involves the folktales of the cowboy, Pecos Bill.

Directions for Ideas That Work

CAPTURING EVERYDAY SOUNDS: A student or a pair of students may enjoy using a tape recorder to capture some everyday musical sounds. Going on a "listening walk," these students may tape the ticking of a clock, the whirr of a lawn mower, the whistle of a tea kettle, the sound of falling rain hitting a surface, the roar of a car, the chatter of a squirrel, the ripple of a brook or crash of a waterfall, the sound of laughter, or the call of a bird.

Back in the classroom, the recording could be played for students as they try to identify the sources of the sounds on the tape. A writing assignment might follow in which the students write an original story on any topic in which they incorporate at least one of the sounds from the tape recording. (Since student writing usual relies heavily on the sense of sight, this activity will help students recognize that sounds, setting, and scents can add enrich their writing.)

Attending performance events

It can also be a special treat for a student to attend some sort of live musical performance. This might be a concert in the school auditorium provided by the school choir, a "Tiny Tots" concert offered to students at a university or concert hall setting, or a special holiday offering such as "The Nutcracker Ballet." Many orchestras and dance groups hold special matinee performances for children where the program's content and length are especially designed to fit the attention span and interests of a young audience. Such special events provide an excellent introduction to live performance.

When deciding about student attendance at special events, adults must assess the appropriateness of the material, the length of the presentation, the lateness of the hour, etc. A fidgety or noisy child or group of children can ruin a performance for other audience members.

Students need to have instruction on appropriate audience behavior. Even though events may take place in the same setting, such as a school gymnasium, the cheering, shouting, and climbing up and down the bleachers that are standard behaviors for spectators at a basketball game are not the appropriate manners for students listening to the school orchestra perform, and students need to learn this.

In addition to being part of an audience in an auditorium or concert hall, parents have many opportunities for helping their children enjoy dance and music in less formal settings. Orchestras may hold open rehearsals at summer festivals. Some communities hold jazz festivals where performing groups are located at a variety of sites with intervals so that the audience can move from one place to another. On the Fourth of July or other special occasions, a community orchestra may perform outdoors while audience members enjoy family picnics. Alert teachers will advertise these opportunities to parents of their students through school newsletters.

Creative movement

Creative movement need not take the form of dance lessons. Many of the resources listed in this chapter suggest ideas for students to respond to music at home and at school in a variety of ways, including learning sign language to help tell a musical story.

The teacher may choose a piece of music and have the students listen to it. Then the teacher may replay a portion inviting one or more class volunteers to move in ways inspired by the music. "The Carnival of the Animals" might be an excellent piece for such an activity. This could be followed by a discussion of the composer and the particular piece of music.

Directions for Ideas That Work

THE WIND-UP TOY: Pretending is a favorite activity of many children. Show the students how a wind-up toy moves in a very precise and measured way. Then have a student volunteer pretend to be a wind-up toy person and demonstrate how he/she would march, bend over, laugh, cry, run, etc. Play a favorite piece of music. The adult or one of the students can pretend to wind-up each student by twisting an imaginary key in the middle of the child's back. One by one the students can join in the movement of toys responding to the music. This might be followed by the presentation of an original puppet show in which one of the puppets is portrayed as a wind-up toy.

Creative teachers and supportive adults will share an enjoyment of music and dance and expand on those opportunities for children to appreciate the many different ways in which music can enrich their lives. Some of the resources listed in the chapters on Holidays Around the World; Games; Poetry; and Folk Tales, Fables, Myths and Legends contain references with musical applications that educators might also wish to consult.

Resource books

Students might be interested in the magazine, "Music Alive," which is published eight times a year for students in grades five through ten and focuses on pop, rock, and classical music.

Air and Space: Young Children Explore the World of Science Through Simple Experiments and Through Language, Math, Art and Movement Experiences.
   Lynn Cohen. Palo Alto, CA: Monday Morning Books, 1988. 64 pp. ISBN 0-912-107-80-4. Filled with creative activities. For preschool through grade 2. [movement; science]

All Ears: How to Use and Choose Recorded Music for Children.
   Jill Jarnow. New York: Viking, 1991. 210 pp. ISBN 0-14-011254-5. Gives useful advice on selecting recorded music. An adult resource book. [music-selection resource]

Alligators and Music.

Donald Elliott. Boston, MA: Harvard Common Press, 1984. 67 pp. ISBN 0-87645-118-0. Provides an introduction to strings, woodwinds, brass and percussion. For grades 6–8. [musical instruments]

Arroz Con Leche: Popular Songs and Rhymes from Latin America.

Selected by Lulu Delacre. New York: Scholastic, 1989. 32 pp. ISBN 0-590-41886-6. Contains children's songs of Latin America. Appropriate for use in preschool through kindergarten. [Latin America; songs]

Beat the Drum.

Josephine Paker. Brookfield, CT: Millbrook Press, 1992. 48 pp. Traces the development of drums in several cultures and gives directions for making simple drums. For use in all elementary grades. [drums]

Black Dance in America: A History Through Its People.

James Haskins. New York: T. Y. Crowell, 1990. 232 pp. ISBN 0-690-04657-X. ISBN 0-06-446121-1 paper. Surveys the history of black dance in America. For grade 6 and up. [African Americans–music; dance]

Black Music in America: A History Through Its People.

James Haskins. New York: T. Y. Crowell, 1987. 198 pp. ISBN 0-690-04460-7. Surveys music such as slave songs, jazz, blues, soul and classical. A teacher resource book. For use in grade 6 and up. [African Americans–music]

Brass.

Elizabeth Sharma. New York: Thomson Learning, 1993. 32 pp. Tells how brass instruments make sounds and gives directions for making a trumpet from a plastic bottle. For students in grade 2 and up. [wind instruments]

Break Dancing.

James Haskins. Minneapolis, MN: Lerner, 1985. 40 pp. Discusses the history of break dancing and gives instructions for some steps. For upper elementary students. [break dancing]

The Cat's Midsummer Jamboree.

David Kherdian and Nonny Hogrogian. New York: Philomel, 1990. 32 pp. A cat enjoys a jamboree in a tree with musical animals. For primary students. [cats; animals]

Celebrate Christmas.

Kathy J. Jones. Carthage, IL: Shining Star Publications, 1985. 144 pp. ISBN 0-86653-279-X. Contains songs and music for children ages six to eleven. [Christmas songs]

Celebrate Special Days.

Phyllis Hand. Carthage, IL: Shining Star Publications, 1985. 143 pp. Contains songs for children ages six to eleven. [holiday music]

Children Around the World: The Multicultural Journey.

Jane Hodges-Caballero. Atlanta, GA: Humanics Learning, 1994. 219 pp. ISBN 0-89334-033-2. Introduces cultures and people through native music, recipes, and games. For use in preschool through grade 4. [games; multicultural music]

Dance.

Louise Tythacott. New York: Thomson Learning, 1995. 48 pp. Discusses dance traditions from around the world. For use with upper elementary grades. [dance]

Dance.

Eleanor Van Zandt. East Sussex, England: Wayland Pub. Ltd., 1988. 48 pp. Surveys dance as an art form. For use in the upper elementary grades. [dance]

Dancing Games for Children of All Ages.

Esther L. Nelson. New York: Sterling Publishing Co. Inc., 1984. Contains more than 40 games for students in kindergarten through fifth grades, with piano accompaniment, lyrics, and instruction for movement activities. [dance; games]

A Day in the Life of a Ballet Dancer.

John Harding. Mahwah, NJ: Troll, 1985. 32 pp. Follows a ballet dancer throughout the day. For use in the elementary grades. [ballet]

Easy Going Games: Using Mismatched Socks, Hoops, and Squares: A Collection of Movement Games to Increase the Motor Skills and Fun of Elementary Age Children and Playful Adults.

Barbara Sher. Whitehorn, CA: Bright Baby Books, 1987. 79 pp. ISBN 0-930681-04-5. Contains ideas for creative movement with young children. For all elementary grades. [games; movement]

Energy and Machines: Young Children Explore the World of Science Through Simple Experiments and Through Language, Math, Art, and Movement Experiences.

Lynn Cohen. Palo Alto, CA: Monday Morning Books, 1988. 64 pp. Filled with creative activities. For use in all elementary grades. [movement; science]

Exploring My World.

Lynn Cohen. Palo Alto, CA: Monday Morning Books, 1986. 64 pp. Shows how young children explore through art, music and movement. For use in the elementary grades. [movement]

Fairy Tales: Musical Dramas for Children (Primary and Special Education.)

Ginger Clarkson. St. Louis, MO: MMB Music, 1986. 42 pp. ISBN 0-918812-49-6. Contains short musical dramas. For use in all elementary grades. [fairy tales; musicals]

Favorite Children's Songs.

> Arranged by Bill Boyd. Winona, MN: Hal Leonard Pub., 1986. 56 pp. ISBN 0-88188-495-2. Filled with children's songs. For use in all elementary grades. [songs]

Favorite Stories of the Ballet.

> James Riordan. Chicago, IL: Children's Press, 1986. 124 pp. ISBN 1-56288-252-X. Contains many ballet stories. For use in grade 4 and up. [ballet]

The Feelings Book: Expressing Emotions Creatively: A Guide for Children and Grownups.

> Evergreen, CO: Cordillera Press, 1988. 72 pp. Discusses how to express emotions through art, literature and music. For all ages. [emotions]

First Steps in Teaching Creative Dance to Children.

> Mary Joyce. Mountain View, CA: Mayfield Pub, 1994. 218 pp. ISBN 1-55934-162-9. Suitable for all elementary students. [dance]

First Time Circle Time: Shared Group Experience for Three, Four, and Five-Year-Olds.

> Cynthia Holley and Jane Walkup. Carthage, IL: Fearon Teacher Aids, 1993. 287 pp. ISBN 0-86653-993-X. Has over two hundred songs and fingerplays around 52 themes. Also includes recipes, arts and crafts. For preschoolers and kindergartners. [cookery; finger plays; songs]

Flutes, Reeds, and Trumpets.

> Danny Staples. Brookfield, CT: Millbrook Press, 1992. 48 pp. ISBN 1-56294-092-9. Traces the development of several instruments and gives directions for making simple instruments. For use in grades 2–6. [wind instruments]

Going to My Ballet Class.

> Susan Kuklin. New York: Bradbury, 1989. 27 pp. ISBN 0-02-751235-5. Follows a little girl through her ballet class. For use in preschool through grade 2. [ballet]

Goodnight Toes! Bedtime Stories, Lullabies, and Movement Games.

> Anne Lief Barlin. Pennington, NJ: Princeton Book Co., 1993. 122 pp. ISBN 0-87127-190-7. The movement games are appropriate for young children. [bedtime stories; lullabies; movement]

The Great Big Book of Rhythm.

> Jackie Weissman. Overland Park, KS: Miss Jackie Music Co., distributed by Gryphon House, 1986. 144 pp. Contains games with movement for children. For use in the primary grades. [rhythm; movement]

I Can Be a Musician.

> Rebecca Hankin. Chicago: Children's Press, 1984. 31 pp. Tells about the different kinds of work musicians do. Suitable for the elementary grades. [musicians]

If You're Happy and You Know It: Eighteen Story Songs, Set to Pictures.

Nicki Weiss. New York: Greenwillow, 1987. 40 pp. ISBN 0-688-06444-2. Contains camp songs and includes piano and guitar music. Suitable for preschool through grade 3. [camp songs; sheet music]

I Like Music.

Barrie Turner. New York: Warwick Press, 1989. 44 pp. Explains several musical instruments. For use in the elementary grades. [musical instruments]

Hear! Hear!: The Science of Sound.

Barbara Taylor. New York: Random House, 1991. 39 pp. Provides an introduction to the science of sound and the ways we make music. For students grade 2 and up. [science; sound]

Homemade Band: Songs to Sing, Instruments to Make.

Hap Palmer. New York: Crown, 1990. 48 pp. ISBN 0-517-57597-3. Includes lyrics for nine songs and describes how to make simple instruments to use in accompaniment. Appropriate for preschool through grade 1. [musical instruments]

How to Grow a Young Music Lover: Helping Your Child Discover and Enjoy the World of Music.

Cheri Fuller. Wheaton, IL: Harold Shaw Publisher, 1994. 194 pp. Includes a bibliography and discography as well as list of video cassettes and computer software. An adult resource book. [parent resources]

I Have Another Language: The Language Is Dance.

Eleanor Schick. New York: Macmillan, 1992. 32 pp. ISBN 0-02-781209-X. In this story a young girl expresses her joy through dancing. Suitable for all elementary grades. [dance]

I Wonder Why Flutes Have Holes: And Other Questions About Music.

Josephine Paker. New York: Kingfisher Books, 1995. 32 pp. ISBN 1-85697-583-5. A picture book in a question-and-answer format. For use in preschool through grade 4. [musical instruments]

Join the Band.

Marjorie Pillar. New York: HarperCollins, 1992. 32 pp. ISBN 0-06-021829-0. A young musician describes what it's like to be in a school band. For primary grades. [band]

Jump for Joy: A Book of Months.

Megan Halsey. New York: Bradbury, 1994. 32 pp. ISBN 0-02-742040-X. Contains playful activities for each month of the year including jumping in January and dancing in December. For primary grades. [months; movement]

Keyboards.

Elizabeth Sharma. New York: Thomson Learning, 1993. 32 pp. ISBN 1-56847-117-3. This book explains how instruments such as organs, accordions, and electric keyboards make music. For upper elementary grades. [keyboards]

Kids & Weekends: Creative Ways to Make Special Days.

Avery Hart and Paul Mantell. Charlotte, VT: Williamson Publishing Co. Inc., 1992. 173 pp. ISBN 0-913589-47-0. Suggests a wide variety of weekend activities including making musical instruments. Suitable for use in the elementary grades. [musical instruments]

Kids in Motion: A Creative Movement and Song Book.

Julie Weissman. Milwaukee, WI: H. Leonard Pub., 1993. 101 pp. ISBN 0-9633279-5-X. ISBN 0-7935-2797-X paper. Suggests activities for children aged three through nine including games, exercises, and songs. [movement; songs]

The Kids' World Almanac of Music from Rock to Bach.

Elyse Sommer. New York: World Almanac, 1992. 275 pp. ISBN 0-88687-521-8. Explains the origins of music and instruments and musical terminology. For upper elementary grades. [music–almanacs]

Let's Do a Poem!: Introducing Poetry to Children Through Body Movement, Dance and Dramatization: Including 98 Favorite Songs and Poems.

Nancy Larrick. New York: Delacorte, 1991. 22 pp. Includes many ideas to combine music, dance, and poetry. For use in the elementary grades. [dance; poetry]

Little Songs of Long Ago: A Collection of Favorite Poems and Rhymes.

Illustrated by Henriette Willebeek le Mair. New York: Philomel, 1988. 63 pp. ISBN 0-85692-185-8. Contains 30 traditional well-known songs. For use in the elementary grades. [poetry; songs]

Lullabies and Baby Songs.

Jannat Messenger. New York: Dial Books, 1988. 24 pp. Contains eleven lullabies with illustrations. For use with preschoolers. [lullabies]

Make Your Own Musical Instruments.

Margaret McLean. Minneapolis, MN: Lerner, 1988. 32 pp. ISBN 0-8225-0895-8. Contains step-by-step instructions for making such simple instruments as a drum and tambourine. For use in grades 5–7. [musical instruments]

Making Music: 6 Instruments You Can Create.

Eddie Herschel Oates. New York: HarperCollins, 1995. 32 pp. ISBN 0-06-021478-3. Describes how to make simple musical instruments from household items. For use in grades 1–5. [musical instruments]

Man's Earliest Music.
Richard Carlin. New York: Facts On File, 1987. 118 pp. ISBN 0-8160-1324-1. An introduction to the music of primitive people. For use in the elementary grades. [music–history]

The Marvelous Music Machine: The Story of the Piano.
Mary Glockama. Englewood Cliffs, NJ: Prentice-Hall, 1984. Gives the history of the piano and tells how one is made. For students in grade 2 and up. [pianos]

Me and My World.
Lynn Cohen. Palo Alto, CA: Monday Morning Books, 1986. 64 pp. This is a useful reference in exploring music and movement with toddlers. [movement]

Meet the Orchestra.
Ann Hayes. San Diego, CA: Harcourt Brace Jovanovich, 1991. 32 pp. ISBN 0-15-200526-9. Shows the role of each instrument in the orchestra. For use in preschool through grade 3. [orchestra]

Midi for Musicians: Buying, Installing and Using Today's Electronic Music-making Equipment.
Brad Hill. Chicago: A Cappella Books, 1994. ISBN 1-55652-221-5. Gives details about computer sound processing. For upper elementary grades. [electronic music]

Mime: Basics for Beginners.
Cindie Straub. Boston, MA: Plays, Inc., 1984. 132 pp. ISBN 0-8238-0263-9. An excellent introduction to mime. For use in grade 6 and up. [mime; movement]

Mini-Mini Musicals.
Jean Warren. Everett, WA: Warren Publishing, 1987. 80 pp. ISBN 0-911019-14-6. Gives directions for working with students to present short, simple musicals. For use in preschool through grade 1. [musicals]

Move Like the Animals.
Stephen Rosenholtz. San Mateo, CA: Rosewood Publishing, 1991. 30 pp. ISBN 0-963079-1-1. Includes movement games based on the Feldenkrais method. For use in preschool through grade 3. [animals; movement]

Movement Improvisation: In the Words of a Teacher and Her Students.
Georgette Schneer. Champaign, IL: Human Kinetics, 1994. 199 pp. ISBN 0-87322-530-9. Discusses improvisation in dance. For use in the elementary grades. [dance; movement]

Movement Time: Early Learning Activities for Parents and Teachers of Young Children.

Jean Warren. Palo Alto, CA: Monday Morning Books, 1984. 80 pp. Contains techniques on exploring movement with children. For use with preschoolers and primary students. [movement; parent resources]

Multicultural Sing and Learn: Folk Songs and Monthly Activities.

Carolyn Meyer. Carthage, IL: Good Apple, 1994. 142 pp. ISBN 0-86653-830-5. This music activity book is designed for use in kindergarten through fifth grade. [multicultural music]

Music.

Neil Ardley. New York: Knopf, 1989. 63 pp. ISBN 0-394-82259-5. Discusses different instruments from very early ones to the present. For students in grade 5 and up. [musical instruments]

Music.

Ting Morris. New York: Franklin Watts, 1993. 32 pp. ISBN 0-531-14269-8. Provides step-by-step instructions for constructing musical instruments from readily available materials. Appropriate for grades 2–4. [musical instruments]

Music!

Genevieve Laurencin. Ossining, NY: Young Discovery Library, 1989. 35 pp. ISBN 0-944589-25-1. Discusses the origins of music and the evolution of musical instruments. For students in all elementary grades. [music–history; musical instruments]

Musical Instruments.

Claude Delafosse. New York: Scholastic, 1994. 1 v. unpaged. ISBN 0-590-47729-3. This book is spiral bound with transparency over-lays to present information on instruments and how they make music. An adult resource book for use with preschool through grade 2. [musical instruments]

Musical Story Hours: Using Music With Storytelling and Puppetry.

William M. Painter. Hamden, CT: Library Professional Publications, 1989. 158 pp. ISBN 0-208-02205-8. Contains ideas for combining music with story time. For use in the elementary grades. [puppets; storytelling]

Music Crafts for Kids: The How-to Book of Music Discovery.

Noel Fiarotta. New York: Sterling Publishing Co. Inc., 1993. 160 pp. ISBN 0-8069-0406-2. Explains how to construct simple musical instruments. For use in grade 3 and up. [musical instruments]

Music from Strings.

Josephine Paker. Brookfield, CT: Millbrook Press, 1992. 48 pp. ISBN 1-56294-283-2. Traces the development of stringed instruments and offers directions for making simple instruments. For use in grades 2–6. [stringed instruments]

Music Through Children's Literature: Theme and Variations.

Donna B. Levene. Englewood, CO: Teacher Ideas Press, 1993. 117 pp. ISBN 1-56308-021-4. Includes bibliographical references and discographies. An adult resource book. [themes]

Native Artists of North America.

Reavis Moore. Santa Fe, NM: John Muir Publications, 1993. 47 pp. ISBN 1-56261-147-X. Gives brief biographies of five talented Native Americans and discusses their contributions to art, music and dance. For use in grades 4–7. [Indians of North America]

Of Swans, Sugarplums and Satin Slippers: Ballet Stories for Children.

Violette Verdy. New York: Scholastic, 1991. 90 pp. ISBN 0-590-43484-5. Provides the stories of six well-known ballets. Appropriate for grades 2–5. [ballet]

On the Move: A Handbook for Exploring Creative Movement With Young Children.

Ginger Zukowski and Ardie Dickson. Carbondale, IL: Southern Illinois University Press, 1990. 81 pp. ISBN 0-8093-1542-4. Good discussion of movement education. An adult resource. [movement]

Orchestranimals.

Vlasta van Kampen and Krene C. Eugen. New York: Scholastic, 1989. 40 pp. ISBN 0-590-73163-7. Animal musicians introduce a symphony orchestra. For use in preschool through grade 2. [animals; orchestra]

The Orchestra: An Introduction to the World of Classical Music.

Alan Blackwood. Brookfield, CT: Millbrook Press, 1992. 92 pp. ISBN 1-56294-202-6. Traces the history and development of the orchestra and describes various instruments. For use in grades 3–6. [orchestra]

The Oxford First Companion to Instruments and Orchestras.

Kenneth and Valerie McLeish. Oxford, England: Oxford University Press, 1984. 32 pp. ISBN 0-19-321438-5. An introduction to musical instruments. For use in the elementary grades. [musical instruments]

A Parent's Guide to Band and Orchestra.

Jim Probasco. White Hall, VA: Betterway Publications, 1991. 136 pp. Tips for parents whose children are joining a band or orchestra. [band; orchestra; parent resource]

Playdancing: Discovering and Developing Creativity in Young Children.

Diane Lynch-Fraser. Pennington, NJ: Princeton Book Co., 1991. 122 pp. ISBN 0-87127-152-4. Contains information for preschool and elementary movement education as well as a bibliography. [movement]

Play Me a Story.

Jane Rosenberg. New York: Knopf, 1994. 45 pp. ISBN 0-67984-391-4. A collection of poems that suggest images which might be evoked by pieces of classical music. For use in the elementary school. [poetry]

Rattles, Bells, and Chiming Bars.

Karen Foster. Brookfield, CT: Millbrook Press, 1992. 48 pp. ISBN 1-56294-284-0. Traces the development of percussion instruments from various cultures and suggests projects for making instruments. Suitable for use in grades 2–6. [multicultural instruments; percussion instruments]

Sally the Swinging Snake/ Songs to Enhance the Movement Vocabulary of Young Children.

Hap Palmer. Freeport, NY: Educational Activities, 1987. 20 pp. Songs and a cassette tape. Appropriate for use in elementary grades. [movement]

Science Fun With Drums, Bells, and Whistles.

Rose Wyler. New York: Julian Messner, 1987. 44 pp. ISBN 0-671-63783-5. Contains directions for experiments with sound. Suitable for grades 2–4. [percussion instruments; science; sound]

The Science of Music.

Melvin Berger. New York: T. Y. Crowell, 1989. 153 pp. ISBN 0-690-04647-2. Discusses instruments, records, tapes, discs, and playback equipment. For use in grades 5–9. [science; sound recordings]

Science Projects for Young People.

George Barr. New York: Dover, 1986. 153 pp. ISBN 0-486-25235-3. Explains methods of doing simple scientific research involving sound and music. For students in grade 5 and up. [science]

Scott Gustafson's Animal Orchestra: A Counting Book.

Scott Gustafson. Chicago: Contemporary Books, 1988. 29 pp. ISBN 0-86713-030-X. Uses members of the animal orchestra to teach about music. For preschoolers and kindergartners. [animals; counting books]

Scrap Materials.

Mike Roussel. Vero Beach, FL: Rourke Enterprises, 1990. 32 pp. ISBN 0-86592-487-2. Describes various craft projects including making musical instruments. Suitable for grades 2–6. [crafts; musical instruments]

Shimmy Shake Earthquake: Don't Forget to Dance Poems.

Collected by Cynthia Jabar. Boston, MA: Little, Brown, 1992. 28 pp. A collection of poems that represent a broad ethnic background and the rhythms and sounds of dance. Suitable for the elementary grades. [dance; poetry]

Shoes of Satin, Ribbons of Silk, Tales from the Ballet.
Antonia Barber. New York: Kingfisher Books, 1995. 79 pp. ISBN 1-85697-593-2. Presents the stories of ten well-known ballets. For use in grades 3–6. [ballet]

Sing and Learn.
Carolyn Meyer and Kel Pickens. Carthage, IL: Good Apple, 1989. ISBN 0-86653-476-8. Contains activities for children ages three to nine with a theme for each month of the year. [months]

Sing Us a Story: Using Music in Preschool and Family Storytimes.
Bronx, NY: H. W. Wilson, 1994. 215 pp. ISBN 0-8242-0847-1. Filled with games and stories using music as well as bibliographic references. [games; parent resources]

Songs and Stories from the American Revolution.
Compiled by Jerry Silverman. Brookfield, CT: Millbrook Press, 1994. 71 pp. ISBN 1-56294-429-0. Contains folk music and patriotic songs. Suitable for use in grades 3–6. [folk music; history]

Sound and Music.
David Evans. New York: Dorling Kindersley, 1993. 28 pp. Explores sound and how to make simple musical instruments from everyday objects. Suitable for use in the elementary grades. [musical instruments]

Sound and Music.
Barbara Taylor. New York: Franklin Watts, 1991. 32 pp. Contains activities that show how and why various musical instruments produce sound. Appropriate for the elementary grades. [musical instruments; sound]

Sound, Noise, & Music.
Mick Seller. New York: Gloucester Press, 1993. 32 pp. ISBN 0-531-17408-5. Suggests experiments and projects for exploring sound waves and how they produce noise or music. Suitable for grades 5–8. [sound]

Sound Waves to Music.
Neil Ardley. New York: Gloucester Press, 1990. 32 pp. Contains various projects involving sound, some with applications to music. Suitable for the elementary grades. [sound]

Step It Down: Games, Plays, Songs and Stories from the Afro American Heritage.
Bessie Jones and Bess Lomax. Athens, GA: University of Georgia Press, 1987. 233 pp. ISBN 0-8203-0960-5. Contains many Afro-American songs and games. For use in the elementary grades. [African Americans; games; songs]

Storytime Theme-a-saurus: The Great Big Book of Story Teaching Themes.
Jean Warren. Everett, WA: Warren Publishing, 1995. 57 pp. ISBN 0-911019-56-1. Contains folktales and fables with hands-on activities that include

movement and music. For use with preschool through grade 1. [folklore; movement]

This Is Rhythm.

Ella Jenkins. Bethlehem, PA: Sing Out Corp., 1993. ISBN 1-881322-02-5. Includes games with music. For use in elementary grades. [games; rhythm]

The Usborne First Book of the Piano.

John C. Miles. London: Usborne, 1988. 64 pp. An introduction to the piano. For all elementary students. [pianos]

Weather and Seasons: Young Children Explore the World of Science Through Simple Experiments and Through Language, Math, Art, and Movement Experiences.

Lynn Cohen. Palo Alto, CA: Monday Morning Books, 1988. 64 pp. Filled with creative activities. For use in elementary grades. [movement; seasons; weather]

What Instrument Is This?

Rosmarie Hausherr. New York: Scholastic, 1992. 38 pp. ISBN 0-590-44644-4. Identifies instruments, discusses how they are made and the sounds they make as well as the styles of music for which they are best suited. For use in grades K–3. [musical instruments]

Other resources

African Folksongs for Children.

New Rochelle, NY: Spoken Arts, 1986. 1 sound cassette, 43 minutes, SAC:1163. Contains children's songs from Ghana. For use in the elementary grades. [Africa–songs; Ghana]

Baby's Morningtime.

Los Angeles, CA: Hi-tops Video, Video Treasures, Inc., 1990. 1 videocassette, 25 min., MO 22710. A collection of poems set to music and sung by Judy Collins. For preschoolers. [lullabies; poetry]

Ballet for Preschoolers.

Kathy Blake. Antrim, NH: Butterfly Video, 1987. 1 videocassette, 60 min. Explores ballet for very young children. [ballet]

Cowboy Poems & Country Music.

Chuck Cusimano. Trinidad, CO: Cusimusico, 1995. 1 sound cassette, 30 minutes. Contains cowboy stories and music. For use in the elementary grades. [cowboys; country music]

Creative Dance for Preschoolers.

Kathy Blake. Antrim, NH: Butterfly Video, 1986. 1 videocassette, 60 minutes. Explores creative dance and movement. [dance]

11 Sing, Stretch, and Shape Up Songs.

Racine, WI: Western Publishing Co., 1987. 1 videocassette, 30 minutes. Contains exercises for children. For use in the elementary school. [movement]

Even More Baby Songs.

Los Angeles, CA: Hi-Tops Video, 1989. 1 videocassette, 32 minutes. Features ten songs for infants to children aged six. [lullabies]

Fiesta! Mexico and Central America: A Global Awareness Program for Children in Grades 2–5.

Carthage, IL: Fearon Teacher Aids, 1993. 1 book, 240 pp and 1 sound cassette, 50 minutes. Uses folk and fine art, classical and folk music and dances to help teach an appreciation of cultures. For use in the elementary grades. [dance; Mexico; Central America]

Flutterby.

Stephen Cosgrove. Los Angeles, CA: Price, Stern, Sloan; Serendipity, 1984. 1 sound cassette and 30-page book. A read-along book about a flying pony. For preschoolers and primary grades. [horses; storytelling]

Jazz Dance for Kids (6 - 11).

Kathy Blake. Antrim, NH: Butterfly Video, 1987. 1 videocassette, 60 minutes. Shows how to dance to jazz. [dance; jazz]

Kiddieworks: Aerobic Activities for Children.

Judith Scott. New York: Caedmon, 1985. 1 sound diskette, 49 minutes. Demonstrates a variety of exercises for children. For use in the elementary grades. [movement]

Leonard Bernstein's Young People's Concerts.

New York: Sony Classical, 1993. 1 videocassette, 160 minutes. In three programs, Leonard Bernstein defines mode, the sonata form, and the versatility of the orchestra. The New York Philharmonic plays excerpts from classical music. Suitable for the elementary grades. [orchestra]

Making Music With Children Ages 5–7.

John Langstaff and Elizabeth Lloyd Mayer. Berkeley, CA: Langstaff Video Project, 1993. 1 videocassette, 60 minutes. Working with a group of young children, an educator shows how to add movement to songs and chants. For use in the elementary grades. [movement]

Musical Encounter: The Orchestra and Its Parts.

Produced by Cheryll Flaningam. Lincoln, NE: Great Plains National Instructional Television Library, 1991. 1 videocassette, 30 minutes. Various sections of the orchestra play short pieces and performers answer questions. Suitable for the elementary grades. [orchestra]

Reading, Writing, and Rhythm.

Felice Kane. Princeton, NY: Felice Kane, 1991. 1 sound cassette. Teaches language usage and punctuation through songs. For students in grade 2 and up. [language]

The Snowman: Easy Piano Picture Book.

Story and pictures by Raymond Briggs, music and words by Howard Blake. London, England: Faber & Faber, 1986. Tells the musical story of a snowman. For preschoolers and primary grades. [snowmen]

Songs and Games for Toddlers.

Bob McGrath and Katharine Smithrim. Toronto, Ont: A & M Records of Canada, 1985. 1 sound diskette. Contains songs appropriate for two- and three-year-olds. [songs]

Songs from Mother Goose.

Racine, WI: Golden Book Video, 1987. 1 videocassette, 30 minutes, #13795. Contains 48 songs from Mother Goose. For preschoolers and kindergartners. [Mother Goose; songs]

Tap Dance for Preschoolers.

Kathy Blake. Antrim, NH: Butterfly Video, 1987. 1 videocassette, 60 minutes. Explores and explains tap dance steps. [dance]

The Thrill of the Orchestra.

Produced by William Cole Hueter. Boca Raton, FL: SIRTS, 1987.
1 videocassette, 24 minutes. Discusses the history of the orchestra. For children aged six to nine. [orchestra]

Toddler Tunes and Tales.

Produced by Miriam Goodman and Donna P. Hall. San Francisco, CA: Quality Time Video, 1986. 1 videocassette, 45 minutes. Includes music and movement for children aged two to four. [movement]

The World of Ballet.

Davina Parmet. Kansas City, MO: Andrews and McMeel, 1992. One book, 36 pp. and one sound cassette, 36 minutes. Explains about ballerinas, including their costumes, positions and music. For use in the elementary grades. [ballet]

8

Holidays Around the World

*H*oliday! The very word seems to lift the spirits of adults and bring a smile to the face of almost any child. Whatever the holiday, it holds special promise for satisfying times both in the home with family and friends and in the elementary language arts classroom.

Because of the increasing diversity in our schools, teachers need to demonstrate sensitivity around holidays realizing that students represent many different races, religions, and cultures. If an activity seems inappropriate for a given child, an alternative should be offered in such a way that no child is made to feel uncomfortable.

The first major holiday of the school year is Halloween. And one of the cheeriest and least controversial of the Halloween symbols is the Jolly-Jack-o'-lantern. A pumpkin can be a great source of fun and learning.

Directions for Ideas That Work

JOLLY JACK-O'-LANTERNS: Depending on your class size, bring in enough pumpkins so that students can group comfortably at a table around a pumpkin in teams of about five students each. The first day, the five students can "get to know" their pumpkin.

Each group should name the pumpkin, lift it and guess its weight, estimate its circumference, and make a guess as to the number of seeds it contains. One member of each group should be responsible for writing down this information on a prepared worksheet. This will involve an interesting group process and considerable discussion as students debate over the best name and as they try to reach consensus on estimating the pumpkin's weight, circumference, and its number of seeds.

On day two, give students a piece of paper and ask them to draw their pumpkin with the face they would like to have cut into it as their pumpkin is turned into a Jack-o'-lantern. Beneath the drawing, have students write a short story involving their pumpkin. It could be a story about the pumpkin while it was still growing in the farmer's field or it could be a story about Halloween night.

On day three, have the student groups meet again and share their stories with one another. They should look at the various drawings for possible cut-out faces and reach consensus on the face they want for their Jack-o'-lantern. This may involve choosing the eyes from one drawing and the mouth from another.

On day four, the teacher will need an adult volunteer to assist with each group. First the adult should help the students to weigh the pumpkin and write down its weight to the nearest ounce or gram. The adult should then oversee the measurement and recording of the circumference of the pumpkin to the nearest quarter inch or millimeter. Next, the adult should use a knife to cut the top from the pumpkin. Then students should take turns hollowing out the pumpkin. The seeds should be set aside to be counted and dried.

One of the students should use a magic marker to draw the selected face on the pumpkin and the adult should do the carving. A student could place a candle in the pumpkin which could be fastened in place by putting a straight pin through the bottom of the pumpkin and right up into the wax candle. When everyone is ready, the adults could light the candles on the pumpkins in a darkened room and all the students can admire them.

Many interdisciplinary activities can follow. In mathematics, groups could discuss how close they came to guessing the weight of the pumpkin, its circumference, and its number of seeds. Did the biggest pumpkin have the most seeds? Research can be done on world records for size and weight of pumpkins. Cooking activities might also be included.

At Thanksgiving, there are many choral readings involving the gobble-gobble of turkeys. There may be research and art projects about the first Thanksgiving and what the early settlers learned about raising crops from the Native Americans.

Directions for Ideas That Work

A "HANDY" TURKEY: Give each student a piece of art paper. At the top of the paper have a student place his or her hand flat on the paper with the fingers spread slightly apart. Using the other hand, the student should trace his or her hand-print. With only a little imagination, the thumb will resemble a turkey's neck and head and the spread fingers will look like tail feathers. Students can then add details and color their turkeys using crayons, colored pencils, markers, etc. Beneath the "handy" turkey, invite students to write a humorous poem or story that features a turkey.

Illus. 8.1. Handy turkey: By tracing her hand, a child has the simple, basic shape of a turkey, with the thumb serving as the turkey's head and the outspread fingers as its tail feathers.

During the winter season, the class members might enjoy making a special treat for the birds. To lead into the activity, the teacher might put up a bulletin board featuring colored pictures of birds. Working with partners, students could choose one of the birds and do a short research paper including information on where the bird is found throughout the year and throughout the world.

Records, tapes and computer programs are available that feature bird songs. The teacher might play one of these so that students have a chance to hear the song or call that their birds make. A local birder might be willing to come to class and discuss the birds that are found locally and especially any that are around during the winter season.

Directions for Ideas That Work

A HOLIDAY TREAT FOR THE BIRDS: Gather or purchase enough pine cones so that there is one for every member in the class. Also cut a twenty-inch length of ribbon for each class member. First have the students take a length of ribbon and thread it among the bracts at the thick end of the cone and tie a knot. Next the students tie the two end of the ribbon together. This "loop" can now be hung from a schoolyard or backyard tree or at some other site where birds are common.

Students will then take pieces of suet purchased from a butcher shop and push the suet in among some of the bracts of the cone. Using a wooden coffee stirring stick, students can spread peanut butter onto the other bracts of the cone. The students can take the cones home and hang them as a holiday treat for the birds.

As a follow-up activity, each student might write a legend to explain something about a bird such as how the peacock got its brilliant tail, why the robin has a red breast, why the blue jay has a crest on its head, or how the toucan got its strange beak. Allow time for students to share their original legends.

Illus. 8.2. Holiday feeder: Treats for the birds can be made in school, at home, or with a group of scouts. Yarn threaded around the cone will hold the cone securely to a tree limb or fence post. Peanut butter and suet spread into the bracts of the cone make tasty treats for the winter birds.

Around the winter holidays, students might also enjoy bringing to class a favorite recipe that the child's family associates with a holiday. Each student could have one page in a class recipe booklet that is duplicated and sent home for all the families in the class to enjoy.

If cooking facilities exist at the school, cooking activities provide many cross-curricular opportunities involving reading, following directions, and using math skills. Adult volunteers help to make these cooking activities go more smoothly for a class of students.

At Valentine's Day, students may plan a class program featuring choral readings, poetry, or a puppet show. The students may want to invite another class to come to the program.

Directions for Ideas That Work

BROKEN-HEARTED INVITATIONS: Get a list of the names of the students being invited to the class Valentine program. Assign a guest's name to each of the home-room students. Give each home-room student an envelope and have the student write his or her guest's name on the envelope.

Next give each student a red heart. Have each home-room student write an invitation on the heart asking the guest to attend the program. Each invitation can be original, but be sure each home-room student includes the sentence, "If you don't come to our program, I'll be broken-hearted."

When the invitation is complete, each student glues the red invitation to apiece of oak tag board or light weight cardboard and allows it to dry thoroughly. Finally the student takes a scissors and cuts the invitation apart leaving tabs and indentations like jig-saw puzzle pieces. All the pieces are put inside the envelope with the guest's name on it ready to be delivered.

Each recipient will need to put the puzzle together in order to read the invitation.

Illus. 8.3. Broken-hearted invitations: Write a message on a sheet of paper, glue it to tagboard or cardboard, and cut it out into simple jig-saw shapes. Be sure not to lose any before you seal all the pieces into an envelope. The recipient has great fun putting the puzzle pieces together and reading your message.

Many opportunities will arise naturally for cross-curricular activities while studying Holidays Around the World. For example, if you are studying about island countries such as Japan, students might do some research on special holidays that are celebrated in Japan. Other students might be discussing the countries which border the United States to the north and south. Learning about the holidays of people in these countries will enrich a unit of study.

Some holidays commemorate the lives of important figures in American history such as Martin Luther King, Jr., Abraham Lincoln, and George Washington. They provide many opportunities for linking social studies and the language arts.

Some holidays involve gift giving. Hand-made gifts are fun to make and are often treasured above all others.

Directions for Ideas That Work

SPECIAL PAPER WEIGHTS: If possible, students might go on a hike and each collect a unique rock. The rock might have an usual shape or special colors in it. The rock should be no bigger than a child's fist. Back at school, students should thoroughly scrub their rocks and allow them to completely dry.

Tempera paints can then be used to turn the rock into a creature that could serve as a desk paper weight. One rock might be painted to look like a spotted lady bug while another is a striped beetle, a frog, or a fish. When the paint is dry, a coat of shellac gives a finished appearance.

Illus. 8.4. Paper Weights: Gather rocks, wash them, and let them dry. Then imagination goes to work! One will turn into a spotted lady bug and another into a striped beetle. These paper weights are fun to make and own.

Each student should use a square of note paper to write a paragraph explaining about the paper weight. For example, "Here's a special beetle called 'Stripe.' Stripe will sit on your desk and hold your papers in place. He's a loyal pet that makes no noise, requires no food or water, and will give you years of service."

For Mother's Day or Father's Day, students might prepare a special book as a gift.

Directions for Ideas That Work

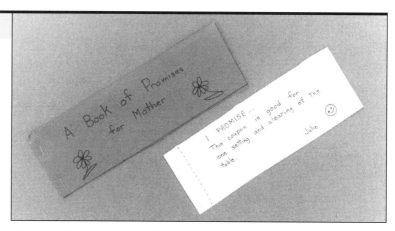

A BOOK OF PROMISES: Cut different colors of construction paper into strips that are about nine inches by three inches. Allow the students to select several strips of paper. On the top strip of paper, a student writes, A Book of Promises, for *xxxxxxx*, from *xxxxxxx*, filling in the name of the person for whom the book is intended and the name of the giver.

On each strip, the child then writes a promise that the child will fulfill when mother or father tears off a coupon from the book and gives it to the child. Tasks might include: Set the table, Take out the garbage, Wash the dishes, Wash the car, etc.

Illus. 8.5. Book of Promises: For Mother's Day or Father's Day, a book of promises is a great gift. Each student can come up with simple tasks that will be valued at home. Writing skills will be put to use, and the cover of the Book of Promises can be decorated to suit the special occasion.

When all of the coupons are complete, the child may want to design and decorate a cover page before stapling the coupon book together.

Since some holidays are religious in nature, the resources listed here may be a good complement to activities that are also taking place in the church or synagogue. Other special days include patriotic holidays such as the Fourth of July, and unusual days such as April Fool's Day. Any of these might be interesting to explore in the elementary language arts classroom.

When you consult the resources in the chapter, perhaps more often than in any other section of the book, you may be led almost immediately to dip into other chapters of this book. Remember that resources are listed only once although they might apply to several different topics.

The chapters on Arts and Crafts; Folktales, Fables, Myths, and Legends; Storytelling and Puppetry; Creative Dramatics; Music and Movement; and Games, for example, all contain resources that might be appropriate and helpful for one of your Holidays Around the World activities.

Resource books

About Martin Luther King Day.
Mary Virginia Fox. Hillside, NJ: Enslow Publishers, 1989. 64 pp. ISBN 0-89490-200-8. Gives a history of Martin Luther King Day. Appropriate for use in grades 4–7. [King, Martin Luther, Jr.]

America's Birthday: The Fourth of July.
Tom Shachtman. New York: Macmillan, 1986. 46 pp. Contains descriptions and photos of celebrations of the Fourth of July. For use in all elementary grades. [Fourth of July]

Arbor Day Magic.
James W. Baker. Minneapolis, MN: Lerner, 1990. 48 pp. Explains magic tricks that can be used around the theme of Arbor Day. For all elementary grades. [Arbor Day; magic]

Autumn Festivals.
Mike Rosen. New York: Bookwright, 1990. 32 pp. Discusses festivals and holidays held during the harvest season around the world. [autumn; harvest]

Bear Child's Book of Special Days.
Anne F. Rockwell. New York: Dutton, 1989. 32 pp. ISBN 0-525-44508-0. For each month of the year, Bear Child explains the significance of important days. For preschool through grade 1. [months]

Birthday Magic.
James W. Baker. Minneapolis, MN: Lerner, 1988. 48 pp. ISBN 0-8225-9536-2. Explains ten magic tricks that have a birthday theme. Suitable for grades 2–5. [birthdays; magic]

Blue Monday and Friday the Thirteenth.

Lila Perl. New York: Clarion, 1986. 96 pp. Discusses the popular superstitions that are associated with certain days of the week and year. Suitable for elementary grade students. [days, special]

Bolivia.

Robert Pateman. New York: Marshall Cavendish, 1995. 128 pp. ISBN 0-7614-0178-4. Provides a description of lifestyles, art, food, and festivals of Bolivia. Appropriate for grades 3–5. [Bolivia]

The Book of Holidays Around the World.

Alice Van Straalen. New York: Dutton, 1986. 192 pp. Contains a chronology of events to celebrate through each day of the year. Suitable for the elementary grades. [multicultural holidays]

Brazil, An Awakening Giant.

Mark L. Carpenter. Minneapolis, MN: Dillon Press, 1987. 125 pp. ISBN 0-87518-366-2. Discusses the holidays, folkways, and people of Brazil. Suitable for grade 5 and up. [Brazil]

Canada, Good Neighbor to the World.

Adam Bryant. Minneapolis, MN: Dillon Press, 1987. 191 pp. ISBN 0-382-39498-4. Discusses the holidays, traditions, people, history, and geography of Canada. Appropriate for elementary grades. [Canada]

Celebrating Earth Day.

Janet McDonnell. Chicago: Children's Press, 1994. 31 pp. ISBN 0-516-00689-4. Mr. Webster's class plans an Earth Day party. Includes activities. Appropriate for preschool through grade 2. [Earth Day]

Celebrating Kwanzaa.

Diane Hoyt-Goldsmith. New York: Holiday House, 1993. 32 pp. ISBN 0-8234-1048-X. ISBN 0-8234-1130-3 paper. Shows how a Chicago family celebrates this African American holiday. Appropriate for grades 3–7. [African Americans; Kwanzaa]

Celebration: The Story of American Holidays.

Lucille Recht Penner. New York: Macmillan, 1993. 79 pp. ISBN 0-02-770903-5. Discusses the origins of thirteen holidays and provides directions for handicrafts and recipes. For all elementary grades. [crafts; United States]

Christmas.

Jane Duden. New York: Crestwood House, 1990. 48 pp. Describes the history of the Christmas holiday and ways in which it is celebrated. Suitable for the elementary grades. [Christmas]

Christmas Holiday Grab Bag.

Judith Bauer Stamper. Mahwah, NJ: Troll, 1993. 48 pp. ISBN 0-8167-2908-5. Describes the origins of Christmas customs and suggests holiday activities. For grades 2–5. [Christmas]

Christmas Magic.

James W. Baker. Minneapolis, MN: Lerner, 1988. 48 pp. Contains ten magic tricks based on a Christmas theme. For all elementary grades. [Christmas; magic]

Columbus Day.

Dennis B. Fradin. Hillside, NJ: Enslow Publishers, 1990. 48 pp. ISBN 0-89490-233-4. Discusses the achievements of Columbus that led to celebrating the anniversary of his landing in the New World. For grades 1–4. [Columbus Day]

Columbus Day.

Vicki Liestman. Minneapolis, MN: Carolrhoda Books, 1991. 52 pp. ISBN 0-87614-444-X. Describes the voyages made by Columbus and gives a history of this holiday. For use in preschool through grade 3. [Columbus Day]

Columbus Day.

Cass R. Sandak. New York: Crestwood House, 1990. 8 pp. Discusses the highlights of Columbus Day and the reasons for the celebration. For use in the elementary grades. [Columbus Day]

Crafts for Kwanzaa.

Kathy Ross. Brookfield, CT: Millbrook Press, 1994. 47 pp. ISBN 1-56294-412-6. Explains how to make crafts and decorations. Suitable for use in preschool through grade 3. [crafts; Kwanzaa]

Cuba.

Sean Sheehan. New York: Marshall Cavendish, 1995. 128 pp. ISBN 1-85435-691-7. Describes the lifestyles, art, food and festivals of Cuba. For use in the elementary grades. [Cuba]

Days of Awe: Stories for Rosh Hashanah and Yom Kippur.

Adapted by Eric A. Kimmel. New York: Viking, 1991. 47 pp. ISBN 0-670-82772-X. Provides stories about two major Jewish holidays, Rosh Hashanah and Yom Kippur. For students in grades 4–7. [Rosh Hashanah; Yom Kippur]

Draw 50 Holiday Decorations.

Lee J. Ames with Ray Burns. New York: Doubleday, 1987. 74 pp. ISBN 0-385-26770-3. Gives step-by-step directions for drawing such symbols as Easter baskets, Fourth of July rockets, and a Valentine cupid. For use with elementary school-aged children. [drawing]

Earth-friendly Holidays: How to Make Fabulous Gifts and Decorations from Reusable Objects.

George Pfiffner. New York: Wiley, 1995. 128 pp. ISBN 0-471-12005-7. Describes how to make handicrafts and contains bibliographical references. For use in grades 3–7. [crafts; recycled materials]

Easter.

Cass R. Sandak. New York: Crestwood House, 1990. 48 pp. ISBN 0-89686-499-5. Discusses the origins and symbols of Easter and describes how the holiday is celebrated. For grades 5–6. [Easter]

El Salvador.

Erin Foley. New York: Marshall Cavendish, 1995. 128 pp. ISBN 1-85435-696-8. Discusses the lifestyles, art, food and festivals of El Salvador. For use with upper elementary students. [El Salvador]

The Family Read-Aloud Christmas Treasury.

Alice Low. Boston, MA: Little, Brown, 1989. 136 pp. ISBN 0-316-53371-8. Contains the works of 54 poets and authors in a holiday collection. For elementary-school-aged children. [Christmas; parent resources]

Father's Day.

Laura Alden. Chicago, IL: Children's Press, 1994. 31 pp. ISBN 0-516-00693-2. Tells how we celebrate Father's Day. For preschool through grade 2. [Father's Day]

Festival of Esther: The Story of Purim.

Maida Silverman. New York: Simon & Schuster, 1989. 26 pp. ISBN 0-671-67200-2. Explains the history of the holiday and includes a traditional song and a recipe for hamantashen cookies. For grades 1–5. [Purim]

Fiesta! Cinco de Mayo, Dias de Fiesta.

June Behrens. Chicago, IL: Children's Press, 1986. 30 pp. Tells the history of this holiday which celebrates the victory in 1862 of the Mexican army over the French. For use with elementary students. [Cinco de Mayo]

Fiesta U.S.A.

George Ancona. New York: Lodestar Books, 1995. 48 pp. ISBN 0-525-67498-5. Describes the holidays, social life and customs of Hispanic Americans. For grades 3–5. [Hispanic Americans]

Fourth of July.

Lynda Sorensen. Vero Beach, FL: Rourke Press, 1994. 24 pp. ISBN 1-57103-069-7. Discusses the holiday on which we celebrate our independence. For all elementary grades. [Fourth of July]

Great Big Holiday Celebrations.

Compiled by Elizabeth McKinnon. Everett, WA: Warren Publishing, 1991. 221 pp. ISBN 0-911019-43-X. Contains activities for celebrating major holidays with children. For all elementary grades. [Christmas; Easter]

Haiti.

Roseline Ng Cheong-Lum. New York: Marshall Cavendish, 1995. 128 pp. ISBN 1-85435-693-3. Describes the lifestyles, art, food and festivals of Haiti. Suitable for the elementary grades. [Haiti]

Halloween.

Dennis Brindell Fradin. Hillside, NJ: Enslow Publishers, 1990. 48 pp. ISBN 0-89490-234-2. Discusses the history of Halloween and the ways in which it is celebrated. For grades 1–4. [Halloween]

Halloween.

Cass R. Sandak. New York: Crestwood House, 1990. 48 pp. Gives the history and customs of Halloween. For use in elementary grades. [Halloween]

Halloween Holiday Grab Bag.

Judith Bauer Stamper. Mahwah, NJ: Troll, 1993. 48 pp. ISBN 0-8167-2904-2. Discusses the origins of Halloween customs and symbols, and suggests activities. For grades 2–5. [Halloween]

Halloween Magic.

James W. Baker. Minneapolis, MN: Lerner, 1988. 48 pp. ISBN 0-8225-2228-4. Contains ten magic tricks on a Halloween theme. For grades 2–5. [Halloween; magic]

Hanukkah.

Dennis Brindell Fradin. Hillside, NJ: Enslow Publishers, 1990. 48 pp. ISBN 0-89490-259-8. Tells about Hanukkah, its history, and the ways in which it is celebrated. For grades 1–4. [Hanukkah]

Hanukkah, the Festival of Lights.

Jenny Koralek. New York: Lothrop, Lee & Shepard, 1990. ISBN 0-688-09329-9. Gives information about the festival of Hanukkah. Suitable for preschool through grade 4. [Hanukkah]

Happy Holiday Riddles to You!

Joanne E. Bernstein and Paul Cohen. Niles, IL: Whitman, 1985. 32 pp. ISBN 0-8075-3154-5. Contains one hundred riddles about holidays. For grades 1–5. [riddles]

Happy Thanksgiving!

Carol Barkin and Elizabeth James. New York: Lothrop, Lee & Shepard, 1987. 80 pp. ISBN 0-688-06800-6. Contains ideas for projects, recipes, and activities to celebrate Thanksgiving. For use in grades 4–7. [Thanksgiving]

Happy New Year.

Emily Kelley. Minneapolis, MN: Carolrhoda, 1984. 48 pp. ISBN 0-87614-269-2. Tells how the New Year is celebrated in such places as Ecuador, Japan, and China. For preschool through grade 4. [New Year's]

Harvest Festivals Around the World.

Judith Hoffman Corwin. Morristown, NJ: Julian Messner, 1995. 48 pp. ISBN 0-671-87240-0. Provides a description of many harvest festivals. For grades 2–5. [harvest]

Holiday Art Projects.

Jerome C. Brown. Belmont, CA: Fearon Teacher Aids, 1984. 18 pp. ISBN 0-8224-5190-5. Gives information about various holiday handicrafts. For use in grades 3–12. [crafts]

Holiday Crafts: More Year-Round Projects Kids Can Make.

Alan Bridgewater. Blue Ridge Summit, PA: Tab Books, 1990. 262 pp. ISBN 0-8306-7409-8. ISBN 0-8306-3409-9 paper. Gives instructions for making crafts related to holidays such as New Year's, Valentine's Day, and Halloween. For use in the elementary grades. [crafts]

Holiday Gifts and Decorations Kids Can Make (for Practically Nothing).

James C. Brown. Belmont, CA: Davis S. Lake Publishers, 1986. 108 pp. ISBN 0-8224-3595-0. Contains many suggestions for holiday crafts. For all elementary grades. [crafts]

The Holiday Handbook.

Carol Barkin. New York: Clarion, 1994. 240 pp. ISBN 0-395-65011-9. Discusses secular holidays by seasons, and describes their origins and the ways they are celebrated. For use in the elementary school. [seasons]

Holiday Hoopla: Songs & Finger Plays: New Songs to Favorite Tunes, Finger Plays and Action Verses.

Kathy Darling. Palo Alto, CA: Monday Morning Books, 1990. 64 pp. ISBN 1-878279-15-7. Contains ideas for the holiday activities to use with young children. For preschoolers. [finger plays; music]

Holidays and Celebrations.

Ruth Goring. Vero Beach, FL: Rourke Publications, 1995. 48 pp. ISBN 0-86625-542-7. Describes holidays and festivals of the United States and Latin America. For use in grades 2-6. [Central America; South America; United States]

Holidays of the World Cookbook for Students.

Lois Sinaiko Webb. Phoenix, AZ: Oryx, 1995. 297 pp. ISBN 0-89774-884-0. A collection of 388 recipes from 136 countries with an introduction that describes various holidays. For use with grade 5 and up. [cookery]

Ideas for Special Occasions.

Compiled by Beryl Leitch, Margaret Crowther, and Jenny Mulherin. New York: Marshall Cavendish, 1991. 48 pp. ISBN 1-85435-407-8. Gives step-by-step instructions for ways to celebrate holidays through handicraft projects and foods. For use in grades 4–8. [crafts]

Independence Day.

Willma Willis Gore. Hillside, NJ: Enslow Publishers, 1993. 48 pp. ISBN 0-89490-403-5. Tells of the origins of the holiday as well as how it has been celebrated in the past and today. For use in grades 1–4. [Fourth of July]

Independence Day Magic.

James W. Baker. Minneapolis, MN: Lerner, 1990. 48 pp. Explains magic tricks around the theme of Independence Day. For upper elementary students. [Fourth of July; magic]

Jewish Holiday Fun.

Judith Hoffman Corwin. New York: Julian Messner, 1987. 64 pp. ISBN 0-671-60127-X. Suggests ways to celebrate Jewish holidays through cooking, crafts, and other activities. For grade 3 and up. [Jewish holidays]

Kids' Holiday Fun: Great Family Activities Every Month of the Year.

Penny Warner. New York: Meadowbrook Press, 1994. 214 pp. ISBN 0-671-89981-3. Contains many suggestions for handicrafts. For use in grades 1–8. [crafts]

Kwanzaa.

A. P. Porter. Minneapolis, MN: Carolrhoda Books, 1991. 48 pp. ISBN 0-87614-668-X. ISBN 0-87614-545-4 paper. Describes the origin and the practices of this African-American holiday. For use in preschool through grade 3. [Kwanzaa]

Kwanzaa.

Janet Riehecky. Chicago: Children's Press, 1993. 31 pp. Introduces this holiday through which African Americans celebrate their cultural heritage. For use in all elementary grades. [Kwanzaa]

Las Navidades: Popular Christmas Songs from Latin America.

Selected by Lulu Delacre. New York: Scholastic, 1990. 32 pp. ISBN 0-590-43549-3. This is a bilingual collection of popular Christmas songs from Latin America with illustrations and chord symbols. For use in kindergarten through grade 6. [Christmas; songs; Spanish language]

Let's Celebrate: Jokes About Holidays.

Peter and Connie Roop. Minneapolis, MN: Lerner, 1986. 32 pp. ISBN 0-8225-0989-X. Filled with jokes and riddles. For grades 1–4. [humor]

Let's Celebrate Summer.

Rhoda Nottridge. Hove, England: Wayland Pub. Ltd., 1994. 32 pp. Describes a variety of summer festivals. For use in the elementary grades. [summer]

Lincoln's Birthday.

Dennis Brindell Fradin. Hillside, NJ: Enslow Publishing, 1990. 48 pp. ISBN 0-89490-250-4. Discusses the achievements of Lincoln that led to the holiday celebrating his birth. Suitable for grades 1–4. [Lincoln, Abraham]

Make It Special: Cards, Decorations and Party Favors for Holidays and Other Special Occasions.

Esther Rudomin Hautzig. New York: Macmillan, 1986. 86 pp. ISBN 0-02-743370-6. Contains suggestions for craft projects and for making cards and decorations. Suitable for grades 3–7. [crafts]

Martin Luther King Day.

Linda Lowery. Minneapolis, MN: Carolrhoda Books, 1987. 56 pp. ISBN 0-87614-299-4. Recounts the life of Martin Luther King, and discusses the holiday in his honor. Suitable for preschool through grade 3. [King, Martin Luther, Jr.]

Martin Luther King, Jr., Day.

Lynda Sorensen. Vero Beach, FL: Rourke Press, 1994. 24 pp. ISBN 1-57103-068-9. Describes the life of Martin Luther King, Jr. from 1929 to 1968. For all elementary grades. [King, Martin Luther, Jr.]

Memorial Day.

Lynda Sorensen. Vero Beach, FL: Rourke Press, 1994. 24 pp. ISBN 1-57103-071-9. Describes how and why we celebrate Memorial Day. For use in the elementary grades. [Memorial Day]

Menorahs, Mezuzas, and Other Jewish Symbols.

Miriam Chaikin. New York: Clarion, 1990. 102 pp. ISBN 0-89919-856-2. Tells about Jewish holiday symbols and rituals. For grade 5 and up. [Jewish holidays]

Mother's Day.

Willma Willis Gore. Hillside, NJ: Enslow Publishers, 1993. 48 pp. ISBN 0-89490-404-3. Tells about this national holiday on which sons and daughters honor their mothers. For grades 1–4. [Mother's Day]

A Mother's Manual for Holiday Survival.

Kathy Peel and Judie Byrd. Pomona, CA: Focus on the Family Pub., 1991. 135 pp. ISBN 1-56179-040-0. Contains ideas for family fun during special occasions. An adult resource book. [parent resources]

Muslim Festivals.

M. M. Ahsan. Vero Beach, FL: Rourke Enterprises, 1987. 48 pp. Discusses customs and traditional Islamic festivals and celebrations. For students in upper elementary grades. [Islamic celebrations]

My First Book of Jewish Holidays.

Maida Silverman. New York: Dial Books, 1994. 32 pp. ISBN 0-8037-1427-0. Provides an introduction to ten important Jewish holidays. For preschool through grade 8. [Jewish holidays]

My First Fourth of July Book.

Harriet W. Hodgson. Chicago, IL: Children's Press, 1987. 31 pp. ISBN 0-516-42907-8. Contains poems about picnics, fireworks, and parades. For preschool through grade 2. [Fourth of July]

My Very Own Thanksgiving: A Book of Cooking and Crafts.

Robin West. Minneapolis, MN: Carolrhoda Books, 1993. 63 pp. ISBN 0-87614-723-6. Gives information about the holiday and supplies a collection of recipes and crafts. For preschool through grade 4. [cookery; crafts; Thanksgiving]

New Year's Poems.

Selected by Myra Cohn Livingston. New York: Holiday House, 1987. 32 pp. ISBN 0-8234-0641-5. Contains poems by a variety of poets on the topic of beginning a new year. For preschool through grade 3. [New Year's; poetry]

Nicaragua.

Jennifer Cott. New York: Marshall Cavendish, 1995. 128 pp. Describes the lifestyles, art, food and festivals of Nicaragua. For upper elementary grades. [Nicaragua]

175 Easy-to-Do Halloween Crafts: Creative Uses for Recyclables.

Sharon Dunn Umnik, ed. Honesdale, PA: Boyds Mills Press, 1995. 63 pp. ISBN 1-56397-372-3. Gives step-by-step directions for making masks, cards, and other Halloween items. For grades 1–5. [crafts; Halloween; masks]

Our National Holidays.

Karen Borneman Spies. Brookfield, CT: Millbrook Press, 1992. 48 pp. ISBN 1-56294-109-7. Discusses patriotic holidays, and holidays that honor famous people, as well as special American holidays such as Thanksgiving. For use in grades 2–4. [patriotism; United States]

Our St. Patrick's Day Book.

Sandra Ziegler. Elgin, IL: Child's World, 1987. 32 pp. ISBN 0-89565-344-3. A kindergarten class is involved in activities to celebrate St. Patrick's Day. For preschool through grade 2. [St. Patrick's Day]

Paper-Cutting Stories for Holidays and Special Events.

Valerie Marsh. Fort Atkinson, WI: Alleyside Press, 1994. 63 pp. ISBN 0-917846-42-7. Combines storytelling and holidays. For use in the elementary grades. [storytelling]

Patriotic Holidays.

Cass R. Sandak. New York: Crestwood House, 1990. 48 pp. ISBN 0-89686-501-0. Discusses the origin of patriotic holidays such as the 4th of July, Presidents' Day, and Armistice Day. For grades 5–6. [patriotic holidays]

Poems for Jewish Holidays.

Selected by Myra Cohn Livingston. New York: Holiday House, 1986. 32 pp. ISBN 0-8234-0606-7. Contains poems about Judaism and its fasts and feasts. For preschool through grade 4. [Jewish holidays; poetry]

Presidents' Day.

Laura Alden. Chicago: Children's Press, 1994. 29 pp. ISBN 0-516-00691-6. Describes why we celebrate the birthdays of George Washington and Abraham Lincoln. For use in preschool through grade 2. [President's Day]

Projects for Christmas & Holiday Activities.

Mary Ann Green. Ada, OK: Garrett Educational Corp., 1989. 31 pp. A collection of arts and crafts activities for Christmas. For grades 3–5. [Christmas; crafts]

Projects for Spring & Holiday Activities.

Celia McInnes. Ada, OK: Garrett Educational Corp., 1989. 31 pp. Arts and crafts activities, games, and recipes relating to spring. For grades 3–5. [crafts; spring]

Projects for Winter and Holiday Activities.

Celia McInnes. Ada, OK: Garrett Educational Corp., 31 pp. Contains a variety of holiday activities related to the winter season. For grades 3–5. [winter]

Puerto Rico.

Patricia Marjorie Levy. New York: Marshall Cavendish, 1995. 128 pp. ISBN 1-85435-690-9. Describes the lifestyles, art, food and festivals of Puerto Rico. For use in the elementary grades. [Puerto Rico]

Ramadan and Id Al-Fitr.

Dianne MacMillan. Hillside, NJ: Enslow Publishers, 1994. 48 pp. ISBN 0-89490-502-3. Explains some of the rituals of Islam. For grades 1–4. [Ramadan; Id Al-Fitr]

Special Day Celebrations.

Elizabeth McKinnon. Everett, WA: Warren Publishing, 1989. 125 pp. ISBN 0-911019-224-3. Filled with activities for celebrating special days throughout the year. For preschool through grade 1. [days, special]

Spring Festivals.

Mike Rosen. New York: Bookwright Press, 1991. 32 pp. Shows ways that different cultures around the world celebrate spring. For all elementary grades. [spring]

Somoans!: Festivals and Holidays.

June Behrens. Chicago, IL: Children's Press, 1986. 31 pp. Describes holidays in Western and American Somoa. For use in upper elementary grades. [Somoa]

Sound the Shofar: The Story and Meaning of Rosh Hashanah & Yom Kippur.

Miriam Chaikin. New York: Clarion, 1986. 87 pp. ISBN 0-89919-427-3. Describes the ways in which these holidays were celebrated throughout history and today. For use in grades 3–7. [Rosh Hashanah; Yom Kippur]

St. Patrick's Day.

Janet Riehecky. Chicago: Children's Press, 1994. 31 pp. ISBN 0-516-00696-7. Explores the holiday commemorating the Irish saint. For use in preschool through grade 2. [St. Patrick's Day]

St. Patrick's Day Magic.

James W. Baker. Minneapolis, MN: Lerner, 1990. 48 pp. Explains magic tricks around the theme of St. Patrick's Day. For use in upper elementary grades. [St. Patrick's Day; magic]

Summer Festivals.

Mike Rosen. New York: Bookwright, 1991. 32 pp. Discusses the various festivals and holidays relating to summer that are celebrated around the world. For all elementary grades. [summer]

Tet: Vietnamese New Year.

Dianne MacMillan. Hillside, NJ: Enslow Publishers, 1994. 48 pp. ISBN 0-89490-501-5. Discusses this Vietnamese holiday. For use in grades 1–4. [New Year's; Tet; Vietnam]

Thanksgiving.

Jane Deeden. New York: Crestwood House, 1990. 48 pp. Explains the historic events that shaped this holiday and the ways in which it is celebrated. For all elementary grades. [Thanksgiving]

Thanksgiving.

Lynda Sorensen. Vero Beach, FL: Rourke Press, 1994. 24 pp. ISBN 1-57103-072-7. Discusses the Thanksgiving holiday. For use in the elementary grades. [Thanksgiving]

Thanksgiving Fun.

Beth Murray. Honesdale, PA: Boyds Mills Press, 1993. 32 pp. ISBN 1-56397-280-8. Contains craft ideas, recipes, and games suitable for Thanksgiving. For use in grades 2–7. [crafts; Thanksgiving]

This Place Is Crowded.

Vicki Cobb. New York: Walker & Co., 1992. 32 pp. ISBN 0-8027-8145-4. Describes home life, education, and holidays in Japan. For use in grades 2–4. [Japan]

Through the Year in Japan.

Elizabeth Fusae Thurley. London, England: Batsford Academic & Educational, 1985. 72 pp. Shows Japanese life through a seasonal cycle of national holidays and festivals. For use in the elementary grades. [Japan]

The Uninvited Guest, & Other Jewish Holiday Tales.

Nina Jaffe. New York: Scholastic, 1993. 72 pp. ISBN 0-590-44653-3. Contains traditional tales related to the major holidays. For elementary grades 3–5. [Jewish holidays]

Valentine's Day.

Dennis B. Fradin. Hillside, NJ: Enslow Publishers, 1990. 48 pp. ISBN 0-89490-237-7. Gives the history of Valentine's Day and discusses the ways in which it is celebrated. For grades 1–4. [Valentine's Day]

Valentine's Day.

Cass R. Sandak. New York: Crestwood House, 1990. 48 pp. Tells the history and customs of Valentine's Day. For all elementary grades. [Valentine's Day]

Veteran's Day.

Lynda Sorensen. Vero Beach, FL: Rourke Press, 1994. 24 pp. ISBN 1-57103-070-0. Discusses why and how Veteran's Day became a holiday. For use in the elementary grades. [Veteran's Day]

We Celebrate Easter.

Bobbie Kalman. New York: Crabtree Pub. Co., 1985. 56 pp. ISBN 0-86505-042-2. ISBN 0-86505-052-X paper. Discusses the religious and secular symbols of Easter and includes ideas for projects. For grades 3–4. [Easter]

We Celebrate New Year.

Bobbie Kalman. New York: Crabtree., 1985. 56 pp. ISBN 0-86505-041-4. ISBN 0-86505-051-1 paper. Describes how New Year's is celebrated throughout the world. For grades 3–4. [New Year's]

We Celebrate Valentine's Day.

Bobbie Kalman. New York: Crabtree, 1985. 57 pp. ISBN 0-86505-047-3. ISBN 0-86505-057-0 paper. Discusses Valentine's Day and gives ideas for a variety of activities. For grades 3–4. [Valentine's Day]

The Whole Christmas Catalogue for Kids.

Louise Betts. New York: Mallard Press, 1988. 158 pp. Discusses the significance of Christmas and gives instructions for making ornaments, decorations, and gifts. For elementary school aged children. [Christmas; crafts]

Whole Language for the Holidays.

Flora Joy. Carthage, IL: Good Apple, 1992. 138 pp. ISBN 0-86653-689-2. Includes stories, poems, patterns, and activities. For preschool through grade 4. [poetry]

Winter Festivals.

Mike Rosen. New York: Bookwright Press, 1990. 32 pp. Shows how winter is celebrated around the world. For all elementary grades. [winter]

A World of Holidays.

Louisa Campbell. New York: Silver Moon Press, 1993. 60 pp. ISBN 1-881889-08-4. Looks at many of the holidays we celebrate. For preschool through grade 4.

Zimbawe, A Treasure of Africa.

Al Stark. Minneapolis, MN: Dillon Press, 1986. 160 pp. ISBN 0-87518-308-5. Tells about the people, traditions, history, geography and holidays of Zimbabwe. For grade 5 and up. [Zimbabwe]

Other resources

The magazine, *Holidays & Seasonal Celebrations*, is published four times a year by the Teaching & Learning Company. It is filled with ideas for teachers of students pre-K to grade three.

Chinese New Year.

Fabian-Baber Communications. Bala Cynwyd, PA: Schlessinger Video Productions, 1994. 1 videocassette, 30 minutes. For grades K–4. Discusses music, folktales, arts and crafts and explores the symbols of Chinese New Year. Suitable for the elementary grades. [Chinese New Year; crafts; New Year's]

Christmas.

Fabian-Baber Communications. Bala Cynwyd, PA: Schlessinger Video Productions, 1994. 1 videocassette, 30 minutes. For grades K-4. Discusses music, folktales, arts and crafts and explores the Christmas holiday and holiday symbols. [Christmas]

Cinco de Mayo.

Fabian-Baber Communications. Bala Cynwyd, PA: Schlessinger Video Productions, 1994. 1 videocassette, 30 minutes. Discusses music, folktales, arts and crafts and explores the symbols of Cinco de Mayo. For grades K–4. [Cinco de Mayo]

Easter.

Fabian-Baber Communications. Bala Cynwyd, PA: Schlessinger Video Productions, 1994. 1 videocassette, 30 minutes. Discusses music, folktales, arts and crafts and explores symbols of Easter. For grades K-4. [Easter]

The First Thanksgiving.

Linda Hayward. New York: Random House, 1992. 1 book, 48 pp., and 1 sound cassette, 24 minutes. Shows the Pilgrims' amazing adventures during the first Thanksgiving. For use in the elementary grades. [Thanksgiving]

Halloween.

Fabian-Baber Communications. Bala Cynwyd, PA: Schlessinger Video Productions, 1994. 1 videocassette, 30 minutes. Discusses music, folktales, arts and crafts and explores the symbols of Halloween. For grades K–4. [Halloween]

Halloween Night.

Carolyn Brachen. New York: Bantam Books, 1989. 1 book, 24 pp., and 1 sound cassette, 10 minutes. Tapekit on Halloween. For use in the elementary grades. [Halloween]

Independence Day.

Fabian-Baber Communications. Bala Cynwyd, PA: Schlessinger Video Productions, 1994. 1 videocassette, 30 minutes. Discusses music, folktales, arts and crafts, and explores the symbols surrounding Independence Day. For grades K–4. [Fourth of July]

Kwanzaa.

Fabian-Baber Communications. Bala Cynwyd, PA: Schlessinger Video Productions, 1994. 1 videocassette, 30 minutes. Discusses music, folktales, arts and crafts, and explores the symbols of this African-American holiday. For grades K-4. [Kwanzaa]

Kwanzaa: Stories & Songs.

Opalanga, storyteller. Denver, CO: Olukano Productions, 1995. One sound cassette. A professional story teller shares stories and songs. For all elementary grades. [Kwanzaa; storytelling]

A Multicultural Christmas.

Warren Colman. Niles, IL: United Learning, 1993. 1 videocassette, 22 minutes. Shows how five families celebrate Christmas in Scandinavia, South Korea, Mexico, Ethiopia, and as an Oneida Indian. For all elementary grades. [Christmas; multicultural celebrations]

Rosh Hashanah.

Fabian-Baber Communications. Bala Cynwyd, PA: Schlessinger Video Productions, 1994. 1 videocassette, 30 minutes. For grades K–4. Discusses music, folktales, arts and crafts and explores the symbols of Rosh Hashanah and Yom Kippur. Appropriate for the elementary grades. [Rosh Hashanah; Yom Kippur]

Thanksgiving Day.

Gail Gibbons. Ancramdale, NY: Live Oak Media, 1985. One book, 32 pp., and 1 sound cassette, 10 minutes. A tapekit about the first Thanksgiving and the ways in which we celebrate it today. For primary grades. [Thanksgiving]

The Thirteen Days of Halloween.

Carol Greene. Chicago, IL: Children's Press, 1990. One book, 29 pp. and one sound cassette, 5 minutes. A tapekit with sing-alongs. For use in the elementary grades. [Halloween]

Valentine's Day.

Fabian-Baber Communications. Bala Cynwyd, PA: Schlessinger Video Productions, 1994. One videocassette, 30 minutes. For grades K–4. Discusses music, folktales, arts and crafts, and explores the symbols of Valentine's Day. For use in the elementary grades. [Valentine's Day]

9

Doing Research and Writing Reports

*I*n a whole language elementary classroom, reading and writing go hand-in-hand. Even the youngest students will try to write messages, using the letters they know and the sounds they can hear when the word is said. This "temporary spelling" can be a challenge for teachers and parents to decipher, but it is a huge step toward literacy, and the child's efforts should be applauded.

Gradually, students acquire more reading and writing skills. They may keep journals on the books they have read and on other activities and important events in their lives. They write stories and letters. They learn more about sentence structure, grammar, and punctuation.

The temporary spelling gives way to formal spelling. And over time, students learn how to build paragraphs from sentences, and essays from paragraphs. They recognize the difference between a rough draft and a final draft, and between a piece of writing in progress and one that is ready for publication.

Students also gradually learn about writing reports. Some of these will be very simple and others will be more formal and complex. Sometimes students will need to talk with experts, read magazine articles, and use books and reference materials in order to find the information that they need. They learn when to paraphrase, when to quote, and how to credit their sources of information.

Learning to carry out research is an integral part of the elementary school language arts program and an excellent way to foster cross-disciplinary studies. Students will no doubt write many papers in the language arts class, especially as they respond to literature. But there also will be opportunities for report writing in other disciplines.

Students may be required to write papers to accompany a science fair project; to prepare a biography on an important figure in American history; to find out more about the life and work of an artist or musician; to tell about the people, products and geography of a country; or to explain the contributions of a famous mathematician.

Sometimes the student carries out research simply to satisfy his or her own curiosity or as a natural part of a continuing interest or hobby. For example, if the student wishes to add another fish to an existing aquarium at home, he or she will want to find out which fish are compatible with others, special water temperature requirements, etc. If a student glimpsed an unusual bird at a bird feeder, or during a hike, he or she may wish to try to identify it. Speaking to a knowledgeable expert in the field would be an excellent way to research these questions. At other times, the research is related to a school assignment. Perhaps in social studies, the student will be asked to give an oral report on what has been learned or take part in a panel discussion using researched information to present one side of an issue. To be successful, the student needs to find sources of information and take notes.

There are skills and techniques which will make doing research easier and more satisfying. Depending on the grade level, teachers will find themselves introducing or reviewing these skills. The librarian or media specialist will be a valued partner. Approached as an exploration of resources, research can be an exciting undertaking.

In schools where there are specialists in various subject areas, it is helpful to use some valuable planning time so that teachers can coordinate their efforts. The language arts teacher and social studies teacher, for example, could work closely together on a project involving a state history. The science teacher might request help from the language arts teacher in the report writing skills necessary for a paper to accompany an experiment.

Some of the resources which follow are especially intended for teachers and librarians. Many would be appropriate for parents who are trying to assist their children in learning to use a library effectively and in developing and improving research and report writing skills. Some are intended directly for student use.

When teachers work together, they can set a reasonable time schedule for projects and can also work with the school librarian to help gather together a collection of materials that will be especially helpful to students doing research within a broad field. If this is a major writing assignment, information on the general topics, the specific requirements, and the due date should be shared with parents, also. Informed parents can encourage students to meet their deadlines.

Before beginning to write a school report, first the student must be guided in selecting a manageable topic. If, for example, the student is supposed to do a short research paper on anything of interest from that time period in American history when the young colonies were struggling for independence, the student needs to consider broad areas first and then focus in on a narrower subject.

After doing some preliminary reading, a specific topic may attract interest. The student at this point may find that he or she has some questions which could be answered during the course of the research.

Directions for Ideas That Work

BRAINSTORMING TO SELECT A TOPIC: First, the teacher might lead a brainstorming session at the chalkboard. At this point, the purpose is to get up on the chalkboard as many ideas as possible, but even during this brainstorming process, the teacher might model the narrowing of topics. For example, one student might suggest, "Important People During the Revolution." Later someone might say, "Benjamin Franklin." By writing "Important People" as a major classification, and then listing "Franklin" under it, the students can visually observe a narrowing of the topic.

The following might be a piece of what would emerge from a short brainstorming session at the chalkboard:

Important Places	**Important People**	
Freedom Trail	Samuel Adams	Thomas Paine
Independence Hall	Benjamin Franklin	John Adams
Valley Forge	Thomas Paine	Benedict Arnold
Concord	Thomas Jefferson	Paul Revere
Lexington	George Washington	General Howe
Independence Hall	Marquis de Lafayette	Cornwallis
Bunker Hill	Abigail Adams	Braddock

Acts and Resolutions	**Important Events**	
Sugar Act of 1764	Boston Massacre	Boston Tea Party
The Stamp Act	First Continental Congress	
The Townshend Acts	Second Continental Congress	
The Intolerable Acts	Declaration of Independence	

After this initial group brainstorming, allow time for clusters of four to six students to gather around a table, each with paper and pencil, and help one another to select and write down a research topic. Encourage the groups to help each member to continue to narrow down the topic until it seems manageable, and to include some questions that they hope to answer as they carry out their research.

Once each of the students has a manageable topic, and some questions on which to focus, some time should be invested in teaching about or reviewing information on how to make the best use of libraries. The classroom teacher would be wise to enlist the help of the librarian or media specialist in this undertaking.

Directions for Ideas That Work

GETTING TO KNOW YOUR LIBRARY/MEDIA CENTER: Choose a time when the library will not be heavily in use by other classes and when the librarian is not busy with scheduled story hours. Before going to the library/media center, have students select a partner. Explain that the partners will draw a slip of paper with a subject written on it from a box. The students are to find out whatever they can to share with the rest of the class about their subject and how materials related to it might be located in the library and used in their research project. Students should take any necessary notes to help them when they orally report back to their classmates.

Subjects on the slips of paper will vary depending on the size of your library, but might include: The card or computer catalog, encyclopedias, reference books, magazines & periodicals, indexes, newspapers, electronic resources, Internet sources, vertical file of pamphlets, maps, video tapes & sound cassettes, biographies & special collections, *Readers' Guide to Periodical Literature,* almanacs and yearbooks, atlas and/or geographic dictionary.

Back in class, after the partners have had an opportunity to explore the library and to find out about their topic which was on the slip of paper they drew, the teacher should display a map of the library and allow time for the partners to take turns explaining to their classmates where to find specific materials and how the material might be of help in doing their research reports.

Some libraries use the Library of Congress Classification system for their holdings, but most school libraries use the Dewey Decimal System. Since students may use the local public library as well as the school library in conducting their research, it is worth while for the teacher to be thoroughly familiar with both and to share information that will be helpful to student researchers.

A field trip to the town's library or one of its branches, or inviting a city librarian to visit the class and discuss the local library in depth might both be good ideas for assisting a class of students to be prepared to carry out their research.

Assuming that the school and local library use and are connected to a computerized database that relies on the Dewey Decimal Classifications, a work session in the school library might be planned during which each student should demonstrate the ability to use the Dewey system.

Directions for Ideas That Work

A DEWEY DECIMAL SCAVENGER HUNT: Give students a sheet in which the following is printed:

000 - 099	General Works	**500 - 599**	Pure Science
100 - 199	Philosophy	**600 - 699**	Technology
200 - 299	Religion	**700 - 799**	The Arts
300 - 399	Social Studies	**800 - 899**	Literature
400 - 499	Language	**900 - 999**	History
B	Biography		

Ask students to find one book in their library from each of the categories above and to write at the bottom of their sheet of paper the name of the book, author, and Dewey Decimal Classification number.

Some students will be adept at using a card catalog or, more likely, a computerized catalog of the library's holdings. But a review might be in order. A few brainstorming sessions at the chalkboard would be helpful. What descriptive words would likely yield information if the students wanted to know more about the first Model T Ford? What descriptive words would you use to find a book on outlining? Such a brief review may save the students hours of frustration.

Some class time will need to be used to explain to students ways of taking notes on the materials they consult. If you wish students to use note cards, they'll need to see some examples of how to do this. Students may also need help in deciding when to quote material and when to put the information they find into their own words.

Once students have gathered sufficient information to be in a position to write the first drafts of their papers, more instruction will be needed to help them choose an organizational pattern for their paper and to write an outline. How might a paper begin and end? Will the bulk of the information be in chronological order? Will similar types of information be grouped regardless of time?

Depending on the age and skill level of students, the teacher might or might not want them to complete a bibliography to accompany their research papers. Even the youngest researchers should learn to write down the name of any book that they use in their research. Older students can be expected to master a simple bibliographic form. If the teacher has taught a format that students should follow in bibliographies, the following activity will provide a check on whether or not students have mastered it.

Directions for Ideas That Work

PUTTING THINGS IN ORDER: Choose some books and articles. On a worksheet, enter the bibliographic data in a random format. Allow the students to work in small teams to re-write the material into proper form for bibliographical entries. Your random material might look like this:

> The Fiddlehoppers: Crickets, Katydids, and Locusts
> Franklin Watts
> Danbury Connecticut 1995 64 pages
> Phyllis J. Perry

Your student teams would re-write the material into the format you have taught them, such as:

> Perry, Phyllis J. The Fiddlehoppers: Crickets, Katydids, and Locusts. Danbury, CT: Franklin Watts, 1995. 64 pp.

You might want to include examples of magazine articles, books with more than one author, and encyclopedia articles in your random materials.

Besides research papers, students will have the need to make other reports. One of the commonest assignments is to prepare a book report to share with the class. Some of the resource books suggest novel ways of sharing information about books in addition to the more traditional reports.

Learning to do research and to write reports of various kinds are important skills that students need to master. For some topics in which they are interested, students may interview experts in person, over the telephone, or on-line, or, in some instances, they may carry out original research. Most often, however, they will be consulting a variety of print materials, both primary and secondary resources. What they learn about effectively using and organizing their research materials will help them in all content fields.

Resource books

Activities Almanac: Daily Ideas for Library Media Lessons.

H. Thomas Walker and Paula K. Montgomery, eds. Santa Barbara, CA: ABC-CLIO, 1990. 283 pp. Contains ideas compiled from a monthly column of *School Library Media Activities*. Good adult resource. [library skills; media center activities]

Asking Questions, Finding Answers.

Dianne Draze. San Luis Obispo, CA: Dandy Lion Publishers, 1990. 70 pp. For students in grades 4–7. [library skills]

Basic Library Skills

Carolyn Wolf and Richard Wolf. Jefferson, NC: McFarland, 1986. 2nd ed. 141 pp. ISBN 0-89950-895-2. Gives an introduction and orientation to the library. For use in all elementary grades. [library skills]

Basic Media Skills Through Games.

Irene Wood Bell and Jeanne E. Weickert. Englewood, CO: Libraries Unlimited, 1985. 2 volumes. Contains games designed to help teach library skills. For use in the elementary grades. [library skills; media center activities]

Better Than Book Reports: More Than 40 Creative Projects for Responding to Literature, Grades 2–6.

Christine Boardman Moen. New York: Scholastic Professional Books, 1992. 128 pp. Give ideas for different kinds of book reporting. For grades 2–6. [book reports]

Brainstorms and Blueprints: Teaching Library Research As a Thinking Process.

Barbara K. Stripling and Judy M. Pitts. Englewood, CO: Libraries Unlimited, 1988. 181 pp. ISBN 0-87287-638-1. For older students, provides a useful reinforcement of library skills. Good adult reference book. [library skills]

Building Reference Skills in the Elementary School.

M. Ellen Jay and Hilda L. Jay. Hamden, CT: Library Professional Publications, 1986. 187 pp. ISBN 0-208-02098-5. Techniques for librarians. [library skills]

Check It Out! The Book About Libraries.
Gail Gibbons. San Diego, CA: Harcourt Brace Jovanovich, 1985. 32 pp. ISBN 0-15-216400-6. Provides an introduction to libraries. Suitable for the primary grades. [libraries]

Choose, Use, Enjoy, Share: Library Media Skills for the Gifted Child.
Phyllis B. Leonard. Englewood, CO: Libraries Unlimited, 1985. 153 pp. Filled with information on using library skills. Suitable for use in the elementary grades. [library skills]

Computers.
Norman S. Barrett. New York: Franklin Watts, 1985. 32 pp. Explains the use of computers in schools. For students in the elementary grades. [computer skills]

Destinations: How to Use All Kinds of Maps.
Carlienne Frisch. New York: Rosen Pub. Group, 1993. 48 pp. ISBN 0-8239-1607-3. Explains how to interpret and use information from maps. For students in grades 5 and up. [map reading skills]

Developing Library Skills.
Esther Lakritz. Carthage, IL: Good Apple, 1989. 108 pp. ISBN 0-86653-481-4. An activity book for students in grades 4–8 on library skills. [library skills]

Dewey Dynamite.
Sherry R. Crow. San Antonio, TX: Book Lore (distributed by ECS Learning Systems, Inc.), 1987. 32 pp. Can be used with individuals or groups, grades 3-6, in presenting research skills using the Dewey Decimal System. [Dewey Decimal Classification; library skills]

Educating the Public Library User.
John Lubans, Jr., ed. Chicago: American Library Association, 145 pp. Offers information on using public libraries. A useful reference book. [libraries]

Find It Fast: How to Uncover Expert Information on Any Subject.
Robert I. Berkman. New York: Perennial Library, 1990. 330 pp. ISBN 0-06-273294-3. Explains how to locate information. A useful adult reference book. [library skills]

Find It! The Inside Story at Your Library.
Claire McInerney. Minneapolis, MN: Lerner., 1989. 55 pp. ISBN 0-8225-2425-2. Tells how to use the resources that can be found in a library. For grade 4 and up. [library skills]

First Encyclopedia of Science.
Brian J. Ford. New York: Random House, 1993. 153 pp. ISBN 0-679-83698-5. Contains over four hundred alphabetical entries. For grades 2–6. [science–encyclopedias]

First Research Projects.

Nancy Polette. San Antonio, TX: Book Lore (distributed by ECS Learning Systems, Inc.), 1984. 32 pp. Suggests beginning research projects for students in grades K–3. [library skills; research projects]

The Grolier Library of International Biographies.

Grolier Educational Corp. staff. Danbury, CT: Grolier Educational Corp., 1996. 10 volumes. Includes biographies in categories such as explorers, politicians and national leaders. Suitable for intermediate grades. [biography]

A Guide to Independent Research.

Phyllis J. Perry, ed. Mobile, AL: GCT Publications, 1990. 66 pp. ISBN 0-937659-33-9. Explains how to approach research and tells about reference tools in the library. Suitable for grades 4–9. [library skills; research projects]

The Guinness Book of Answers: The Complete Reference Handbook.

Beatrice Frie and Honor Head, eds. Enfield, Middlesex: Guinness Books, 1989. 596 pp. A useful reference book containing unusual records and facts. [almanacs]

Helping Your Child Use the Library.

Kathryn Perkinson. Washington, D.C.: U.S. Department of Education, Office of Educational Research & Improvement, 1993. 24 pp. Tips on using the library. Suitable for elementary grades. [library skills; parent resources]

Help Is on the Way for—Group Reports.

Marilyn Berry. Chicago: Children's Press, 1986. 46 pp. Contains ideas for organizing and completing group reports. For grade 3 and up. [group reports]

Help Is On the Way for—Library Skills.

Marilyn Berry. Chicago: Children's Press, 1985. 46 pp. Gives an orientation to library skills. For grade 3 and up. [library skills]

Help Is On the Way for—Outlining Skills.

Marilyn Berry. Chicago: Children's Press, 1985. 46 pp. Gives helpful hints on note taking and outlining. For grade 3 and up. [note taking]

Help Is On the Way for—Written Reports.

Marilyn Berry. Chicago: Children's Press, 1984. 46 pp. For grades 3–6. Discussing finding a topic, doing research, making an outline and writing a final draft. [term papers]

Holidays: Lessons and Activities for Library Media Centers.

H. Thomas Walker and Paula K. Montgomery, eds. Santa Barbara, CA: ABC-CLIO, 1990. 285 pp. Contains ideas previously published in *School*

Library Media Activities Monthly. Suitable for use in the elementary grades. [holidays; media center activities]

Hooked On Independent Study! A Programmed Approach to Library Skills for Grades 3 Through 8.

Marguerite Lewis. West Nyack, NY: Center for Applied Research in Education, 1990. 248 pp. ISBN 0-87628-405-5. Goes into detail about library research skills. For grades 3–8. [library skills; research projects]

Hooked On Research! Ready-to-Use Projects & Crosswords for Practice in Basic Library Skills.

Marguerite Lewis. West Nyack, NY: Center for Applied Research in Education, 1984. 252 pp. ISBN 0-87628-407-1. Filled with ideas on doing library research. For grades 3–8. [library skills; research projects]

How to Become an Expert: Discover, Research, and Build a Project in Your Chosen Field.

Maurice Gibbons. Tucson, AZ: Zephyr Press, 1991. 136 pp. ISBN 0-913705-55-1. Contains reproducible pages and provides step-by-step guidance in carrying out investigations. For grades 5–8. [research projects]

How to Be a Better Writer.

Elizabeth A. Ryan. Mahwah, NJ: Troll, 1992. 96 pp. ISBN 0-8167-2462-8. ISBN 0-8167-2463-6 paper. Gives practical tips on making an outline, writing paragraphs, and write a conclusion. For grades 5–9. [writing skills]

How to Write Better Book Reports.

Elizabeth A. Ryan. Mahwah, NJ: Troll, 1992. 79 pp. ISBN 0-8167-2458-X. ISBN 0-8167-2459-8 paper. Suggests faster and easier ways to prepare book reports. For grades 5–9. [book reports]

How to Write a Term Paper.

Nancy Everhart. New York: Franklin Watts, 1994. 142 pp. ISBN 0-531-11200-4. Explains step-by-step how to write a paper. For grades 6–12. [term papers]

How to Write Book Reports.

Harry Teitelbaum. New York: Macmillan, 1995. 95 pp. ISBN 0-02-860300-1. Gives tips on writing interesting book reports. For use in the elementary grades. [book reports]

How to Write Term Papers & Reports.

L. S. Baugh. Lincolnwood, IL: VGM Career Horizons, 1993. 259 pp. ISBN 0-8442-5645-5. ISBN 0-8442-5899-7 paper. A handbook for adult reference. [term papers]

How to Write Your Best Book Report.

Elizabeth James and Carol Barkin. New York: Lothrop, Lee & Shepard, 1986. 71 pp. ISBN 0-688-05744-6. ISBN 0-688-05743-8 paper. Explains how to write an effective book report. For grades 3–7. [book reports]

The Independent Learner's Sourcebook: Resources and Materials for Selected Topics.

Robert McCaughan and Phyllis M. Cunningham. Chicago: American Library Association, 1987. 306 pp. Explains research methodology. Good adult reference book. [research projects]

Knowing Where to Look: The Ultimate Guide to Research.

Lois Horowitz. Cincinnati, OH: Writer's Digest Books, 1984. 436 pp. ISBN 0-89879-329-7. A handbook for adults. [library skills; research projects]

The Know It All: Resource Book for Kids.

Patricia R. Peterson. Tucson, AZ: Zephyr Press, 1989. 144 pp. Used like a dictionary, it contains definitions, examples, and illustrations. Suitable for use in the intermediate grades. [research projects]

Let's Go to the Library.

Lisl Weil. New York: Holiday House, 1992. 32 pp. ISBN 0-8234-0829-9. Tells what goes on in a library and gives a brief history of libraries. For use in preschool through grade 3. [libraries]

Libraries.

Patricia Fujimoto. Chicago: Children's Press, 1984. 47 pp. Explains how to use a library. For use in the elementary grades. [libraries; library skills]

Library Media Skills: Strategies for Instructing Primary Students.

Alice R. Seaver. Englewood, CO: Libraries Unlimited, 1991. 147 pp. Filled with resources for teaching information skills to primary grade students. [library skills]

Library: Your Teammate.

Philly Murtha. Mankato, MN: Creative Education, 1985. 32 pp. Provides a teenage orientation to the library. [libraries]

Media Skills Puzzlers.

Ruth Toor and Hilda K. Weisberg. Berkeley Heights, NJ: Library Learning Resources, Inc., 1984. 126 pp. ISBN 0-931315-00-X. Uses puzzles to help develop media skills. Suitable for the elementary grades. [library skills; media center activities; puzzles]

My Hometown Library.

William Jaspersohn. Boston, MA: Houghton Mifflin, 1994. 47 pp. ISBN 0-395-55723-2. Describes how resources and services in a library have changed over the years. For use in the elementary grades. [libraries]

The Mysteries of Research. (2nd ed.)

Sharron Cohen. Fort Atkinson, WI: Alleyside Press, 1996. 143 pp. ISBN 0-917846-76-1. Teaches research and reference skills. For grade 4 and up. [library skills; media center activities; mysteries]

The New York Public Library Book of How and Where to Look It Up.
Sherwood Harris, ed. New York: Prentice Hall, 1991. 382 pp. ISBN 0-671-89264-9. Explains research methodology. Good reference tool. [library skills]

The New York Public Library Student's Desk Reference.
New York: Prentice Hall, General Reference, 1993. 513 pp. Presents information in a question and answer format. Useful reference book for intermediate grades and up. [library skills]

On Line Searching in the Curriculum: A Teaching Guide for Library Media Specialists and Teachers.
Beverly Hunter and Erica K. Lodish. Santa Barbara, CA: ABC-CLIO, 1989. 219 pp. Explains how to do online library searches. An adult reference book. [computer skills; library skills]

The Perfect Term Paper: Step by Step.
Donald J. D. Mulkerne. New York: Anchor Press/Doubleday, 1988. 158 pp. ISBN 0-385-24794-X. A research manual for teachers and adults. [term papers]

Picture Encyclopedia for Children.
John Paton, ed. New York: Grosset & Dunlap, 1987. 380 pp. Contains over 750 alphabetical entries. For use in the elementary grades. [encyclopedias]

Putting It in Writing: Friendly Letters, Business Letters, Complaints and Requests, School Reports, Thank Yous, Essays.
Steven Otfinoski. New York: Scholastic, 1993. 144 pp. ISBN 0-590-49459-7. Gives advice, models, and examples. A good reference suitable for grades 4–7. [letters; writing skills]

Ready for Reference: Media Skills for Intermediate Students.
Barbara Bradley Zlotnick. Englewood, CO: Libraries Unlimited, 1984. 274 pp. Introduces reference skills. For grades 3–6. [library skills]

Ready-to-Use Library Skills Games: Reproducible Activities for Building Location and Literature Skills.
Ruth V. Snoddon. West Nyack, NY: Center for Applied Research in Education, 1987. 185 pp. ISBN 0-87628-721-6. Contains games designed to teach library skills. Suitable for the elementary grades. [library skills; media center activities]

Reference Puzzles and Word Games for Grades 7-12.
Carol Smallwood. Jefferson, NC: McFarland, 1991. 190 pp. ISBN 0-89950-623-2. Contains ideas for library activities. Grades 7–12. [media center activities; word games]

Research Book of the Fifty States.
Nancy Polette. San Antonio, TX: Book Lore (distributed by ECS Learning Systems, Inc.), 1991. 32 pp. ISBN 1-879287-03-X. Contains activities which

can be used in connection with any states. For students in grades 4–7. [media center activities; states (U.S.)]

The Research Book for Gifted Programs.

Nancy Polette. O'Fallon, MO: Book Lures, 1984. 170 pp. ISBN 0-913839-28-0. Explains independent study methods. For use in grades K–8. [gifted and talented programs; library skills]

Research Made Easy: A Guide for Students and Writers.

Robert D. Matzen. New York: Bantam, 1987. 248 pp. An introduction to doing library research. For use in grade 4 and up. [library skills]

Research to Write.

Maity Schrecengost. Ft. Atkinson, WI: Alleyside Press, 1994. 52 pp. ISBN 0-917846-37-0. Hints on report writing. For use in grades 3–6. [term papers; writing skills]

Researching People.

Maity Schrecengost. Ft. Atkinson, WI: Alleyside Press, 1996. 32 pp. ISBN 0-917846-69-9. Introduction to research using library reference tools best suited for biographical reports. For use in grades 5–9. [term papers; biography]

Savvy Student's Guide to Library Research.

Judith M. Pask and Robert J. Kovac. West Lafayette, IN: Purdue University, 1990. 84 pp. This orientation to the library is suitable for college-aged students. [library skills]

Scholastic Dictionary of Idioms.

Marvin Terban. New York: Scholastic Reference, 1996. 245 pp. ISBN 0-590-27549-6. Contains more than 600 phrases, in alphabetical order listing definitions and origins. A useful reference book for grade 4 and up. [dictionaries; idioms]

Scholastic's A+ Junior Guide to Book Reports.

Louise Colligan. New York: Scholastic, 1989. 88 pp. A guide to report writing. For use in grade 4 and up. [book reports]

School Power: Strategies for Succeeding in School.

Jeanne Shay Schumm. Minneapolis, MN: Free Spirit Publishing, 1992. 123 pp. ISBN 0-915793-42-3. Suggests necessary study skills including taking notes. For students in grade 5 and up. [study skills]

Search: A Research Guide for Science Fairs and Independent Study.

Connie Wolfe. Tucson, AZ: Zephyr Press, 1988. 94 pp. Explains how to organize research. For use in grade 4 and up. [study skills]

Smart Learning: A Study Skills Guide for Teens.

William J. Christen and Thomas Murphy. Bloomington, IN: Grayson Bernard Publishers, 1992. 111 pp. ISBN 0-9628556-5-0. Provides strategies for study, note taking, and writing. For grade 6 and up. [study skills]

So You Have to Write a Term Paper!

Nancy Everhart. New York: Franklin Watts, 1987. 124 pp. Goes through the steps of choosing a topic, carrying out research, taking notes, making an outline, writing a draft and editing. For grade 6 and up. [term papers]

Study Starters: Basic Strategies for Academic Success.

Diane P. Kostick. Carthage, IL: Good Apple, 1994. 154 pp. ISBN 0-86653-797-X. Suggests strategies for becoming an effective and efficient learner. For grades 5–9. [study skills]

Teaching Basic Reference Skills With—the New Book of Knowledge.

Grolier Ed. Corp. Staff. Danbury, CT: Grolier Educational Corp., 1994. 84 pp. Explains how to get information from an encyclopedia. Includes 50 pages of worksheets for duplication. For use in the intermediate grades. [library skills; encyclopedias]

Teaching Writing: A Workshop Approach.

Adele Fiderer. New York: Scholastic Professional Books, 1993. 112 pp. ISBN 0-590-49202-0. Suggests ways to approach composition for grades 2–6. [writing skills]

10,000 Ideas for Term Papers, Projects, Reports, and Speeches.

Kathryn Lamm. New York: ARCO, 1995. 4th ed. An alphabetical listing of topics. [term papers; themes]

Tracking the Facts: How to Develop Research Skills.

Claire McInerney. Minneapolis, MN: Lerner, 1990. 64 pp. ISBN 0-8225-2426-0. Explains how to use a library, interview people, do computer searches, and outline material. For grade 4 and up. [library skills, interviews]

Using Resources.

Joan L. Poole. Austin, TX: Steck-Vaughn, 1994. 32 pp. Contains hints on study skills for adults. [study skills]

What Should I Write My Report On? 499 Thematic Research Ideas for Reports.

J. A. Senn. New York: Scholastic Professional Books, 1993. 88 pp. ISBN 0-590-49648-4. A handbook for students in grades 4–8. [term papers; themes]

What You Need to Know About Developing Study Skills, Taking Notes, and Tests, Using Dictionaries, and Libraries.

Marcia J. Coman and Kathy L. Heavers. Lincolnwood, IL: National Textbook Co., 1991. 91 pp. Information on how to develop study skills. For grade 4 and up. [library skills; study skills]

Word for Word I.

Susan Hovis and Bonnie Domin. Tucson, AZ: Zephyr Press, 1988. 80 pp. A compilation of ten activity units that combine creative thinking and research skills. For use in the elementary grades. [creative thinking; library skills]

Word for Word II.

Susan Hovis and Bonnie Domin. Tucson, AZ: Zephyr Press, 1990. 80 pp. A compilation of ten activity units combining creative thinking and research skills. For use in the elementary grades. [creative thinking; library skills]

You Mean I Have to Stand Up and Say Something?

Joan Detz. New York: Atheneum, 1986. 86 pp. ISBN 0-689-31221-0. Suggestions on how to give oral reports. For grades 5–9. [oral reports]

The Young Writer's Handbook.

Susan J. Tchudi. New York: Scribner's, 1984. 156 pp. Explains how to write and edit reports. For grade 4 and up. [writing skills]

Other resources

Check It Out: The Book About Libraries.

Story Time Associates. Englewood, CO: Story Time Associates, 1993. 1 videocassette, 8 minutes. Based on the book by Gail Gibbons for primary through intermediate grade students. [libraries]

How to Study Smart.

Joyce Lynn Lee. Chicago, IL: Encyclopedia Britannica Educational Corp., 1990. 1 videocassette, 23 minutes. Encourages exploring and using library resources. For use in the elementary grades. [study skills]

How to Use Children's Magazine Guide.

Patti Sinclair. New Providence, NJ: R.R. Bowker, 1994. 1 videocassette, 15 minutes. Three students learn how to locate magazine articles. For use in intermediate grades. [library skills]

How to Use the Library.

Mark Shaeffer. Bronx, NY: H. W. Wilson, 1989. 1 videocassette, 20 minutes, plus 12 page guide. Shows how to do research and use the periodical index. For use in the intermediate grades. [library skills]

Information Please!

David Creech. Bohemia, NY: Rainbow Educational Video, 1995. 1 videocassette, 16 minutes, plus teacher's guide. A boy visits the library to make a report and finds out what is available to him. For use in the elementary grades. [libraries; research projects]

Using Reference Materials.

Salina, KS: School Specialty Supply, Inc. Three transparency duplicating books. Reference tools, grades 1–3. Study skills, grades 4–6. Basic library skills, grades 4–6. [library skills; study skills]

Using Your Library to Write a Research Paper.

Roslyn, NY: Video Aided Instruction, Inc., 1992. 4 videocassettes, 285 minutes. Videos show how to select a topic, find sources of information, take notes and organize material, and write the paper. For use in the intermediate grades. [library skills; study skills]

Writing a Report.

A. W. Peller & Associates. Hawthorne, NJ: Educational Materials, 1990. Teacher's guide and four films or four cassettes. "I've Got An Idea!" "Where Do I Go From Here?" "What's Your Point?" "Polishing It Up." For use in the intermediate grades. [term papers; writing skills]

10

Indoor Educational Games

*C*hildren enjoy playing games both alone and with friends at home and at school. Effective pre-planning can ensure that these games are fun and also exciting learning opportunities. The teacher may have a special learning game set up at an interest center where students rotate through the center during the week so that each child has an opportunity to play the game.

Some students play together well with a minimum of bickering and hard feelings. For others, games can quickly deteriorate into debates about the rules, whose turn it is, etc. When introducing a new game, it is very helpful to have an adult volunteer who can play with the students several times until the players fully understand the rules and procedures. Then most students can play happily without adult supervision.

Many teachers keep a special box of games that are brought out so that on those days when there is inclement weather and students cannot go outside for recess or go out to play after eating their lunches, they have favorite games to play indoors.

Gaming situations provide many opportunities for learning. Depending on the type of game, students may gain in expressive and verbal skills, geography and map skills, math facts and reasoning skills, word spellings and meanings, understanding spatial relationships, devising strategies, in increasing manipulative ability and memory.

Directions for Ideas That Work

ATTACHING WORDS: This game can be played in a variety of ways. The directions that follow are for teams of two players. The game requires only pencil and paper. Team AB sets the length of the words to be used in the first game. For example, Team AB may choose "five letter words."

A timer is set for five minutes. Player A then writes down a five-letter word at the top left corner of a sheet of paper. Player B must add a five-letter word by attaching it vertically onto the first word and beginning the new word with the last letter which was written on the paper.

If Player A writes "table," Player B attaches a five-letter word that begins with the letter "e" such as "eaten." Player A now adds a new word beginning with the last letter written by Player B, such as "never."

T A B L E
A
T
E
N E V E R

Team CD begins at the same time as Team AB. Players C and D also alternate in making five-letter attached words. After five minutes, the teams count up the number of five letter words they were able to attach. The team with the most words (spelled correctly) wins. The losing team sets the word length for the next games, such as "seven-letter words" and sets the timer.

The suggested games are not always language arts games. When students play games designed to increase their knowledge of geography, to give practice in math skills, or to develop an awareness of ecology and endangered species for example, there are still important verbal and reasoning components.

In addition to reinforcing various subject matter skills, games also teach students social skills such as taking turns, following rules, being a good winner or loser, observing conventions, and being responsible for handling and putting playing pieces away with care. All of these gaming skills stand the child in good stead in other life situations.

Very young students may take a game and use the pieces quite creatively in ways not originally intended. For example, a child may use a set of Chinese Checkers to simply make interesting marble patterns on the playing board. A deck of cards may be shuffled somewhat clumsily by a young child who then draws cards at random to see which king is the first to collect all the cards in his suit. The pie-shaped pieces in Trivial Pursuit may be manipulated to make a pie with slices of alternate colors.

It is possible that some adults and some children may find this creativity of a young child very disturbing. There is an urge on the part of some observers to "correct" the child and "explain" that this is not the way this game was designed to be played!

Actually, such creative uses of gaming materials involve children in learning to match, to observe colors and shapes, etc. And many young children take great satisfaction in manipulating some gaming materials that they see being used by admired older siblings and adults. Not to fear. When they are mature enough, young children will learn to play the game "correctly."

Sometimes young students can play a game, more or less as intended, if some rules and constraints are removed. For example, in playing Scrabble Crossword Cubes, young students may simply make unconnected words or may take as long as they need to make words without the pressure of the timer.

Most people prefer winning to losing, or at least like to win once in a while. Games that have an element of luck as well as skill allow many students to have the real satisfaction of sometimes winning the game. There are also a number of games where there are no winners or losers, and these can be satisfying to all participants.

Not all games require boards, cards, die, or playing pieces. Many can be prepared from simple objects such as string, buttons, old newspapers and magazines, and egg cartons.

Directions for Ideas That Work

EGG CARTON ALPHABET: The young student who likes to work alone, will enjoy this alphabet game. Cut and hook together parts of three egg cartons to form 26 compartments. Label each of the compartments with a letter of the alphabet. Have the student look through old magazines and find small pictures that begin with each letter of the alphabet. The child will use a blunt scissors to cut out pictures and will try to find a picture for every compartment.

For a variation, the child might cut words from a newspaper that begin with each of the letters of the alphabet and place them in the labeled compartments.

One type of game that is popular with many students is learning and performing a magic trick. Many books are available that will teach students how to perform a trick that will amaze their classmates. Some of these books suggest tricks associated with holidays, and these magic feats might be presented at a class party.

Directions for Ideas That Work

THE OBEDIENT STRAW: To do the Obedient Straw trick, a student will need a plastic drinking straw, a pin, and a glass of water. Use the pin to prick a double row of tiny holes in the straw about two inches from one end. (This needs to be done privately before showing the trick, and the holes must be so tiny that they will not be noticed.)

The performing student tells the class that she has an "Obedient Straw" which will only allow someone to drink from it if she so commands. With the pin-pricked-end of the straw out of the water, the performer asks a classmate to try to take a sip.

Little or no water will come up from the straw.

Then the performer picks up the straw and speaks to it seriously saying, "Straw, I command you to let my thirsty friend have a drink of water." The performer replaces the straw in the glass, but this time is sure to put the pin-pricked end of the straw down into the water. The classmate will now be able to drink from the "Obedient Straw."

Illus. 10.1. The Obedient Straw: A student demonstrates the obedient straw magic trick. Students have fun with showmanship and develop their confidence and oral language skills as they perform feats of magic. The explanation following the trick provides areas for further science investigations

Other students are fascinated by codes. The teacher might write a coded message on the chalkboard which students see when they arrive in the morning. Students can be trying to solve the code while classmates are hanging up coats, removing snow boots, and other morning tasks. The teacher might remind the class in code, "We'll do our puppet shows this afternoon." One simple code is to have each letter of the alphabet represented by the letter than follows it. In such a code, the teacher's message would be, "XF'MM EP PVS QVQQFU TIPXT UIJT BGUFSOPPO."

If a class enjoys this type of activity, students can prepare a short coded message for their classmates. Several of these might be collected, typed, duplicated, and shared with class members.

Some students delight in crossword puzzles and others in jig-saw puzzles. A word of caution is needed here. The attention span of some students is quite short. If less than half-way through completion, a student gets tired of working at the jig-saw puzzle, what then? Few classrooms have sufficient space so that several puzzles can be left out undisturbed.

A solution to the problem might be to select puzzles with a small number of large pieces that will more appropriately challenge and fit with the young student's attention span. There are special puzzle sheets which can be placed on a table where more complicated puzzles are to be worked. These sheets can be rolled up and put away between puzzle-working times, keeping the partially completed puzzle intact.

Some puzzles require no materials at all. If a class has been studying a group of animals, for example, they may want to make up animal riddles with three clues which their classmates can try to guess.

Directions for Ideas That Work

ANIMAL RIDDLES: Students choose an animal and think of three clues. They write the animal's name and the clues on a 4 x 6 inch card. During puzzle time, students can take turns reading their riddles and clues while classmates try to guess.

A student might write: What animal is found in Australia, eats eucalyptus leaves, and has a pouch? Answer: koala bear. The student who successfully answers, reads his or her riddle next, or picks a student who hasn't had a turn to read. Variations might be riddles about famous historical figures, riddles about numbers.

In another variation, a teacher or volunteer might cut and draw some basic animal shapes, cutting a large hole where the animal's face would be. Then the teacher calls a child to the front of the room. The teacher slips one of the cut-out animal shapes in front of the child and holds it up without letting the child see the animal shape. By asking questions that can be answered yes or no, the child tries to discover which animal shape is being held up.

The child might ask such questions as: Am I a mammal? Do I live in Africa? Am I a wild animal? Am I bigger than a lion? Do I eat plants? Am I ever in a circus? Do I live in trees?

Illus. 10.2. Animal riddles: Holding a simple outline of an animal, such as the tiger pictured here, allows a student to practice forming questions to help discover the animal's identity.

In other chapters of this book, students will learn more about Holidays Around the World. If students become interested in the special foods and customs of a country, they may also want to learn about the games that children play in other parts of the world. Some of these games are unique, while others will be much like games already familiar to students.

Directions for Ideas That Work

BREAK THE PIÑATA: Making a Mexican piñata can provide a great party game. A paper bag can be used for the "body." Put wrapped candy or other small treats in a paper bag and hold it closed with a twist tie. Fill a plastic bucket with about three inches of water. Sprinkle in wall paper paste, stirring constantly as you pour, until the mixture is about the thickness of pancake batter. Tear strips of newspaper about two inches by ten inches until you have a big pile.

A few students at a time can work on the piñata. They will dip a torn strip of newspaper into the wheat paste mixture and lay the strips around the bag of candy. After the bag is completely covered, you can add strips of paper to complete the shape of the piñata. If, for example, the bag of candy is to be the animal's body, you can tape on four paper towel tubes for legs, using masking tape. Then students can paper mache over the tubes and securely fasten the legs to the body. A crushed ball of newspaper can be attached to the candy bag to make the animal's head. And then the head can be covered in papier mache. You could add ears, wings, etc.

After the papier mache animal dries, it can be stood on a table. Students now cut one-inch squares of different colored crepe paper. Put a scoop of paste in several clean jar lids. Fold a square of crepe paper over the eraser end of a pencil. Dip the eraser in the paste. Press the crepe paper onto the papier mache animal and remove the pencil eraser. Repeat, putting the squares of colored crepe paper close together until the entire animal is covered.

On the game day, string the piñata up high in the gym. Blindfold students and let them take turns trying to break the piñata by hitting it with a stick. When it breaks open, the wrapped candy inside will fall and scatter, and the students can have a candy scramble.

When you are studying about a part of the United States, or a period of history, you might interest students in making toys or games common to a particular area such as an Appalachian spinning top, or you might use some of the resources to learn about games that were common in the nineteenth century.

In studying mathematics, students will enjoy working with magic squares or playing board games that introduce math as it is used in astronomy. And, of course, there are many language art games available to reinforce knowledge about such topics as contractions and homonyms.

You can create a multi-purpose board game on traveling to the planets in which students meet obstacles such as meteors and in which they rocket toward their destination in space by correctly answering questions which you prepare on fact cards. The same game can be used with many different decks of cards so that you provide practice and reinforce whatever skills you want to target in a given week.

An enormous number of computer games are available with graphics and sound effects that fascinate students. The range of quality in these materials is tremendous. Space does not permit a listing of a large number of computer games in the present book, but the potential should be explored. As with all educational materials, teachers will need to read reviews and try out games and activities to determine which are appropriate for their classrooms.

The possibilities for gaming situations are truly limitless, and can be a great source of learning and satisfaction to students in the elementary language arts classroom.

Illus. 10.3. Appalachian top: Bringing in toys, songs, and foods associated with various parts of the U.S. or of the world, deepens understanding of cultures and enriches the classroom. These two students play with an Appalachian spinning top.

Resource books

A B C Folder Games: Patterns for Easy-to-Do Reading Games.

Lillian Liebermann. Palo Alto, CA: Monday Morning Books, 1991. 64 pp. Reproducible educational games suitable for Pre K–2. [alphabet games]

A B C Games.

Robert Lopshire. New York: T. Y. Crowell, 1986. 57 pp. Encourages a student to choose a person, animal, or thing that belongs with the object named in alphabetical sequence. For use in the elementary grades. [alphabet games]

Alphabet Puzzle.

Jill Downie. New York: Lothrop, Lee & Shepard, 1988. 56 pp. ISBN 0-688-08044-8. Provides practice in word association by having the student look through page windows with letters of the alphabet. For use in preschool through grade 1. [alphabet puzzles]

The Amazing Book of Chess: Learn to Play the World's Most Popular Game of Skill.

Gareth Williams. Edison, NJ: Chartwell Books, 1995. 125 pp. Introduction to chess. For use in the elementary grades. [chess]

The Amazing Puzzle and Trick Book.

Pamela Shaw-Hesketh. New York: Derrydale Books, distributed by Crown Publications, 1990. 31 pp. Contains easy puzzles and tricks. For use in the elementary grades. [magic; puzzles]

Anno's Math Games III.

Mitsumasa Anno. New York: Philomel, 1991. 103 pp. Picture puzzles involve abstract thinking, geometry, and topology. For use in the elementary grades. [math games; puzzles]

Anno's Peekaboo.

Mitsumasa Anno. New York: Philomel, 1987. 32 pp. ISBN 0-399-21520-4. Shows how to play peekaboo with a variety of people and animals. For use with preschoolers. [animals]

Are We There Yet?: Car Games, Word Puzzles, Brain Teasers, Sing Alongs.

Editors of Rand McNally. Chicago: Rand McNally, 1985. 46 pp. Contains games for travelers, some of which can be played in the classroom. For use in elementary grades. [brain teasers; word games]

Around the World: The Great Treasure Hunt.

David Anson Russo. New York: Simon & Schuster Books for Young Readers, 1995. 1 vol. unpaged. ISBN 0-689-80281-1. Readers join Sir Gordon Goodfellow as he travels around the world in search of twelve golden goblets hidden in pictures. For grades 2–5. [geography games]

Bear All Year: A Guessing Game Book.

Harriet Ziefert. New York: Harper & Row, 1986. 13 pp. The child looks at a picture, guesses what the bear will do, then folds out the page which shows the answer. For preschoolers. [guessing games]

Board and Card Games.

Ruth Oakley. New York: Marshall Cavendish, 1989. ISBN 1-85435-082-X. Contains descriptions of a variety of games that students play around the world. For use in grades 4–8. [board games; cards; multicultural games]

Brain Twisters.

Paul Hayes. Milwaukee, WI: Penworthy Publishing, 1987. 32 pp. ISBN 0-88625-149-4. Filled with challenging games. For grades 2–6. [brain teasers]

Can You Find It?

Bernard Most. San Diego, CA: Harcourt Brace, 1993. 1 volume unpaged. ISBN 0-15-292872-3. Contains fifteen word-play puzzles. For preschoolers through grade 3. [puzzles]

Card Games for Children.

Len Collis. New York: Barron's, 1989. 95 pp. ISBN 0-8120-4290-5. Describes games that can be played with one, two, three, or more players. For preschoolers and up. [cards]

Cards for Kids: Games, Tricks, and Amazing Facts.

Elin McCoy. New York: Macmillan, 1991. 150 pp. ISBN 0-02-765461-3. Contains explanations of a variety of card games and tricks. For grades 1–7. [cards]

Card Tricks.

Vanessa Bailey. New York: Franklin Watts, 1990. 32 pp. Filled with tips for doing card tricks. For use in the elementary grades. [cards]

CDC ?

William Steig. New York: Farrar, Straus & Giroux, 1984. 63 pp. ISBN 0-374-31015-7. Describes how to create simple, coded messages using letters, numbers, and symbols. For use in the elementary grades. [codes]

Chess for Children.

Ted Nottingham. New York: Sterling Publishing Co. Inc., 1993. 126 pp. ISBN 0-8069-0452-6. Explains how to play chess by using the Lincolnshire system. For use in grade 3 and up. [chess]

Chess for Juniors: A Complete Guide for the Beginner.

Robert M. Snyder. New York: David McKay, Co., 1991. 237 pp. ISBN 0-8129-1867-3. Provides an introduction to chess, giving rules, moves, strategies, and describing the playing pieces. For use in the elementary grades. [chess]

Citymaze! A Collection of Amazing City Mazes.

Wendy Madgwick. Brookfield, CT: Millbrook Press, 1995. 1 v. unpaged. ISBN 1-56294-561-0. Contains maze puzzles. For grade 3 and up. [mazes]

Codes & Ciphers: Hundreds of Unusual and Secret Ways to Send Messages.

Christina Ashton. Cincinnati, OH: Betterway Books, 1993. 110 pp. ISBN 1-55870-292-X. Explains how readers can make and use secret codes and provides some history of codes. For grade 6 and up. [codes]

The Complete Book of Children's Activities.

Melanie Rice. New York: Kingfisher Books, 1993. 120 pp. ISBN 1-85697-907-5. Contains creative activities and educational games. For use in the elementary grades.

Crazy Eights and Other Card Games.

Joanna Cole and Stephanie Calmenson. New York: Morrow Junior Books, 1994. 76 pp. ISBN 0-688-12199-3. Explains how to hold, shuffle, deal, and play card games such as Aces Up and Go Fish. For grade 2 and up. [cards]

Crosswords for Spelling: Student Pleasing Puzzles for Practice and Fun.

Christine Thornton. Belmont, CA: David S. Lake Publishers, 1985. ISBN 0-8224-2354-5. Contains crossword puzzles. For grades 4–6. [crosswords]

Demi's Opposites: An Animal Game Book.

Demi. New York: Grosset & Dunlap, 1987. 48 pp. Verses and illustrations of animals showing opposites such as empty/full, curly/straight. For preschoolers and primary grades. [animals]

Doubletalk: Codes, Signs, & Symbols.

Helene Hovanec. New York: Bantam, 1993. 62 pp. ISBN 0-553-37218-1. Contains a collection of puzzles using codes, signs and symbols to solve the problems. For grade 6 and up. [codes; puzzles]

Do You Wanna Bet?: Your Chance to Find Out About Probability.

Jean Cushman. New York: Clarion, 1991. 102 pp. ISBN 0-395-56516-2. Shows that events and activities such as coin flips and card playing are dependent on an interplay of chance and probability. For grades 3–7. [probability]

The Dragon Thanksgiving Feast: Things to Make and Do.

Loreen Leedy. New York: Holiday House, 1990. 30 pp. ISBN 0-8234-0828-0. Using dragons at a feast, instructions are given for activities and games related to Thanksgiving. For preschool through grade 3. [dragons; Thanksgiving]

Eco-Games.

Stuart A. Kallen. Edina, MN: Abdo & Daughters, 1993. 31 pp. ISBN 1-56239-201-8. ISBN 1-56239-414-2 paper. Gives instructions for making and playing games with the spotlight on the environment, recycling, and ecology. For the elementary grades. [ecology]

Eye Spy: A Mysterious Alphabet.

Linda Bourke. San Francisco, CA: Chronicle Books, 1991. 1 v. unpg. ISBN 0-8118-1076-3. The reader is challenged to discover answers to picture puzzles using homonyms or homophones. For use in preschool through grade 3. [word games]

Factivities.

Karen Gleason. Carthage, IL: Good Apple, 1991. 140 pp. ISBN 0-86653-601-9. Games based around fascinating facts for students in grades kindergarten through fifth. [games]

The Farmer in the Dell, a Singing Game.

Mary Marki Rae. New York: Viking Penguin, 1988. 24 pp. ISBN 0-14-050788-4. Tells the old folk song game. For preschool through grade 1. [songs]

52 Simple Ways to Have Fun With Your Child.

Carl Dreezler. Nashville, TN: Oliver-Nelson Books, 1991. 142 pp. Describes games to play with children. For use in the elementary grades. [parent resources]

Find Demi's Dinosaurs: An Animal Game Book.

Demi. New York: Grosset & Dunlap, 1989. 38 pp. ISBN 0-448-19020-6. A game book to increase the young student's visual discrimination. For preschool through grade 3. [dinosaurs]

Find Demi's Sea Creatures: An Animal Game Book.

Demi. New York: Putnam & Grosset, 1991. 38 pp. Children increase perception while looking for marine animals. Some pages fold out. For preschool through grade 3. [marine life]

A Gallery of Games.

Catherine Marchon-Arnaud. New York: Ticknor & Fields, 1994. 56 pp. ISBN 0-395-68379-3. Provides instructions for making unusual versions of familiar games. For grade 3 and up. [games]

Games.

Godfrey Hall. New York; Thomson Learning, 1995. 48 pp. ISBN 1-56847-345-1. Discusses traditional games from around the world. For use in the elementary grades. [multicultural games]

Games and Giggles Just for Girls.

Paul Meisel, illustrator. Middleton, WI: Pleasant Co. Publications, 1995. 92 pp. ISBN 1-56247-232-1. Contains an assortment of word searches, crossword puzzles and word games. For grades 3–6. [crosswords; girls; word games]

Games from Long Ago.

Bobbie Kalman. New York: Crabtree, 1995. 32 pp. ISBN 0-86505-482-7. ISBN 0-86505-521-1 paper. Describes games, along with rules and how to play them, which were popular in the nineteenth century. For grades 2–9. [games–history of]

Games Magazine Junior Kids' Big Book of Games.

Karen C. Anderson, ed. New York: Workman Pub., 1990. 173 pp. ISBN 0-89480-657-2. Contains over 125 games, picture puzzles, mazes, logic defiers, etc. For grades 1–7. [mazes; puzzles]

Games With Papers and Pencils.

Ruth Oakley. Freeport, NY: Marshall Cavendish, 1989. ISBN 1-85435-083-8. Contains a collection of instructional games. For grades 3–8. [paper-pencil games]

Games With Sticks, Stones & Shells.

Ruth Oakley. Freeport, NY: Marshall Cavendish, 1989. ISBN 1-85435-079-X. Gives background and instruction on such games as hopscotch, jacks, and marbles. For grades 3–8. [games–history of]

Geographunny: A Book of Global Riddles.

Mort Gerberg. New York: Clarion, 1991. 64 pp. ISBN 0-395-52449-0. ISBN 0-395-60312-9 paper. A collection of riddles involving the knowledge of geography. For use in the elementary grades. [geography; riddles]

Global Alert!

Thomas Christie. Carthage, IL: Good Apple, 1992. 108 pp. ISBN 0-86653-692-2. Uses games and other activities to raise understanding of environmental problems. For grades 5–8. [ecology]

Hands Around the World: 365 Creative Ways to Build Cultural Awareness and Global Respect.

Susan Milord. Charlotte, VT. Williamson Publishing Co. Inc., 1992. 158 pp. ISBN 0-913589-65-9. Contains a wide variety of games. For grades 1–8. [multicultural games]

Happy Day!: Things to Make and Do.

Judith Conaway. Mahwah, NJ: Troll, 1987. 47 pp. ISBN 0-8167-0842-8. Gives instructions for making toys and games from easily available materials. For grades 1–5. [toys]

Hide and Snake.

Keith Baker. San Diego, CA: Harcourt Brace Jovanovich, 1991. 34 pp. ISBN 0-15-233986-8. The reader tries to find a snake hiding among familiar objects. For preschool through grade 3. [snakes]

How to Create Adventure Games.

Christopher Lampton. New York: Franklin Watts, 1986. 87 pp. Gives instructions for writing BASIC computer games programs. For use in grade 6 and up. [computer games]

How to Win at Trivial Pursuit and Other Knowledge Games.

Robert J. Heller. New York: Rinehart & Winston, 1984. 118 pp. Gives tips on playing knowledge games. For use in grade 4 and up. [knowledge games]

Illusions Illustrated: A Professional Magic Show for Young Performers.

James W. Baker. Minneapolis, MN: Lerner, 1984. 120 pp. ISBN 0-8225-9512-5. Provides ten illusions for a complete magic show. For grade 6 and up. [magic]

I Spy: A Game to Read and Play.

Caitlin Haynes. New York: Random House, 1993. 30 pp. Reader tries to guess what is being described. Features *Sesame Street* characters. For preschool to grade 1. [guessing games]

It's for You: An Amazing Picture-Puzzle Book.

John Talbot. New York: Dutton Children's Books, 1995. 1 vol. unpaged. ISBN 0-525-45402-0. Contains picture puzzles, some involving math. For grades 4–5. [puzzles]

It's Magic.

Henry Gordon. Buffalo, NY: Prometheus Books, 1989. 92 pp. ISBN 0-87975-545-8. Describes easy conjuring tricks. For grade 5 and up. [magic]

The Kids' Book of Chess.

> Harvey Kidder. New York: Workman Pub., 1990. 96 pp. ISBN 0-89480-767-6. Gives the history of chess, describes the pieces and the strategy of the game. For grades 3–7. [chess]

The Kids Can Do It Book.

> Jeri Robins, Meg Sanders, and Kate Crocker. New York: Kingfisher Books, 1993. 80 pp. ISBN 1-85697-860-5. Instructions for indoor and outdoor games and activities including cooking and dice games. For preschool through grade 4. [cookery]

Kids' Games: Traditional Indoor and Outdoor Activities for Children of All Ages.

> Phil Wiswell. Garden City, NY: Doubleday, 1987. 164 pp. ISBN 0-385-23405-8. Contains instructions for 130 traditional indoor and outdoor games, including word, strategy, and memory games. For preschool and up. [word games]

Let's Play Cards: Great Card Games for Kids.

> Jude Goodwin. Louisville, KY: Devyn Press, 1989. 102 pp. ISBN 0-910791-65-1. Describes many card games suitable for children in the elementary grades. [cards]

Logic Brain Boosters.

> Becky Daniel. Carthage, IL: Good Apple, 1992. 60 pp. ISBN 0-86653-652-3. Contains logic puzzle which involve deductive skills. For grades 1–4. [logic puzzles]

Macfroggy Teaches BASIC.

> Amy Barger and Andrew Barger. Madison, WI: Medical Physics Pub., 1993. 127 pp. ISBN 0-944838-39-1. Explains how to program puzzles and games on a Macintosh using commands in BASIC. For grades 5–10. [computer games]

The Magic Globe: An Around-the-World Adventure Game.

> Heather Maisner. Cambridge, MA: Candlewick Press, 1995. 29 pp. ISBN 1-56402-853-4. Contains geographic picture puzzles. For grades 2–5. [geography games]

Magic Tricks for Children.

> Len Collis. Hauppauge, NY: Barron's Educational Series, 1989. 95 pp. ISBN 0-8120-4289-1. Provides routines for young magicians. For grade 3 and up. [magic]

Many Stars and More String Games.

> Camilla Gryski. New York: Morrow, 1985. 80 pp. ISBN 0-688-05793-4. Gives step-by-step instructions for telling stories using string patterns. For grade 3 and up. [storytelling; string games]

Math Around the World: Math/Geography Enrichment Activities for Middle Grades.

Betty Bobo and Lynn Embry. Carthage, IL: Good Apple, 1991. 138 pp. ISBN 0-86653-600-0. Math and geography games and activities for students in grades 4–6. [geography games; math games]

Measuring Up! Experiments, Puzzles, and Games Explore Measurement.

Sandra Markle. New York: Atheneum Books for Young Readers, 1995. 44 pp. ISBN 0-689-80618-3. For use in the elementary grades. [measurement]

More Magic Tricks You Can Do.

Judith Conaway. Mahwah, NJ: Troll, 1987. 47 pp. ISBN 0-8167-0864-9. Contains descriptions of how to do sixteen simple tricks using matchboxes, scarves, coins, etc. For grades 1–5. [magic]

Mrs. Mustard's Name Games: Including the Common and the Curious, the Famous and the Infamous, the Long and the Short of It.

Jane Wattenberg. San Francisco, CA: Chronicle Books, 1993. 45 pp. ISBN 0-8118-0259-0. The reader tries to identify over one hundred personal names using an illustrated rebus format. For use in the elementary grades. [names]

My Book of Christmas Games.

Kathleen Thompson. Milwaukee, WI: Raintree, 1987. 24 pp. An illustrated collection of games and activities. For use in the elementary grades. [Christmas games]

Number Mysteries.

Cyril Hayes and Dympna Hayes. Milwaukee, WI: Penworthy Publishing, 1987. 32 pp. ISBN 0-88625-145-1. This book is filled with mind bending number activities. For grades 2–6. [numbers]

1001 Things to Do With Kids.

Caryl Waller Krueger. Nashville, TN: Abingdon Press, 1988. 314 pp. ISBN 0-687-29192-5. Filled with ideas for indoor games and outdoor activities for kids. For use in the elementary school. [games]

Pass It On!: All About Notes, from Secret Codes and Special Inks to Fancy Fold and Dead Man's Drops.

Sharon Bailly. Brookfield, CT: Millbrook Press, 1995. 64 pp. ISBN 1-56294-588-2. Gives instructions for inks, codes and personal seals. For grades 4–6. [codes]

Pergamon's Chess for Children.

Martin J. Richardson, ed. New York: Pergamon Press, 1984. 77 pp. Provides an introduction to chess. For use in the elementary grades. [chess]

Perplexing Puzzlers.

Ann Fisher. Carthage, IL: Good Apple, 1992, 76 pp. ISBN 0-86653-677-9. Contains 65 challenging puzzles in mathematics and the language arts arranged in a monthly/seasonal format. For grades 4–8. [math games; puzzles; seasons]

Picture Puzzles.

Dympna Hayes. Milwaukee, WI: Penworthy Publishing, 1987. 32 pp. ISBN 0-88625-147-8. A book of puzzles. For grades 2–6. [puzzles]

Play by Play: A Book of Games and Puzzles.

Fred Winkowski. New York: Little, Brown, 1990. 1 vol. unpaged. Filled with word games. For use in the elementary grades. [puzzles]

Playing Smart: A Parent's Guide to Enriching, Offbeat Learning Activities for Ages 4-14.

Susan K. Perry. Minneapolis, MN: Free Spirit Pub., 1990. 211 pp. ISBN 0-915793-22-9. Contains unusual activities for kids. For preschool through grade 8. [parent resources]

Pocket Book of Chess.

Raymond D. Keene. New York: Simon & Schuster Books for Young Readers, 1988. 192 pp. Describes chess, the basic moves, its history, and some of its great champions. For use in the elementary grades. [chess]

Power Up: Experiments, Puzzles, and Games Exploring Electricity.

Sandra Markle. New York: Atheneum, 1989. 40 pp. ISBN 0-689-31442-6. Uses games and puzzles to help teach science. For grades 3–7. [electricity]

Primary Puzzlers.

Ann Fisher. Carthage, IL: Good Apple, 1993. 140 pp. ISBN 0-86653-720-1. Provides more than 110 mazes, graphs, and word puzzles arranged by month. For use in the elementary school. [mazes; word puzzles]

Problem Solving.

Lakshmi Hewavisenti. New York: Gloucester Press, 1991. 32 pp. Colorful puzzles and games involving problem solving. For use in the elementary grades. [problem solving]

Protecting Our Planet: Activities to Motivate Students to a Better Understanding of Our Environmental Problems: For Intermediate Grades.

Ava Deutsch Drutman and Susan Klam Zeikerman. Carthage, IL: Good Apple, 1991. 138 pp. ISBN 0-86653-589-6. Contains many activities on environmental themes. For grades 4-8. [ecology]

Puzzle Farm.

Susannah Leigh. Tulsa, OK: EDC Publishing, 1991. 32 pp. ISBN 0-88110-555-4. Contains puzzles featuring farm animals and chores. For preschool and up. [farms; puzzles]

Puzzles.

Kate Petty. New York: Glouster Press, 1986. 31 pp. Gives directions for programs for creating ten puzzles on an Apple computer. For use in the elementary grades. [computer games; puzzles]

Puzzle Town.

Susannah Leigh. Tulsa, OK: EDC Publishing, 1991, 32 pp. Contains picture puzzles from Usborne. For use in the elementary grades. [puzzles]

Razzle Dazzle!: Magic Tricks for You.

Larry White and Ray Broekel. Niles, IL: Albert Whitman & Co., 1987. 48 pp. ISBN 0-8075-6857-0. Contains instructions on how to do twenty tricks. For grades 3–8. [magic]

The Search for the Mystery Planet: Space Math.

Time-Life Editors. Alexandria, VA: Time-Life for Children, 1993, 63 pp. A collection of stories, poems, riddles and games which introduce mathematics as it is used in astronomy. For use in the elementary grades. [astronomy; poetry; math games]

Shapes & Solids.

Lakshmi Hewavisenti. New York: Gloucester Press, 1991. 32 pp. Involves investigations and rearrangement of geometric figures to demonstrate mass and volume. For use in the elementary grades. [shapes]

The Shapes Game.

Paul Rogers. New York: Holt, 1990. 26 pp. ISBN 0-8050-1280-X. Introduction to geometry. Basic shapes are introduced through simple riddle verses. For preschool through grade 2. [shapes]

Smithsonian Surprises: An Educational Activity Book.

Sarah D. Toney. Washington, D.C.: Smithsonian Institution Press, 1985. 95 pp. ISBN 0-87474-909-3. Filled with creative activities. For grade 1 and up. [creative games]

The Super Colossal Book of Hidden Pictures.

Selected by editors of Highlights for Children. Honesdale, PA: Boyds Mills Press, 1994. 192 pp. The reader is challenged to find objects hidden in illustrations. For use in the elementary grades. [hidden pictures]

Super String Games.

Camilla Gryski. New York: Morrow Junior Books, 1987. 80 pp. ISBN 0-688-07685-8. Contains step-by-step directions for making twenty-six string figures from around the world. For grade 3 and up. [string games]

Super Toys & Games from Paper.

F. Virginia Walter. New York: Sterling Publishing Co. Inc., 1993. 104 pp. ISBN 1-895569-06-0. Includes detailed instructions for making games. For use in the elementary grades. [toys]

Theme Adventures: Bright Ideas to Turn Any Day Into a Classroom Celebration.

Veronica Terrill. Carthage, IL: Good Apple, 1992. 120 pp. ISBN 0-86653-662-0. Creative activities and games to use with preschoolers through grade two students. [theme adventures]

Thinker Task Cards: Independent Activities to Stimulate Creative Thinking.

Lisa Rogulic-Newsome. Carthage, IL: Good Apple, 1992. 118 pp. ISBN 0-86653-681-7. Each task starts with a fact and then poses a question. For use in the elementary grades. [creative games]

Thinking Numbers: Math Games and Activities to Stimulate Creative Thinking.

Bob Bernstein. Carthage, IL: Good Apple, 1989, 92 pp. ISBN 0-86653-506-3. An activity book of math games for students in grades 2–7. [math games]

Tricks and Stunts to Fool Your Friends.

Sheila Anne Barry. New York: Sterling Publishing Co. Inc., 1984. 128 pp. Describes how to do some easy tricks. For use in the elementary grades. [magic]

Too Many Rabbits & Other Fingerplays: About Animals, Nature, Weather & the Universe.

Kay Cooper. New York: Scholastic, 1995. 46 pp. ISBN 0-590-45564-8. Filled with fingerplays about animals and science topics. For use in preschool through grade 1. [animals; finger plays; nature; weather]

Top Secret!: Codes to Crack.

Burton Albert, Jr. Niles, IL: A. Whitman, 1987. 32 pp. ISBN 0-8075-8027-9. An illustrated exploration of 28 secret codes. For grades 4–7. [codes]

What to Do After You Turn Off the TV: Fresh Ideas for Enjoying Family Time.

Frances Moore Lappe. New York: Ballantine, 1985. 197 pp. Contains ideas for family activities. For use with children in the elementary grades. [parent resources]

Wildlife Challenge: An Entertaining and Informative Game Book Designed to Educate the Reader About Wildlife and the Environment.

Lucy Moreland. Little Rock: AR: August House, 1992. 157 pp. ISBN 0-87483-255-1. Contains multiple choice questions in a game format giving information about animals and plants in the wild. For use in the elementary grades. [animals; plants]

Winning Checkers.

R. W. Pike. Holden, MA: C & M Publishing, 1992. 53 pp. ISBN 0-9635300-0-3. Teaching techniques on successfully playing checkers. For grades 3–8. [checkers]

Word Games.

Gyles Doubeney Brandreth. New York: Harper & Row, 1987. 127 pp. Filled with a variety of word games. For use in the elementary grades. [word games]

Word Games.

Anne Hayes, ed. Niagra Falls, NY: Durkin Hayes Publishing, 1990. 32 pp. RPI Learning Consultants, Ltd. Contains different types of word games. For grades 1–4. [word games]

Word Teasers.

Dympna Hayes. Milwaukee, WI: Penworthy Publishing, 1987. 31 pp. ISBN 0-88625-148-6. Filled with word games. For grades 2–6. [word games]

The World's Best Card Tricks.

Bob Longe. New York: Sterling Publishing Co. Inc., 1991. 128 pp. ISBN 0-8069-8233-0. Gives step-by-step instructions for doing 41 card tricks. For use in the elementary grades. [cards]

The World's Best String Games.

Joanmarie Kelter. New York: Sterling Pub. Co. Inc., 1989. 128 pp. Gives easy to follow directions for making string patterns such as Cat's Cradle. For use in the elementary grades. [string games]

Write Now!

Paul Fleisher. Carthage, IL: Good Apple, 1989. 76 pp. ISBN 0-86653-493-8. Contains 47 motivating activities and games involving creative writing. For grades 5–8. [creative writing]

Other resources

5 to Get Ready!

Catherine Slonecki. Freeport, NY: Educational Activities Video, 1991. 1 videocassette, 30 minutes. Uses animals, games, and song to encourage audience participation with activities such as introducing the alphabet, finding mistakes, filling in missing words, and pantomiming. [animals; songs]

Games and Music from Around the World.

Dana Hancock. Norcross, GA: Valentine Productions, 1990. 1 sound cassette, 60 minutes. For grades K–9. [music]

Games for Rainy Days.

Vee Critz. Atlanta, GA: Northstar Entertainment, 1988. 1 sound cassette. Describes education activities and games in math and language arts for school-aged children. [math games; word games]

Halloween: Games, Stories and Songs.
> Kay Lande and Wade Denning. Port Washington, NY: Den-Lan Music Co., 1989. 1 sound cassette and 1 song booklet. A collection of songs, dances, and games for Halloween. For use in the elementary grades. [Halloween]

Kids 'n Cards.
> Carmel Valley, CA: Greystone Productions, 1991. 1 videocassette, 25 minutes. For ages 4 and up. Explains how to play many popular card games. [cards]

Making Codes and Solving Mysteries With Amy Purcell.
> Cambridge, MA: Intervideo, 1992. 1 videocassette, 53 minutes. Ages five to twelve. Explains how to create and decipher codes and several games such as the fingerprint game. [codes]

Show Off!: Cool Stunts, Tricks and Gags to Amaze Your Friends.
> Stamford, CT: Vestron Video, 1987. 1 videocassette, 60 minutes. A guide to kid's magic tricks. For use in the elementary grades. [magic]

The Tyrannosaurus Game.
> Steven Kroll. Ancramdale, NY: Live Oak Media, 1988. 1 book of 37 pp and 1 sound cassette, 10 minutes. Tells how to play a musical dinosaur game. For use in elementary grades. [animals]

Index

To find page numbers for book and other resource materials, see the Subject Index to Actitivity Resources on p. 191.

Title Index

Author Index

Subject Index to Activity Resources

Bold page numbers indicate subject focuses of chapters. Formats of resources that are not books are indicated as follows: sound cassettes (c); computer software (s); CD-ROM (cd); and video (v).